C000285278

THE HoBbIT

AN UNEXPECTED JOURNEY

CHRONICLES

CREATURES & CHARACTERS

HarperCollins*Publishers*
77–85 Fulham Palace Road,
Hammersmith, London W6 8JB
www.tolkien.co.uk

Published by HarperCollins*Publishers* 2013
1

Text Copyright © Daniel Falconer 2013
Foreword Copyright © Andy Serkis 2013
Introduction Copyright © Joe Letteri 2013

© Warner Bros. Entertainment Inc. All rights reserved. THE HOBBIT: AN
UNEXPECTED JOURNEY and the names of the characters, items, events and
places therein are trademarks of The Saul Zaentz Company d/b/a Middle-earth
Enterprises under license to New Line Productions, Inc.
(s13)

'Tolkien'® is a registered trade mark of The J.R.R. Tolkien Estate Limited.

The Hobbit: An Unexpected Journey Chronicles – Creatures & Characters is a
companion to the film *The Hobbit: An Unexpected Journey* and is published with
the permission, but not the approval, of the Estate of the late J.R.R. Tolkien.

The Hobbit is published by HarperCollins*Publishers* under licence from
The J.R.R. Tolkien Estate Limited.

Daniel Falconer asserts the moral right to be identified as the author
of this work

A catalogue record for this book is available from the British Library

ISBN 978 0 00 748726 4

Printed and bound in China

All rights reserved. No part of this publication may be reproduced, stored in
a retrieval system, or transmitted, in any form or by any means, electronic,
mechanical, photocopying, recording or otherwise, without the prior
permission of the publishers.

Cover design by Monique Hamon

Other publications from Weta include:
The Art of the Adventures of Tintin
The Art of District 9, Weta Workshop
Weta, The Collector's Guide
The Crafting of Narnia: The Art, Creatures, and Weapons from Weta Workshop
The World of Kong: A Natural History of Skull Island
The Hobbit: An Unexpected Journey, Chronicles – Art & Design

Visit the Weta Workshop website for news, online shop and much more at
www.wetaNZ.com

This book is dedicated to Eileen Moran, who passed away as
we were completing this volume of *The Hobbit Chronicles*.
Eileen always championed the recognition and celebration of the
achievements of the crew and it is in that spirit that these books
have been created. She will be missed.

THE HOBBIT

AN UNEXPECTED JOURNEY

CHRONICLES

CREATURES & CHARACTERS

FOREWORD BY ANDY SERKIS

INTRODUCTION BY JOE LETTERI | WRITTEN BY DANIEL FALCONER

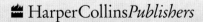 HarperCollins*Publishers*

www.wetaNZ.com

CONTENTS

ACKNOWLEDGEMENTS	6
FOREWORD	8
INTRODUCTION	10
OF HOBBITS	12
OF WIZARDS	28
OF DWARVES	38
OF TROLLS	106
OF ELVES	120
OF STONE GIANTS	136
OF GOBLINS	142
OF GOLLUM	168
OF ORCS	178
OF BEASTS	198
ABOUT THE PENINSULA	218
COLLECTIBLE CREATURES AND CHARACTERS	220
CREDITS	222
CREATURES AND CHARACTERS COMPARATIVE SIZE CHART	224

Acknowledgements

The Hobbit: An Unexpected Journey is a rich film in every aspect, but in no way more so than in its characters. A huge cast was assembled, comprised of returning favourites and new faces, heroes and villains, and backed by a small army of extras and specialized support crew. Many among the film's beings and beasts were composed not of flesh, but pixels, and even those who existed outside of the computer were in some way augmented by prosthetics or digital manipulation, resulting in characters portrayed, it could be fairly claimed, by choir as much as solo performance.

Paying tribute to the many contributors who have breathed this grand cast of fictional beings into life is the aim of this book. We have aspired to tell the stories behind the characters and creatures, illuminating the depth and integrity of thought that has gone into the realization of every aspect of their creation, and through direct quotes permit the artists to relate their experiences in their own words. It is a compilation of observations and anecdotes from across the production, each providing a unique window through which we as an audience can glimpse their view of the making of Middle-earth's inhabitants.

It is therefore with the sincerest gratitude that I take the time here to acknowledge the contributions of those who gave so generously to help in the research and crafting of this book.

There are three visionaries who are first and foremost owed the greatest of thanks, being the creative trio whose vision seemingly knows no bounds and who we must thank for bringing this world into being for the screen: Peter Jackson, Fran Walsh and Philippa Boyens. Zane Weiner, Caro Cunningham and the films' producers have, of course, magnificently supported them in this endeavour. Working both on the films themselves and now researching and crafting this book has been a thrill for me, a lifelong fan of cinema and Tolkien's Middle-earth. Thank you all for the chance to play and delve in this world.

My colleagues in the Weta Publishing team have remained the most diligent, positive and good humoured people anyone could hope to work with. Sincerest thanks to them both. Thanks also to Chris Smith, David Brawn, Terence Caven and the team at HarperCollins*Publishers* UK for their guidance, support and enthusiasm, Marta Schooler of HarperCollins*Publishers* USA, as well as Jill Benscoter, Susannah Scott, Elaine Piechowski, Victoria Selover and Melanie Swartz at Warner Bros. Thanks to Matt Dravitzki at Wingnut Films and Judy Alley at 3 Foot 7 Ltd for their help, advice and patience in managing the flow of assets and approvals to us for this project, and additionally Brigitte Yorke, Amanda Walker, Rachel Gilkison and Anna Houghton.

I'd like to express my sincerest appreciation to Andy Serkis for his input and the kind offer to write the wonderful Foreword to this book, with thanks to Jerry Schmitz and Laurie Wright for facilitating this for us.

This book would not have been possible without the unfettered access we were so generously granted by the wizards of Weta Digital to their amazing work. Thank you to Weta Digital's Dave Gouge, Mahria Sangster, Amy Minty and Natasha Turner for making this possible. Deepest thanks to Weta Digital's Senior Visual Effects Supervisor Joe Letteri for the time he took to write the Introduction, on top of that which he so generously gave us for interviews. Thanks to Diana Godo for her facilitation, and indeed, thanks to all those amazing wielders of digital magic who gave us insights into their mysterious and wonderful world.

Many thank yous to the skilled individuals of the 3 Foot 7 Make-up and Hair Department, Animal, Stunt and Casting teams, and all those from across the production, in New Zealand and abroad, who shared their stories with us.

At home within Weta Workshop, many among our crew gave generously of their valuable time to provide guidance, illuminate complex processes and share stories. And this comes from the very top: Richard Taylor, Tania Rodger and Tim Launder have been stalwart enthusiasts for all our ongoing publishing initiatives and their unfaltering support is deeply appreciated; and Tracey Morgan and Ri Streeter for their tireless support and enthusiastic assistance.

Among the most personal and delightful stories that have come to light as a product of this project have been those shared by *The Hobbit: An Unexpected Journey*'s incomparable cast. I deeply appreciate the friendly and open manner of all who shared them with us: Martin Freeman, Richard Armitage, Sir Ian McKellen, Andy Serkis again, James Nesbitt, Graham McTavish, Ken Stott, Hugo Weaving, Cate Blanchett, Lee Pace, Sir Christopher Lee, Dean O'Gorman, Aidan Turner, Peter Hambleton, John Callen, Mark Hadlow, Jed Brophy, Adam Brown, Stephen Hunter, William Kircher, Sylvester McCoy, Bret McKenzie, Terry Notary, Kiran Shah, and to Ceris Price and Melissa Booth for making this possible. Cheers for helping us pull together an exciting collection of stories about some remarkable people, who have worked together to produce what is the most amazing of films.

Finally, I would like to express my thanks to my patient family, who tirelessly and without complaint put up with a husband and father who was at work when he should have been home, or brought it with him.

Daniel Falconer

FOREWORD

Returning to Middle-earth for me truly was an unexpected journey...

...and pleasure on an unimaginable scale. Although I knew I would be creeping back into the tortured mindset of the creature who seemingly defines my life, my precious Gollum, I was certainly not prepared for a knock on the door and a visit (in the form of an email) from my very own Wizard, Peter Jackson, tasking me with joining him on a new adventure directing the second unit on *The Hobbit*.

Playing Gollum in *The Lord of the Rings* trilogy had taken me beyond the realms of traditional film acting, and introduced me to a vast army of phenomenally talented, brilliant, wonderful minds in the form of concept artists, creature designers, prosthetic and special make-up designers. Of course, it also opened the door to the endless, labyrinthine world of performance capture, with its digital genii, virtual-world creators and animators.

But one of the major thrills of directing was that it afforded me even more time and access to engage and collaborate with the masters of Weta Workshop, and Weta Digital, to study their craft and play with their creations in great detail on a day-to-day basis. These artists and technicians are all storytellers in their own specific fields, and in the pages that follow you will be introduced to a snapshot of the magic that they have woven into *The Hobbit*. From initial concept to fully realized characterization they represent thousands of hours, out of the hundreds of thousands of hours spent imagineering, designing, building and bringing to life Tolkien's world.

As you will see, the arrival on to the screen of hobbits, Dwarves, Elves, Trolls, Goblins, Giants, shapeshifters, Eagles, Wargs and Dragons requires a marriage of many tirelessly forensic minds. Some of these belong to concept artists Alan Lee and John Howe, creature designer Gino Acevedo, performance coach Terry Notary, performance capture guru

Dejan Momcilovic, to name but a very few, whose art and craft are shaped and filtered through the keenest eyes and ears of the master alchemist, Peter Jackson. Peter is then able to wrought these creations with love, truth, humour and a deep understanding of the power of emotionally honest storytelling, into their rightful places in these movies.

I have always marvelled at, and felt extremely privileged to work alongside, the extraordinary wealth of talent in the teams that create this beautifully cared-for work, as they represent a rare and unique devotion and passion for their art, that truly connects us with the story, and I'm sure you will do the same as you delve into the world of this book.

Enjoy the discovery.

Andy Serkis, Actor, Gollum and Second Unit Director

INTRODUCTION

Orcs, Trolls, Eagles and Giants, a Goblin King, vicious Wargs, over-sized rabbits and THE Dragon: Peter Jackson's vision of Tolkien's world is as exciting a place for creatures as one could imagine. Developing believable creatures has been a lifelong passion of mine and it was with great enthusiasm that we began work on *The Hobbit*.

One of the great things about these films is that the creatures we get to create are so integral to the story. In most cases these are not simply 'monsters' but individual characters with distinct personalities that need a wide emotional range including anger, fear and even the ability to pull off a joke or two. No character embodies this range more than Gollum.

Revisiting Gollum after roughly ten years was a real treat. He plays a pivotal role in the saga of the Ring and we see all sides of his character. He is one of the most compelling and fully realized characters in all of Middle-earth. He is capable of incredible malice, but at the same time he engenders sympathy from Frodo and Bilbo, as well as from the audience. This is a tribute to the performance of Andy Serkis and the talent of our animators who bring that performance to life on screen.

As a computer-generated character, Gollum has held up well over the years but there is so much more that we know now that we can apply to make the new version of him more lifelike. We have rebuilt him from the inside out, adding more realism: in the way his muscles move under the skin, the way light is reflected by the moisture in his eyes and a dozen other ways that are subtle, but essential. His role in *The Hobbit* is small but it is arguable that he steals the show in the first film. Not bad for a CG character.

Along with Gollum we have been able to recreate the Trolls, Goblins, Orcs and Great Eagles first seen in *The Lord of the Rings*. All of these have been carefully re-imagined and enhanced while staying true to the originals. Gwaihir, the leader of the Eagles, is the perfect case in point. His role in the film demands that he carry more of a performance so we had to give him more anthropomorphic dimensions than the other Eagles. It was important that we make him, and all of our creatures, much more 'alive' and capable of performance – not just action.

Action and performance is really where our part in the creature process begins. We work with great concept sketches and drawings from Weta Workshop and the 3 Foot 7 Art Department to get inspiration and direction. It's our job to

then take these ideas and bring them into 3D space, as they will be perceived on screen, and make sure they 'work', meaning they conform to the reality of the film world in which they live. We ask questions: 'Do the joints articulate properly? Could the muscles they have bear that much weight? Could they actually run on all fours with that type of skeleton?' Getting these details right goes a long way to making sure our creatures are believable and look like they belong in their scenes. If we get the details right, it opens up the range of performance that is possible.

Our three Trolls (William, Tom and Bert) were all written to have distinct personalities, but their limited screen time meant the audience did not have a lot of time to experience their individuality. To draw out their character, we accentuated design differences with performance cues. Excessive drool and snot was a focus for Tom, who had a cold among his many maladies. One of the ways William is identified as the leader is through the extra jiggle we gave his belly; we imagined he got the lion's share of the food. These details help the characters resonate quickly with the audience, even if they are seen on screen only briefly.

The creatures in *The Hobbit* are not set-dressing or background elements. The Trolls tell jokes, the Goblins have personalities and even the hedgehogs emote. The creatures are front and centre and they carry a good deal of action in the film. Telling the story of *The Hobbit* has been a fantastic opportunity to bring an extraordinary range of creatures to life – both old and new. And we haven't even got to Smaug yet …

Joe Letteri, Weta Digital Senior Visual Effects Supervisor

OF HOBBITS

' *HOBBITS REMAIN A VERY
PLEASANT RACE TO BE AROUND
BECAUSE THEY ARE SO FRIENDLY,
SWEET LOOKING AND FUN LOVING.* '

- Miranda Rivers, New Zealand Casting Director

CONCERNING HOBBITS

Although the book might be called *The Hobbit*, in the film audiences would meet more than just one of Tolkien's beloved hairy footed halflings. As a people in Middle-earth, the pastoral hobbits represent the kind of wholesome, simple values that the author so revered and provide an important contrast to the pretensions and agendas of the other races and characters that populate Tolkien's world. Relaxed and fun loving rather than hard headed or aggrieved like the Dwarves, and humble and earthy rather than aloof or haughty like Elves, Bilbo's fellows toil and play in blissful ignorance of the wider world of Middle-earth. It is why Gandalf enjoys their company so much, and why he chooses Bilbo as the essential fourteenth member of Thorin's Company, much to the doubt and confusion of the Dwarves. The production's own hobbits were drawn from a pool of actors and extras from around New Zealand, many of them rural folk who might in some way resemble modern hobbits as far as their values and attitudes run. It seems New Zealand breeds hobbits rather well.

CASTING HOBBITS

The starting point for casting *The Hobbit* was a gentle discussion about who might play Bilbo, which grew and grew in intensity as the films became a reality. When we started actively casting, it was for a long-list of characters. Some roles were earmarked for New Zealand casting, but otherwise John Hubbard and I, along with our counterparts in the US, Victoria Burrows and Scot Boland, were free to read actors for a large number of roles. When it comes to Tolkien, Peter is keen to 'fly the flag' and cast British actors wherever he possibly can, but it doesn't matter where the actor is from, or if they are associated with another franchise, or a long-running soap, or 'against type', or the hippest thing since sliced bread – the attitude is 'let's try it'.

Martin essentially is a hobbit, and by that I mean he's a wonderful British character who was reluctant to leave the Shire and uproot his idyllic home life. (He doesn't, to the best of my knowledge, have hairy feet.) He was also reluctant to let down his *Sherlock* co-star, Benedict Cumberbatch, and the BBC, by deserting their second series, which clashed with our dates. He's an honourable man and a wonderful actor. Once he'd read, the filmmakers knew they'd found their Bilbo. When the date clash occurred, we went into overdrive to tape alternatives to present to Peter, but the realization grew that Peter, Fran and Philippa would never settle on anyone else in that role and so the plan was hatched to accommodate his *Sherlock* dates, by filming other cast members and editing the movies during his absences. Only Peter could have coped with this huge gap without his lead actor. From all his early years of guerrilla filmmaking, and directing 2nd Unit via a monitor on

The Lord of the Rings, he has developed an amazing capacity to use whatever resources are available to make the best film he can and restrictions such as Martin's availability only make artists like Peter more creative, with exceptional results.

Amy Hubbard, UK Casting Director

Revisiting characters and races that we knew well from *The Lord of the Rings* was comforting and enjoyable on *The Hobbit*. Having worked on the 'Rings' trilogy, we knew hobbits like the backs of our hands. We knew exactly how a hobbit should look and feel. I really enjoyed revisiting Hobbiton and seeing it come back to life.

While it was familiar, there were also some little differences. There are novel elements. The costumes are a little different this time around, for example – more colourful and cheerful – but hobbits remain a very pleasant race to be around because they are so friendly, sweet looking and fun loving. What is true of the people who inhabit Hobbiton in Middle-earth is also true of the real folk we found to play them. They talk a lot and are generally rosy, round and jovial.

Miranda Rivers, New Zealand Casting Director

HOBBIT ACCENTS

The Common Speech of Middle-earth was translated into English by JRR Tolkien. The differences between the various peoples of Middle-earth can be distinguished by the variety of English spoken: true to Tolkien's ideas, we based their accents on varieties of UK English, as established on *The Lord of the Rings* films. Having worked on those films I was asked to establish the 'language-scape' for *The Hobbit*.

We were very lucky to have eight weeks of preparation time before we began shooting the first film. The accents were intended to seem familiar without being immediately localizable or too distracting. Every accent choice was made to serve the character and to tell the story. The actors had dialect sessions every day, to begin with, and as their confidence grew this became every other day. The aim was to prepare them to such a degree that on set they would need little or no coaching and could handle any script changes thrown at them!

Martin Freeman came to Bilbo with his native accent, RP or Standard English – the accent of the Baggins family as established on *The Lord of the Rings*. We had a meeting when he first arrived in New Zealand and talked about Ian Holm's vocal characteristics as Martin had watched his performance and was interested in adopting some of that into his portrayal of the younger hobbit. Peter was keen that Bilbo Baggins be a character of another time and we didn't want him to sound too modern or street-wise. Once Martin had found the character, the voice came with it and he really didn't need much help from us at all.

The Shire hobbits have a Gloucestershire accent. It is an accent that Andrew Jack, the Supervising Dialect Coach on *The Lord of the Rings*, and I chose because it is an easy accent to achieve, easy to understand and is timeless and rustic. The exceptions were the Tooks. If a Took spoke, then they should have a Scottish accent, as established with Billy Boyd's Pippin Took in the previous films.

As Dialect Coaches it's our job to find a means by which the actor can access another accent. For some it's through pictures or through physical representations of the sounds. For others it's simply by ear – listening and repeating. We find what works for each actor. If an actor is very visual, for example, I draw something that is called a mid-sagittal section – basically a head cut in half – and on this I can draw where the tongue is or how it moves when certain sounds are produced. In this way I could show a New Zealand actor that the back of the tongue is in a different place in the mouth when producing an L sound before a vowel in RP (back of the tongue raised for the Kiwi 'dark' L and lowered for the RP 'light' L). A visual representation of this sort is very helpful to some actors.

Concept Artists and Designers are involved in creating the visual world of a film, and we are involved in creating the auditory world. It is another, equally important component in the creation of Middle-earth as a real place. The audience shouldn't be reminded of their everyday world, thus the accents need to be timeless and not immediately localizable. If someone watching the film says, 'Hey, that's Liverpool,' for example, then they've been taken out of Middle-earth.

Roisin Carty, Supervising Dialect Coach

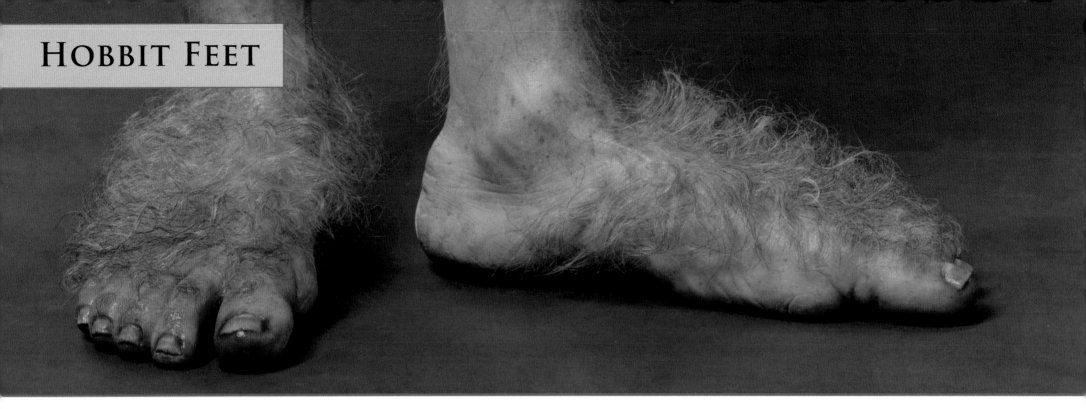

HOBBIT FEET

As described, hobbits have oversized, hair-topped feet and typically go about without shoes. By their nature, they present a technical challenge to replicate on screen, but recent innovations have meant a new approach could be adopted on *The Hobbit*.

'Essentially we created tight-fitting silicone gumboots that moved well and look really cool.'

On *The Lord of the Rings* we used foam latex for many of our hobbits' feet, or silicone in the case of our leads, and all were glued on and blended every day, sometimes more than once.

On *The Hobbit* we employed a totally new system. We used silicone for all our hobbit feet this time, and instead of slippers we had pull-on legs that went up to just below the knee. We also did the exact same thing for our extras as for Martin Freeman's Bilbo. Essentially we created tight-fitting silicone gumboots that moved well and looked really cool.

The big difference has been the advance in silicone technology over the last decade. Readily available platinum cure silicones are now being produced that are incredibly soft while maintaining elasticity and tear strength, and at prices that make them feasible for us.

We also created our new hobbit feet in a way that meant we didn't have a seam line running all the way round the prosthetic to clean up. Instead of coming out of a two-part mould, as in the past, this time we had a collapsible core. Toys, tools, or almost anything cast in plastic have visible seams. That's where

the parts of the mould join and it's exactly what we wanted to avoid on our Prosthetics. Cleaning up and removing that seam is very time-consuming and painstaking work which we'd have to do many hundreds of times. Instead we had a one-part mould, so there was no seam. The core, which mimicked the shape of the real foot inside the cast prosthetic, was collapsible and came out in pieces, leaving basically a silicone sock – the final prosthetic appliance – which we could then pull out without ever having to split open the mould or clean up seams. It's a more complex system to develop in the beginning but was a huge labour saver once we started producing hundreds of hobbit legs. They also didn't need to be glued on when worn, so there was application time saved there, and, unlike our hobbit feet for *The Lord of the Rings*, were 100% reusable.

Jason Docherty,
Weta Workshop Special Make-up and Prosthetics Supervisor

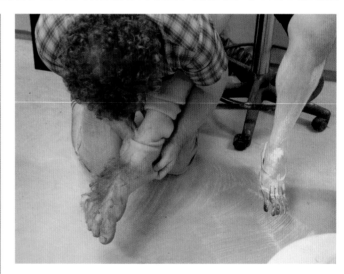

Above: Weta Workshop Special Make-up and Prosthetics Supervisor Jason Docherty fits a hobbit foot on Timothy Bartlett, playing Master Worrywort. Note the internal shoe with toe extensions, covered in talcum powder to make slipping the prosthetic on easier.

Above, left: Prosthetics Artist Marie Kealy with a bundle of painted hobbit feet, ready for hairing.
Above, right: (from left) Prosthetics Assistants Kala Harrison and Heather McMullan, with Additional Make-up Artist Dara Wakely, punch hobbit leg hair in every spare moment on the Hobbiton outdoor set near Matamata, New Zealand.

Above: Prosthetics Artist Jess Reedy applies prosthetic ears.

Our hero hobbits each had silicone prosthetic ears, which were a little more realistic and easier to blend off. The rest wore slip latex ears which we assigned to each individual according to size.

Katy Fray, Senior Prosthetics Artist

Silicone ears require a more complex production process than latex. As with our hobbit feet, we wanted to avoid having to clean seams off every single prosthetic, so we opted for a one- piece mould with a removable core. The core is a basic model of the actor's ear and in this instance we made it out of a different type of silicone for flexibility. The outside of the mould was also silicone, in this case a perfectly clear variety that we encased with a jacket to hold the whole thing together. We sluiced the vinyl barrier in first in order to make sure it got to all the ear's little nooks and crannies and then poured it out. Being a clear mould, we could see what we were doing and know it was getting to all the right spots. With experience you get to know exactly how to get that barrier the right thickness. From there it's a matter of pouring the silicone in and closing the mould.

Unlike the feet, the ears weren't reusable. In Bilbo's case he had one pair of ears for every single day that he shot, meaning we would supply a minimum of five pairs of ears a week. We did this through the entire production. Even if Martin wasn't shooting there was either a double or a stunt double or someone else who needed ears, and of course many, many more if there were hobbit extras on set.

Jason Docherty,
Weta Workshop Special Make-up and Prosthetics Supervisor

One challenge of oversized hobbit feet is the fake toe issue. Extending beyond the actors' own feet, they can flop about unrealistically like clown shoes, or worse, actually fold under and trip up the actor. To solve this we bought toed shoes and built extension mechanisms onto each toe, so the actor puts on a pair of mass-produced, easily changed out shoes with toe extensions and then slips on the silicone hobbit feet over the top. They were quicker to put on, easier to fix, safer and more comfortable than our old hobbit feet from *The Lord of the Rings*.

Jason Docherty,
Weta Workshop Special Make-up and Prosthetics Supervisor

We had around one hundred extras most days at Hobbiton, and one day we had seventy-seven pairs of feet on them, which had to be prepped and hair punched by our prosthetic make-up team. That was a lot of leg hair punching, essentially a strand at a time, so it required everyone to be at it in every free moment. Hobbit legs are necessarily tight and it's inevitable that some hair gets pulled out when they are put on and taken off, so there is maintenance and re-punching. They all had to be disinfected, cleaned and dried ready for the next day too, as we couldn't guarantee each extra would get the same pair back again. Inevitably there's some wear and tear, so to minimise this we had little yellow booties that they would wear over their feet to protect them between takes.

Katy Fray, Senior Prosthetics Artist

HOBBIT HAIR AND WIGS

Even on a project as big as *The Hobbit* there was a limit to how many wigs one could source or hire. We made many wigs, and hired around 250, but through reuse and clever alteration we effectively turned them into between 600 and 700 different wigs. That was essential because there were very few performers in these movies who wore their own hair. Almost everyone, including extras, was wigged.

When my business partner Peter Owen and I set out to make one, we would approach it with the intention to make a head of hair rather than a wig. Most have crowns in them, so they act like a real head of hair. It means we can do anything to them, so the same wigs may be used for many different characters and races and be unrecognizable to the audience. That was essential on *The Hobbit*. We have had wigs that have been straight hair on Elves, been frizzed to sit on the heads of Dwarves, and seen use in Lake-town and Dale as well. Our key make-up artist Angela Mooar kept an excellent record of all our wigs so we always knew where they had been and who they had been used for, in case we needed to go back and reproduce a previous look for a new shot.

Our team was very versatile. Often wigs came in and we had to completely change the colour or shape for whatever reason. Many times we did so in order to reuse a wig for a new character. We have been able to make many of the changes right here in the make-up department rather than send the wigs back to their makers and wait for them to come back again. We have re-knotted, changed hairlines, recoloured, permed and straightened. Often these changes were required to be turned around very quickly. Fortunately we had a team that could respond and jump on anything that needed to be done without it becoming a big deal. I think it is rather unique and worth recognizing because I am not sure the same would be the case everywhere.

Hobbits tend to have curly hair. We have sometimes treated hair so that it takes on a new texture. We did something called pre-curling, in which we wound small sections on wooden rods, tied them off and boiled them for two hours. It was a permanent way of curling the hair. If we were perming, the ammonia in the perm lotion would break down the chains inside the hair and once it was oxygenated it would reform in the new shape. That would be a chemical way of doing it, but we could accomplish what we need mechanically with our rod and boil technique, baking it in an oven afterwards, and it could be controlled to create different effects. Tiny rods combined with a twist gave a frizz, for example. Once pre-curled we knotted the hair into the wig, although we straightened it with water first because it is annoying to try and knot curly hair.

We didn't dye hair with hair dyes. Instead, we used fabric dyes, and for several reasons. Fabric dyes are intended to dye animal fibre, and much like silk or wool, that is what hair is.

Above: Make-up and Hair Designer Peter King uses heated fabric dye to recolour a wig in a matter of seconds.

One of the big advantages is that it can be done very quickly. I would bring a large pot of water to the boil and use acid dyes, mixing my colour from a broad spectrum. The hair went in and within twenty seconds it was done.

The colour is fairly predictable and with experience it is possible to very accurately work out what we'd need to add to compensate for a hue we mightn't like. Blue would help tone down something that was too orange, or some purple would help cut too much yellow. It was very easy to create a new mix and redo the dye if for some reason it didn't go according to plan.

Being such a fast process, we could dye thirty to forty wigs in an hour. If we were using regular hair dyes that would be forty minutes a wig and then they would have to be washed out. If we made a mistake, that would be it and we'd be stuck. Our fabric dye process enabled us to literally get through an entire army in a single day, which meant we could reuse wigs and thereby save a huge amount of money and time.

Every day, every wig came off and the lace at the front was cleaned with isopropyl alcohol, or acetone if it was very dirty and window cleaner if it was very, very dirty. Then we'd block each wig with biased binding tape and hundreds and hundreds of tiny pins. Blocking involves pinning the wig up on head-shaped stands to preserve their shape. It's the only way to make the lace sit down. When gluing lace it has to fit on the head of

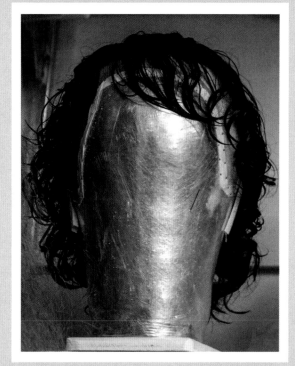

Above: A wig carefully pinned on its block between uses.

the actor. If it is feathery or stretched from not having been blocked properly or simply lying flat overnight then it will pucker and look terrible. We bought more than 300 polystyrene blocks and something in the order of 200 malleable blocks for the lace. Additionally, we had 200 beard blocks because they required the same treatment.

This all meant that once the day's shooting was finished we were usually there for a couple more hours preparing the wigs for the next use. If a wig was intended to look dirty, then we'd leave it that way, but if it was finished then we would wash, condition and comb it into place before placing it in a dryer.

We were constantly repairing any rips or damage, refreshing colour or perming where necessary. Once done, all the wigs would need to be restored to their original condition and returned to England too. I think next I'd quite like to work on a film in which everyone is bald.

Peter King, Make-up and Hair Designer

BILBO BAGGINS

'Bilbo goes through some profound changes over the course of the films, but at the same time remains very much the wholesome hobbit he was in spite of all that he endures and witnesses.'

At the heart of *The Hobbit* is, well, the hobbit, Bilbo Baggins of Bag End. Played by Martin Freeman, Bilbo is the unlikely and often unintentional hero who steps up to save the day, usually much to his own surprise, and certainly that of his travelling companions.

The Hobbit is definitely lighter in tone, generally, than *The Lord of the Rings*. Early on in shooting, I think I was playing, or was wanting to play, *The Lord of the Rings*. Peter gave me the note that this is more like a family story, something that my children will want to come and see, over and over. That note made sense to me, as someone who reads bedtime stories. We were in a certain place, tonally. However, that doesn't mean the stakes aren't high and that the life and death stuff in the story is a gag. It's not, and I couldn't play that if I wanted to.

Bilbo goes through some profound changes over the course of the films, but at the same time remains very much the wholesome hobbit he was in spite of all that he endures and witnesses. As has been noted, the journey reflects Tolkien's in his experiences from leaving home to fight in World War One, something that the vast majority of us can only wonder at, thank God. It's always much more interesting to play an 'arc', as we call it – you want to feel like you've moved a character from A to Z, stopping at all points along the way, but without telling the audience about those stops, if you get my meaning. It should happen by stealth, I think.

I'm very mindful of picking up where those changes occur – for instance, the first time Bilbo goes hungry or has to fight – and making sure that those points are acknowledged. So of course, are Peter, Fran and Philippa. There has to be something different in Bilbo's eyes at the end of the story, while still being him.

Bilbo is the Michael Corleone of Middle-earth!

Martin Freeman, Actor, Bilbo Baggins

Bilbo is a bit of an outsider and in the beginning everyone doubts him, which is something I think Bombur can relate to. Being a big guy makes Bombur a bit of an outsider too, so he probably really likes the kind of tenacity Bilbo demonstrates by constantly defying expectations and proving himself capable of more than everyone thinks. Though he probably doubted him as much as any of the Dwarves to begin with, Bombur has a soft spot for the hobbit and sees his talents.

Stephen Hunter, Actor, Bombur

Nori likes Bilbo. I think he sees something familiar in him. Bilbo is quite cheeky and he says what he thinks. In the beginning Nori bets against him, wagering that he won't come. So, Nori's a little bit annoyed because he loses some gold on that wager, but the hobbit proves himself time and time again.

Nori's one of those characters who will back someone if they've proved themselves to him. If Bilbo hadn't turned out to be useful then Nori would have been all for ditching him. Initially his thought was, 'What do we need a burglar for? I'm a burglar. What do we need another for?' The thing is, Nori's not a particularly good burglar. He's great at lifting things off people and stealing stuff, but in terms of sneaking into places,

he's no Bilbo. He doesn't have a magic ring. Bilbo gets out of situations that leave Nori scratching his head, so there's respect for someone who looks squeaky clean but is actually pretty darned good at being dodgy.

Nori comes to be one of Bilbo's would-be protectors. A lot of people end up protecting him when they come to appreciate he's an essential ingredient in our survival.

Jed Brophy, Actor, Nori

We must have produced over 100 pairs of hobbit feet just for Bilbo Baggins, plus easily 150 or more for the various other hobbits, so I imagine we must have made more than 250 pairs over the course of the shoot. The truth is, when it comes to the exact total, I've lost count. Let's say we made a lot!

Jason Docherty,
Weta Workshop Special Make-up and Prosthetics Supervisor

Hobbit feet have become a lot easier to put on in the last decade! Elijah testified to that. Mine take about eight minutes to put on, with the mighty Heather McMullan and an assistant. They're not too bad to walk in after a couple of days. Running in them over rugged terrain isn't exactly easy, but I didn't have any falls. They're amazing things, though. The detail on them is incredible. People don't know where I begin and latex ends, which has always been an ambition for me.

Martin Freeman, Actor, Bilbo Baggins

In terms of getting into make-up, I'm generally in the chair for an hour and a quarter. My artist, Georgia Lockhart Adams, went through a few dry runs for rehearsal and camera tests, and got to a pretty slick and painless routine that everyone was happy with. I have a wig and false ears, contouring make-up and a bronze skin tone to compensate for the 48 frames, 3D business. You look drained without makeup. And there's a lot of green screen too, which will make you look ill.

We tried a couple of prosthetic noses for Bilbo, which really changed my face and were nixed, I'm happy to say.

Martin Freeman, Actor, Bilbo Baggins

Bilbo's wig initially looked much more like Frodo's. We imagined there might be a family resemblance between the two hobbits, but Frodo's colour was too dark for Martin's complexion. Instead we went through a process of highlighting and re-highlighting until we had something that looked natural and right for the character. It made sense to me that his hair might be sun-bleached from spending time in his beautiful garden. Often we do things for aesthetic reasons and then find ways to justify them within the lore of the world, and usually you can.

Peter King, Make-up and Hair Designer

Above: Martin Freeman is fitted with a wig by Make-up and Hair Artist Georgia Lockhart Adams.

OLD BILBO

While *The Hobbit* is the story of a younger Bilbo Baggins, returning to book-end the tale is an older Bilbo familiar to those who have watched the previous trilogy, providing another bridge between the two film series.

Audiences have met Bilbo before when Sir Ian Holm played him in *The Lord of the Rings*. Of course, I took Ian's Bilbo as a template. What was important to me was not being slavish to it, but inspired by it. I was cast as Bilbo, not Ian Holm, so I didn't want to get too bogged down with 'what would Ian do?'

kind of questions. Suffice it to say, his Bilbo is the 'original' as far as Peter's films go, so I got a lot from watching him closely. Beyond that, I let myself have fun.

Martin Freeman, Actor, Bilbo Baggins

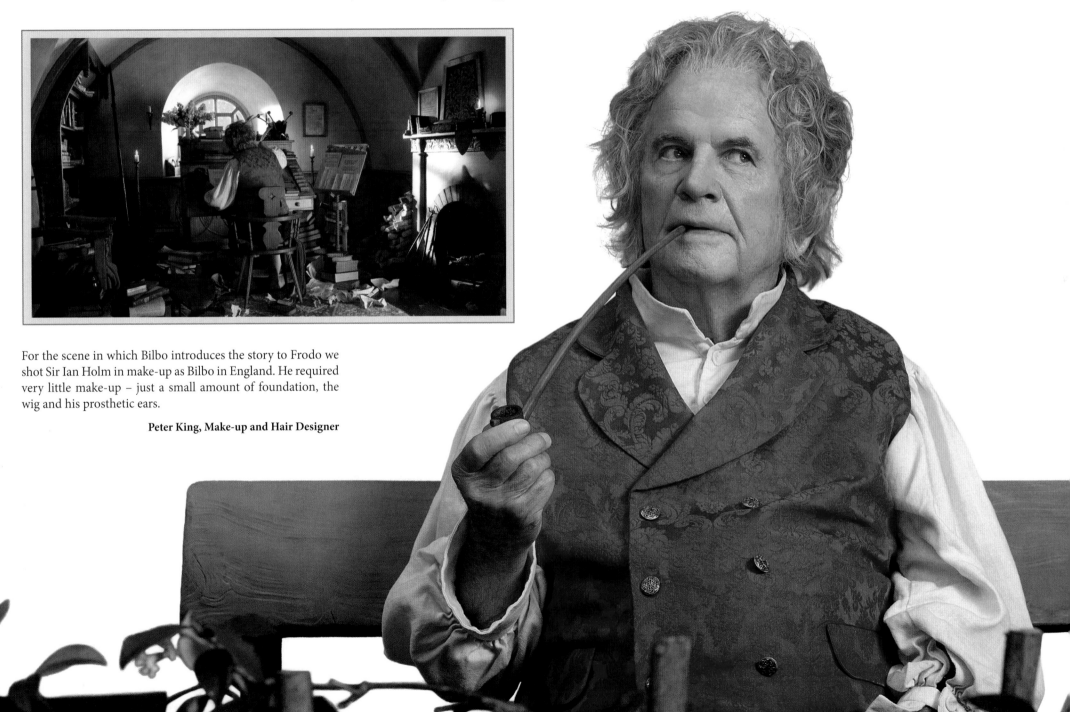

For the scene in which Bilbo introduces the story to Frodo we shot Sir Ian Holm in make-up as Bilbo in England. He required very little make-up – just a small amount of foundation, the wig and his prosthetic ears.

Peter King, Make-up and Hair Designer

OF HOBBITS - FRODO BAGGINS

FRODO BAGGINS

It was a weird and wonderful experience shooting Frodo's scene in London. I worked with Elijah Wood on *The Lord of the Rings* a decade ago, so it was strange being back, putting on his ears and wig and seeing Frodo come back to life again in front of our eyes. 'Frodo is back!'

Peter King, Make-up and Hair Designer

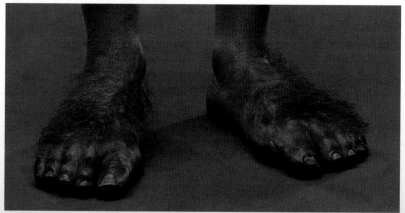

OF WIZARDS

' THE WIZARDS WERE MAIAR, POWERFUL SPIRITS SENT TO MIDDLE-EARTH IN THE DEEP PAST BY THE VALAR, WHO ARE AKIN TO GODS IN MIDDLE-EARTH LORE. '

- Sir Christopher Lee, Actor, Saruman the White

Concerning Wizards

Most enigmatic and little understood of Middle-earth's peoples are its Wizards. Although they might appear to be men, their life spans far outdistance those of even the Dúnedain, most long-lived of human kind. Yet neither are they Elves. The truth is they are far older than most would ever guess and only they and the wisest of the Eldar know their true purpose in the world. Sent to Middle-earth as guardians and keepers of lore, they were meant to teach, council and marshal the peoples of the world against the coming darkness, but in the long years since their arrival some would lose their way, till at the time of Bilbo's adventure only three remain.

Of the Order of Wizards there were five, originally. Three appear in *The Hobbit* films: Saruman the White, whom the Elves called Curunír, Gandalf the Grey, who was known by many names, and Radagast the Brown. Two others are mentioned but don't come into these tales, being the Blue Wizards. No one knows what happened to them and little else is said. The Wizards were Maiar, powerful spirits sent to Middle-earth in the deep past by the Valar, who are akin to Gods in Middle-earth lore.

Sir Christopher Lee, Actor, Saruman the White

GANDALF THE GREY

The architect of Bilbo's participation in the Dwarves' Quest of Erebor is none other than Gandalf the Grey. Always on the move and familiar with all of Middle-earth's peoples, including, of course, the sleepy Shire, Gandalf once again assumes the role of advisor and musterer, this time for a party of ornery Dwarves rather than a Fellowship of many races and, as ever, with a higher purpose in mind. Gandalf cares less for the wealth of Thorin's family than he does about the Dragon that lies curled in the Lonely Mountain and all the evil it could do if not removed from play.

Returning to the role is Sir Ian McKellen, who made Gandalf his own and won over millions in Peter Jackson's first trilogy, donning once again the pointed hat, beard and prosthetic nose and setting out to guide the people of Middle-earth to a greater good, often in spite of themselves.

It's not often in a film that a leading character is entirely on the side of good. Good people usually don't make for interesting film or story subjects. We often like a bit of spice. Often the most attractive characters are those who are not good. Everyone likes Gollum and he is someone to be pitied and feared. So, in that sense, it is good that Gandalf is popular, and for his best qualities. He is a brilliant warrior, although that is not why he is loved. I believe it is his humanity that people respond to, and his sense of humour. It's the fact that he cares about other people and creatures in a way that many other characters don't, being more invested in their own agendas.

Gandalf sees beyond the present and is aware that the equilibrium of Middle-earth is being disturbed. Middle-earth is in danger, though it won't be until Frodo is propelled on his adventure many years later that it becomes obvious to everyone. He sees that things are changing and that he has to bring the people to an understanding of this threat. Dwarves and Elves don't get on and Gandalf can't really understand that. He thinks people should be nice to each other. He gets impatient with them because they don't necessarily do what is right on their own, where he is motivated by what is best for the world.

It's a novelty about these stories. They're about people like Gandalf trying to do good.

Sir Ian McKellen, Actor, Gandalf the Grey

Gandalf and Elrond have known each other for a long time. I think there's a great deal of respect between the two of them. Elrond probably acts to put the brakes on Gandalf a little bit from time to time, but essentially they are both working towards a peaceful world. They are both very mindful of the fact that there are forces around them which could, at any time, reignite and threaten their way of life. I think there's a good deal of respect between the two of them, some humour, and enjoyment of each other's company, but I suspect they don't see each other that much.

He's aware of some things that Elrond isn't. In a sense, he's the meat in the sandwich between Elrond and Thorin and certain sages in Rivendell. He's not divulging exactly what's going on. The disagreement is really about what Elrond feels will happen if Gandalf goes to the Mountain and awakens Smaug. That will just stir things up and they are, at this stage, at peace, but Gandalf has another agenda.

Hugo Weaving, Actor, Elrond

Thorin's relationship with Gandalf is probably the one which is most explored. Thorin has a huge disdain and distrust of Elves, whereas Gandalf is the opposite. It is where these two characters are always divided. Thorin is suspicious of Gandalf. He suspects there is a greater plan in mind and that he is being used for a greater cause, a cause which sees Gandalf always guiding them towards Elves, insisting on Elf help, using Elf Roads.

When Gandalf is with the Company, Thorin can't be a leader. He is disenfranchised momentarily and that is a great annoyance to him. Interestingly, there aren't many characters in Tolkien who question and challenge Gandalf in the way that Thorin does. It was very interesting to play, but ultimately Thorin understands Gandalf's wisdom and benevolence. It is his own stubbornness, mixed with the uncontrollable oncoming Dragon sickness that continues to drive Thorin to be at odds with him. I also believe Thorin's anxiety concerning Gandalf being enamored with the Elves is rooted in a kind of disdain for elitism. The Elves are defined by their superiority – the Firstborn. The Dwarves, conversely, have been defined by their enforced hidden existence – the forbidden race, the secret language, their delayed awakening. All this, and the refusal of Thranduil to assist the Dwarves when Smaug destroyed Erebor and sent them all into exile, inform Thorin's relationship with Gandalf, 'the wand elf'.

Richard Armitage, Actor, Thorin

Never trust a Wizard. They're unpredictable characters and they never show all the cards in their hands. They've got other agendas and you can't help but feel that you're being used to some end you don't understand. That Gandalf drags us to Rivendell is proof that there's something going on. I think many of the Dwarves are suspicious of Gandalf and what his motives are, and some openly question his abilities. It's a pretty bold claim, calling yourself a Wizard, so show me some of that magic, eh?

Jed Brophy, Actor, Nori

Gandalf is a conjurer according to reputation. He's a magician, which is why Dori pushes him, 'Go on, tell us how many Dragons you've killed. Give us a number!' It's one of the best lines I have. He can take or leave the Wizard at the start, but he nonetheless wants to impress him greatly. He offers him tea at Bag End, but when Gandalf asks for wine I think that quite excites Dori. Being (as I imagine him) a restaurateur, he brings Gandalf the best red Bilbo's got.

Mark Hadlow, Actor, Dori

Gloin has been raised in such a way that he respects authority figures. He has likely had some dealings with Wizards or lesser magicians. They're a bit exotic, so while he acknowledges Gandalf's leadership role, there are times when he questions what the Wizard is thinking. He's a bit of a cynic in that sense. There's a contrast there, with him holding fast to a social order, but also mumbling and back-talking among his fellows about where Gandalf keeps taking off to or what he's up to.

When Gandalf drags the Dwarves to Rivendell Gloin is genuinely angry. It undermines Gloin's faith in him, because there is deep-seated hatred between the two races that someone like Gloin finds very hard to let go of. As far as the Dwarves are concerned it signals a reason to mistrust the Wizard's motives and they can't wait to be on their way again.

Peter Hambleton, Actor, Gloin

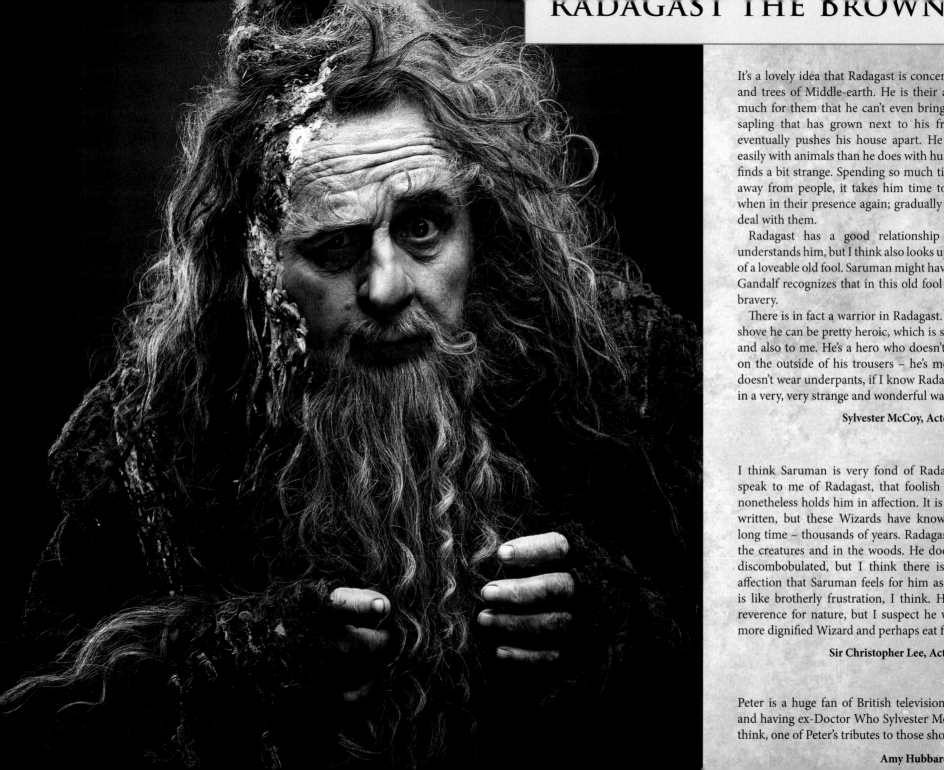

It's a lovely idea that Radagast is concerned with the animals and trees of Middle-earth. He is their advocate. He cares so much for them that he can't even bring himself to pluck the sapling that has grown next to his front door and which eventually pushes his house apart. He communicates more easily with animals than he does with human beings, whom he finds a bit strange. Spending so much time in the wilderness, away from people, it takes him time to warm up, in a way, when in their presence again; gradually remembering how to deal with them.

Radagast has a good relationship with Gandalf, who understands him, but I think also looks upon him as something of a loveable old fool. Saruman might have no time for him, but Gandalf recognizes that in this old fool there is wisdom, and bravery.

There is in fact a warrior in Radagast. When push comes to shove he can be pretty heroic, which is surprising to everyone and also to me. He's a hero who doesn't wear his underpants on the outside of his trousers – he's most likely a hero who doesn't wear underpants, if I know Radagast. He's a superhero in a very, very strange and wonderful way.

Sylvester McCoy, Actor, Radagast the Brown

I think Saruman is very fond of Radagast. He says, 'Don't speak to me of Radagast, that foolish man,' but I think he nonetheless holds him in affection. It is said sternly, as it was written, but these Wizards have known each other a very long time – thousands of years. Radagast spends his life with the creatures and in the woods. He does seem forgetful and discombobulated, but I think there is a certain degree of affection that Saruman feels for him as his fellow Wizard. It is like brotherly frustration, I think. He admires Radagast's reverence for nature, but I suspect he wishes he would be a more dignified Wizard and perhaps eat fewer mushrooms.

Sir Christopher Lee, Actor, Saruman the White

Peter is a huge fan of British television comedy and drama, and having ex-Doctor Who Sylvester McCoy as Radagast is, I think, one of Peter's tributes to those shows he loved.

Amy Hubbard, UK Casting Director

'When push comes to shove he can be pretty heroic.'

The first impression you might get of Radagast is that he's a bumbling fool. He's very old, very eccentric and obviously never washed, but beneath his dishevelled appearance is a fantastic character who is wiser and cleverer than others give him credit for. He comes up trumps all the time in spite of seeming to not know what's going on.

Children should love Radagast. They'll laugh at his bird-muck caked face and rabbit-sled at first, but they'll also come to love him because he's so genuine and endearing. With him caked in poo and dressed in tatters what we are told as an audience is that this character has no agenda. He may be weird and fluffy, but he is selfless and we can trust him. If he had been another clean Wizard I think it would have been easy to mistrust him. It was a stroke of genius on the part of Peter to paint him this way.

Peter King, Make-up and Hair Designer

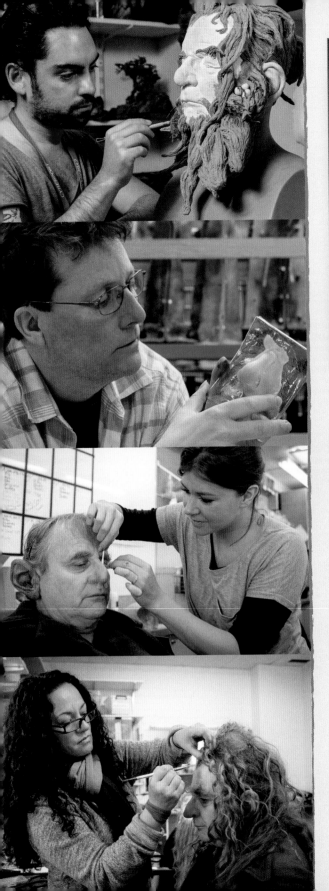

The only abuse we inflicted upon Sylvester McCoy was a nose, ears and a snaggle-tooth. Like Gandalf's, his nose prosthetic was produced in gelatine. Gelatine noses must be a Wizard thing because they all have them. Radagast's nose is quite bulky and points off to one side so it's a little tricky to apply, but creates a very interesting look.

Tami Lane, Prosthetics Supervisor

Radagast's bird poo is actually a silicone prosthetic appliance that is augmented on set with various products to suit. We provide the bulk of the guano with our appliance and the make-up artists provide the character of the splat on set, adding wetness or texture to suit what Peter has in mind.

We also provided a one-sided snaggle-tooth, which is a veneer that the actor wears, sticking out slightly to further throw his appearance out of symmetry.

Jason Docherty,
Weta Workshop Special Make-up and Prosthetics Supervisor

Left, from top: Weta Workshop Designer Johnny Fraser-Allen works on a Radagast hair and prosthetics concept sculpture. Weta Workshop Design and Special Effects Supervisor Richard Taylor inspects a gelatine Wizard nose prosthetic on its vacuum-formed tray at the Workshop before it is sent to the set. Senior Prosthetics Artist Katy Fray applies Sylvester McCoy's gelatine nose. Make-up Artist Frankie Karena blends the lace on Sylvester McCoy's wig.

I was surprised and delighted to be in Peter Jackson's film adaptation, because, as is known, Saruman is not present in the book of *The Hobbit*, so I'm very grateful to be back, playing the part again.

What audiences see of Saruman in *The Hobbit* is Saruman the brave, the good, the noble head of the Order of the Istari, the Wizards, respected by all, including Galadriel and Elrond, who calls him, 'My Lord Saruman'. The others defer to him. He is the head of the White Council and is very much Saruman the White and not the fallen Wizard he will come to be later.

Those familiar with the character from *The Lord of the Rings* should hopefully see little outward difference – he looks the same – although he is somewhat gentler, nobler, and still greatly respected by the other members of the White Council. He is strong, determined, straightforward and formidable, full of knowledge and definitely on the right side, beside his allies on the Council.

And there is occasional humour in Saruman as well, when he refers to yellowing teeth, which is not something we ever saw in *The Lord of the Rings*. Gandalf and Saruman trust each other, something else we did not see last time, as he had already fallen.

Sir Christopher Lee, Actor, Saruman the White

SARUMAN THE WHITE

Saruman as we see him in *The Hobbit* is not the evil Wizard of *The Lord of the Rings*. It was easy to forget that as we were working on him, because that is the image that endures from the original film trilogy, but of course this is the man before the fall. It didn't change much in terms of what we did with him because he had to look the same, but we did give him new nails. Saruman's dark eyebrows are Sir Christopher Lee's own, and even though they are very different to the white of his wig, they keep the severity and strength that are so much a part of the character, so there was never any question of changing those, then or now. Instead, we brought a little darkness into his beard to match. Maybe that little bit of dark is metaphorical, illustrating how the evil will slowly take hold of him?

Peter King, Make-up and Hair Designer

We filmed Sir Christopher Lee in the United Kingdom so that he wouldn't need to travel to New Zealand. We had a stand-in for him in New Zealand, but both had the gelatine nose, beard and wig that people would recognize from *The Lord of the Rings*. As I understand it, the beard and nose were new, but the wig was the very same one he wore in the trilogy. All our Wizards had gelatine noses on *The Hobbit*, just as Saruman and Gandalf did a decade earlier.

Katy Fray, Senior Prosthetics Artist

OF DWARVES

'DWARVES ARE A PROUD PEOPLE.
THEY ARE SHORT IN STATURE BUT THEY
FEEL NO NEED TO BE TALL.'

- Terry Notary, Movement Coach

CONCERNING DWARVES

Much to his own amazement, Bilbo joins the Company of Thorin and elects to undertake a perilous journey to the Lonely Mountain. The original book named thirteen Dwarves in the troop, led by the brooding and regal Thorin Oakenshield. Counting the Wizard Gandalf, that was fifteen characters, an indulgence for any film. Cinema-goers might have forgiven the filmmakers for trimming the Company to a more manageable number for the big screen adaptation of Tolkien's beloved classic, but Peter, Fran and Philippa were intent on honouring Tolkien's Dwarf roster faithfully, and that meant thirteen Dwarves and not one less.

The inherent risk was that many of these characters might be little more than set dressing. Even in the source material, some of the Dwarves were sketched only loosely in terms of character, but instead this challenge became an opportunity as the creative team took apparent delight in developing what could have been a company of Gimli clones into a rich and varied cast of very individual characters, all unmistakably Dwarves, yet each unique and memorable. Amid this motley assemblage of little hairy men there really was a Dwarf for everyone.

How do you bring to life a brotherhood of Dwarves from the pages of the book and give them each individual characters and individual looks? It's intimidating, but Peter Jackson has done it. I think it's a real triumph of the film. Gandalf calls out the names of the Dwarves and we cut to each individual, and there they all are, all very different, very alive, and very real.

James Nesbitt, Actor, Bofur

I think the Dwarves demonstrate a very successful collaboration between three departments coming together and pursuing a common goal, with everyone's work complementing that of his or her colleagues. Weta Workshop produced the early design concepts and manufactured the prosthetics; Tami Lane and her department of make-up artists applied them with such skill every day, managing to maintain consistency and high quality; while Peter King's hair department created incredible wigs and beards that bound and completed each Dwarf so believably. I am very proud of what we accomplished together. Seeing life breathed into these characters by the actors has marked the very gratifying culmination of everyone's efforts.

Richard Taylor,
Weta Workshop Design & Special Effects Supervisor

Casting Dwarves

A character can exist in a script, but they truly become real when given life by an actor. Finding the right actor, or in this case, the right team of performers, was a key step in the process and essential to get right. The daunting challenge of assembling an ensemble of very different actors and supporting performers, diverse in background and experience, would fall to the casting teams. The quest to find the Dwarves had begun.

The Dwarves were the logical place to begin our casting effort on this enormous project. We had a basic outline of the kind of characters we were casting and this information was disseminated to agents around the planet. We were searching in this part of the world while there were people in London, New York and Los Angeles all looking as well.

Nicola Benton, New Zealand Casting Assistant

We read as many actors as we possibly could in the time we had. Auditions can be a type of investment for actors, and I know there are many from this casting process who the filmmakers will treasure in the collective memory bank for future projects. For a few cameos, the filmmakers were interested in approaching specific actors, so there were no auditions for those roles, but for those cast members who would have to form the ensemble and base themselves in New Zealand, don prosthetics and work jolly hard for months on end – those guys had to come through the audition process so they knew exactly what they would be signing up for.

It is a huge commitment after all, coming to New Zealand for so long and acting under intense costume and make-up. People are often shocked at the fact that some actors did have to be talked into this (and previously on *The Lord of the Rings*), but these are human beings who have commitments and maybe families and/or pets. The recalls were a chance for Peter to explain how arduous the costume and make-up would be and how long the shoot would be. He illustrated this by telling them about John Rhys-Davies having to be helicoptered into certain locations sitting on a glorified beanbag, due to the complications of his costume, and Pippin and Merry actors Dominic Monaghan and Billy Boyd having to stand around all day just to commit a couple of looks to camera. Does it really deter the younger actors? No, but some of the mature actors can struggle with the idea of the prosthetics, the long periods away from their home lives and the green-screen element, which, as Peter says, if you are a traditional actor is an uphill challenge. However, they never regret it!

Assembling such a large and diverse cast and creating a successfully functioning ensemble from all around the world really was the filmmakers' achievement. It was like a 'chess game' as they worked out the dynamic of that ensemble. One of my favourite moments on set was sitting with all the Dwarves for lunch. I was like an overexcited child as I finally experienced all thirteen together. So many varied backgrounds – we had great fun piecing together how actors such as LA-based, Scottish actor Graham McTavish came to be cast, and local boy Dean O'Gorman, who was the last of the thirteen to be cast. The camaraderie was so strong, and those guys are hilarious! No matter where they came from, or at what stage they had joined the project, they had become a family. That's a family I'd like to marry into. They are pretty damn hot.

Amy Hubbard, UK Casting Director

Peter, Fran and Philippa weren't concerned where a person might be from so long as they were right for the job. As casting agents swung into action around the world, it was very exciting to be part of the process. It would be much easier from a logistics point of view if we could cast locally, and Peter, Fran and Philippa were enthusiastic to see as many Kiwis in the cast as possible, so we felt that New Zealanders had a very strong chance of being cast in some good roles for these films.

Auditions began. The ability to carry off accents was a tick in anyone's favour, and we were looking for character faces for the most part. Dwarves needn't be the traditional Hollywood beautiful people. We have always been more interested in ugly than pretty! We were looking for people who could embody the essence of these characters. They weren't human so it wasn't like casting the average modern-day movie.

Miranda Rivers, New Zealand Casting Director

The comedic element in Dwarves pushed us in certain directions too. We imagined that someone with comedy or improv history would have an edge, and that certainly turned out to be the case. We also had to keep in mind that we needed people who could work as part of a team because it is such a massive cast. As a casting director, you become very good at reading people, assessing a person's character and attitude, even from across a room.

Liz Mullane, New Zealand Casting Director

A walk around the trailer park outside the studios very quickly conveyed the scale of this operation. You could get lost out there! I had never worked on a film with so many trailers. And the poor prosthetic artists! There were thirteen hero Dwarves, thirteen stunt doubles, thirteen scale doubles, thirteen wide-shot doubles, thirteen riding doubles – five sets of Dwarves! Imagine if they might all be required on one day? Thirteen Dwarves very quickly became sixty-five, so the team-play aspect cannot be understated.

Fortunately, what we got was an amazing collection of enthusiastic people of all types from all over the world, gathered with a collective ambition to make an amazing set of films. They lived together under pretty intense conditions and travelled together for months, but what a great ensemble they have made.

Miranda Rivers, New Zealand Casting Director

It is an unusual situation to be on the road with such a diverse group of characters. We were a very diverse group of actors, coming from so many different places and backgrounds. I tried to let those things inform how the fictional relationships evolved between the Dwarves. Peter is great at casting. It was very easy to feel the hierarchy and camaraderie among us.

Richard Armitage, Actor, Thorin

The Dwarf gang culture has been wonderful to experience and be part of as it developed. Any shot or scene involving all of us is a massive logistical exercise in terms of set-up, but once we're all together and doing our thing as a group there's a fantastic energy. We have lived with these characters for a long time now. It has been amazing watching the culture of this group evolve through the shoot and to see how our arc plays through the journey, seeing how characters have come to be cared about and how invested we have all become in this story. We've become attuned to each other, to the point where we might have a scene involving everyone running and we naturally fall into something you might think was choreographed. It comes from being so familiar and comfortable with this group and who everyone is. When we act together we are able to just let it happen and not get hung up on anything.

Peter Hambleton, Actor, Gloin

Above: Weta Workshop Costume and Armour Technician Bryce Curtis was a willing and enthusiastic test subject for early make-up and body augmentation, transforming him from a six-foot human into a burly, tattooed Dwarf. Below: Application by Weta Workshop Special Make-up and Prosthetics Artist Frances Hawker.

Even before we had any Dwarf actors cast, we had launched into a thorough research and development round, exploring how we might achieve turning regular-proportioned, average-height people into convincing Dwarves, beginning with tests on members of our own Weta Workshop crew.

Bryce Curtis was our first model, but he was in some ways a soft start for us because he suited being a Dwarf so well. We tested oversized arms and hands on him, lowered his waistline and crotch, expanded and inflated his physique and gave him big boots, all in an effort to change his body proportions, truncating him. We gave him a big plaited beard, elaborate tattoos and a bulbous nose. The tests were very successful, but

this was the quintessential Dwarf and we knew that in order to create a full and diverse race, we needed to push it to extremes and also try applying our experiments on subjects who were less naturally Dwarf-like.

We tried out a truly extreme, caricatured make-up on Ben Hawker, which Peter thought was very successful, engaging and endearing. Even when his facial features were pushed so far he still was able to communicate and perform this amazing character. Ben Hawker has the ability to project through heavy make-up. We didn't imagine that our entire Dwarf cast might ever look like this, and in fact as we got deeper into the design process for specific characters we appreciated how important

it would be to let the actors' own features come through the make-up. Fran in particular championed this. It made little sense to cover the younger Dwarves in such heavy and ageing make-up. We still used the opportunity to caricature our Dwarves, but never to the extreme of Ben's tests.

We experimented with more subtle prosthetics on Luke Hawker, another of our staff who acts. We tried a number of variations on Luke, attempting to preserve his inherent good looks while 'Dwarfing' him. How little could we get away with while still making him look like a Dwarf? How do traditionally Dwarvish features alter a handsome face?

Richard Taylor,
Weta Workshop Design & Special Effects Supervisor

Above and Right: Weta Workshop Writer Ben Hawker in an extreme Dwarf make-up prosthetics test. Below: Weta Workshop Special Make-up and Prosthetics Artist Luke Hawker wears experimental prosthetics designed to suggest a younger Dwarf.

SCULPTING DWARVES

Tackling a film version of *The Hobbit*, the first place to start had to be the Dwarves, and like so many projects, the very first design concept was a maquette by Jamie Beswarick. It was a very beautiful sculpture with a quality that I felt we should aspire to capture in the thirteen that we had to bring to life for the film – slightly more caricatured than where we'd ended up going with Gimli, because this time we had a large and diverse range of Dwarves. Some would be more subtle, but some could afford to be quite extreme in their features and their body types. We were creating a race as diverse as our own, and humans come in all shapes and sizes.

Our design team set about creating an amazing collection of early conceptual design work. Daniel Falconer compiled a range of beautiful studies on one page that got Peter and Fran excited around the potential diversity of these characters and this was complemented by a number of other people all having a go, building upon each other's successes with each round.

We continued to work on the Dwarves early in the project, but it really wasn't until a couple of months out from the shoot, when casting was occurring and we started gaining access to the actors, that we really gained some great traction and made excellent headway in coming up with specific looks for each of the characters.

Above: Weta Workshop Designer and Sculptor David Meng sculpts Bombur's neck piece. Inset: The first Dwarf maquette sculpted by Weta Workshop Designer and Sculptor Jamie Beswarick.

Below: Thorin's look continued to evolve on the busts. Some early Plasticine studies had longer beards and elaborate hair-styling.

As our designs took shape we came to appreciate that our Dwarf ensemble would run the full gamut from heavily made up to some with just the most minimal of prosthetic appliances. Our younger Dwarves in particular would have minimal build-up as we didn't want it to interfere with our audience's ability to relate to these characters.

We enjoyed working closely with Peter, Fran and Philippa in those final weeks before the shoot was to begin, getting to know the characters they had developed and settling on specific looks. We ultimately produced more than 800 2D images and a comprehensive maquette collection, culminating in us taking head casts of all the actors and sculpting the prosthetics and hair designs directly on top for Peter's feedback. That is ultimately how we achieved the final leads that informed the way they looked in the films.

Make-up and Hair Designer Peter King joined us in New Zealand at this point, bringing his unique expertise to bear on the discussion, but even at this point we were only halfway there, as we hadn't yet tested the prosthetic prototypes on the actors. Our sculpting team transferred the approved designs into mouldable prosthetics and we began testing. A restriction Peter set, and it proved to be a wise restriction ultimately, was that we weren't able to bring the prosthetics down on to the actors' cheekbones. He wanted them only on the nose, forehead and temples because he didn't want the prosthetics invading the more moveable areas on the face, nor the longer application time required to blend edges on the soft areas of the cheeks. For Gimli, we widened the actor's face with expanded cheeks as part of our effort to make his proportions more Dwarf-like. Although restrictive at one level, not covering our actors' cheeks was a challenge for us to enjoy problem-solving without resorting to adding more silicone.

Part of our process of Dwarfing someone involved altering their head-to-body ratio so that their head seemed larger in comparison with their body. An average-sized human actor would have a 7:1 ratio, while very tall actors like Richard Armitage or Graham McTavish might have 8:1 ratios. Their heads are much the same size as someone shorter, but their limbs are much longer. By making their heads appear larger with prosthetics, we could make it appear that their limbs were proportionally shorter and thereby give the illusion of being Dwarves, 5:1 being the head-to-body ratio ideal we were aiming for. We put each Dwarf in a foam head cowl, but, because we couldn't blend down onto the cheeks, we were left with a dramatic and unnatural step between the head cowl and the back edge of the cheeks. To solve this we put the ears on stalks which would stand up to an inch proud of the actors' temples, using hair to disguise the gap and broaden the head form.

Bombur was the one character with which we were able to break the rule of no application around the cheeks. Peter wanted to see Stephen Hunter transformed by the prosthetics into a character with a huge throat and big round cheeks to complement his great belly girth, so we developed a comprehensive silicone appliance for him that covered most of the actor's face.

Richard Taylor,
Weta Workshop Design & Special Effects Supervisor

A challenge for us as prosthetic sculptors was to find ways of caricaturing our Dwarves to make them distinctive. The beards were the obvious thing, but we tried to give them unique facial characteristics as well and ensure that our prosthetics enhanced their own features. It could easily have become a collection of indistinguishable guys with different coloured beards. We looked at textures and scarring, and for distinctive shapes in the actors' own faces that we could magnify and bring out on the prosthetics. I would take slight indications of where they may not yet be wrinkles, but where they look like they will grow in future, and exaggerate them, over-emphasizing what was there, but not adding anything that wasn't already evidenced.

The one exception was Gloin, who had perhaps 40% imported Gimli DNA in his prosthetic design. We did this to draw those characters together.

Steven Saunders, Weta Workshop Sculptor

Balin is a scholarly, grandfatherly, gentleman-type when we are first introduced to him, but obviously he comes from a long line of impressive warriors and he himself, in his prime, was a warrior of great stature. The scars we put in his make-up tell us he's had a few near misses over the years. He has three or four on his forehead and a severe one through his nose that hint at his warrior past.

Ori's design evolved on the sculpt, starting with a very dramatic nose, but becoming much smaller. Peter also wanted very smooth skin to help make him feel young and innocent.

Greg Tozer, Weta Workshop Sculptor and Designer

Some of the Dwarves' noses we based on the actors' own, enhancing them, enlarging them and building them out. For others we did the opposite, looking for ways to idealize their features, if anything, Thorin being one of these. His prosthetics were very thin and his sculpted facial features very refined.

Jamie Beswarick, Weta Workshop Sculptor and Designer

This page, and opposite: Dwarf prosthetics and hair concept sculpts were done by Weta Workshop sculptors on life-size busts of the actors as part of the development of their specific individual looks.

DWARF PROSTHETICS

'We've run something like 250 of each Dwarf, which works out to around 4.5 tons of silicone, just for the faces of the main Dwarf cast.'

Making prosthetics for a Dwarf begins with a full head cast. Head casting processes haven't changed much in years. Unless an actor is bald we slick their hair back and glue a bald cap over the top. This is to prevent hair being grabbed by the moulding material, so for the same reason we will slick down the eyebrows, and any facial hair.

Traditionally the actual life casting is done using alginate, a water-based impression material. Dentists use it to take casts of people's teeth. We paste this onto the actor's face and head, leaving breathing holes exposed of course, either nostrils or sometimes the mouth as well. It takes about ten minutes to set. We then back the alginate with a layer of plaster bandaging creating a jacket that gives it rigidity and allows it to retain its shape. This is done in two parts – the front and back halves of the mould – so that it can be removed.

Once the plaster is set, we peel it off gently and carefully cut away the alginate in matching halves that go back into the jackets. Usually our actor is inside for between twenty and thirty minutes. Sometimes we might use a silicone impression material instead of alginate, in which case the curing time is another ten minutes or so. Silicone can provide a better cast.

Alginate shrinks, so once the actor is freed we'll pour a plaster positive of their freshly cast head from the new mould,

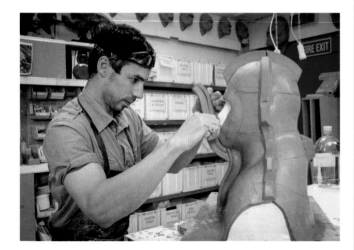

which will be cleaned up and turned into a nice clean master that we can work from, making copies as we need to. This gives us a full head and shoulders to work with to start creating our prosthetic.

We deliver a plaster cast out of the head and shoulders mould which our sculptors then use to develop their prosthetic design at 1:1 scale in Plasticine. Sometimes the sculptors work from Photoshop design concepts but often the design really comes together on the bust, with Peter giving his input and the design evolving.

Once approved, the Dwarf's prosthetics are what we call locked off, then we decide how we're going to do the make-up – how each part will be split up and what materials and fabrication processes we're going to use.

On a Dwarf, we'd take a second head cast and sculpt the head cowl, which wraps around and makes the head look much larger. We sculpt the large ears and then take what we call a snap. A snap is a mould of just one part of the sculpt that we need separately, in this case the face, with the information from the edge of the head cowl and ears on it. We pour another cast of this portion in plaster again and remove any undercuts in parts like the nostrils, or under the lips. We have to do this because we are going to make a one-part mould of the face and these areas would likely catch and lock the mould, making it impossible to get apart. Once that is done, we mould it again and cast out an epoxy version of the face onto which we re-sculpt the face, replicating the locked-off design. This is what is cast to give us our run moulds, out of which we will create all our prosthetic facial appliances.

In the case of the Dwarves, we used an epoxy system because we knew we were going to be running a lot of them. We've run something like 250 of each Dwarf, which works out to around 4.5 tons of silicone, just for the faces of the main Dwarf cast.

Jason Docherty,
Weta Workshop Special Make-up and Prosthetics Supervisor

Each Dwarf wears a foam latex head cowl. When applied this is glued along the leading edge. Reusable latex ears are attached and refeshed after a couple of weeks when they start to look dirty or worn. The head cowl can be used many times as it really just adds volume and isn't seen. Dori used the same one for three months.

On the other hand, the facial appliances are silicone gel-filled with vinyl surfaces. One side features the negative imprint of the actor's face, and this is the surface that is glued on, while the other side faces camera. It has a translucency like skin. The vinyl is clear but the silicone is tinted and flocked, matching any colour we need it to. They move very well on the actors' faces, better than anything we have used before and certainly a step forward from where we were with Gimli a decade ago.

Jason Docherty,
Weta Workshop Special Make-up and Prosthetics Supervisor

Head of Prosthetics and Special Make-up Effects here at Weta Workshop, Jason Docherty conceived and oversaw all the processes by which we were able to achieve our many make-ups for *The Hobbit*. Jason and his wife, Kim, were responsible for the near-faultless production of all the prosthetics through the movie, near 97%, which is a very impressive number considering the complexity of those processes and the massive scale of the operation.

Richard Taylor,
Weta Workshop Design & Special Effects Supervisor

Left: Weta Workshop Moulding Supervisor Michael Wallace laying up a clay matrix for a silicone case head mould. Above: Weta Workshop Design & Special Effects Supervisor Richard Taylor and Special Make-up and Prosthetics Supervisor Jason Docherty with Bifur's facial appliance. Facing Page: Weta Workshop Special Make-up and Prosthetics Artist Kim Docherty amid silicone Dwarf facial appliances.

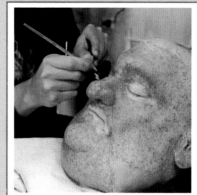

The first day I had all the full prosthetics on, and we did all the tests, I got home and thought, 'I don't know how I'm going to do this.' There was just so much bulk to wear. I was really claustrophobic as a kid and I'd never worn prosthetics, so there was a seed of doubt in my mind that I might completely freak out. But once we had done the head casting, I realized that if I could deal with that then I could deal with prosthetics fine.

To begin with I really noticed the weight of everything I was wearing, because Bombur is significantly bulked out. My arms and shoulders were quite sore and my hands were tight. As we went along costumes and make-up were adjusted according to our feedback. I think my body also got used to it, and I became a lot stronger because of all the training.

Performing under prosthetics has a stage acting quality to it. It's something that Peter was very aware of and he would make a point of telling us to make sure we moved our faces around a lot. And of course what he always does is give you an example, which is always great – he pulls great faces. Obviously, screen acting and stage acting is quite different. With screen acting so much of it is in the eyes and you don't really have to project as much, but with all the stuff we were wearing we had to project a bit more to push the silicone around and perform through the prosthetics. It's something you get used to and it becomes natural.

I had a particular look that was a big eyebrow raise, because it was something you would really notice when it happened. I was always on set with my prosthetic artist to make sure they were lined up properly. If they were slightly wonky it would look like I was permanently puzzled.

Stephen Hunter, Actor, Bombur

All our Dwarves wore silicone prosthetic hands of some kind. The reason that we opted to put them all in prosthetic hands was because once we had increased the size of their heads to such a degree, their hands looked disproportionately tiny and extremely human. Our prosthetic hands were designed to thicken and truncate their digits, broaden the palms of their hands and generally alter the proportions enough to make them look less like miniaturized people.

Richard Taylor,
Weta Workshop Design & Special Effects Supervisor

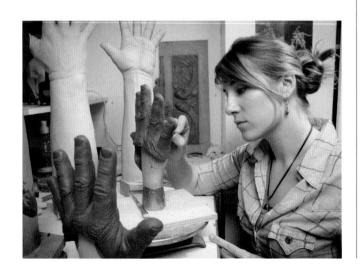

We had different types of Dwarf hand prosthetics. What we called full arms covered everything from the fingertips to the elbow, full hands that encased the hand like a glove but stopped just past the wrist, and what we termed mitts which were the hands minus palms. The palm of the mitt, which it was intended in this case the camera would not see, was mesh, making it easier to grip things. Our fourth hands were fighting mitts, on which the silicone covered only the top, leaving the fingers, palm and bottom completely open, and thereby not inhibiting the gripping of weapons at all – great for fight sequences but not for a close-up. For close-ups, we always used a full arm or full hand.

Dwalin had his sleeves rolled up and his tattoos showing, and Thorin spent quite a lot of time with his forearms exposed too, so they both often had full arms, and there were fighting versions of those too, lacking palms, for the same reason as above.

Because our Dwarf hands were made to be tight fitting and create suction when put on, they didn't need to be glued, just like our hobbit feet, and were easy to swap if torn or damaged.

Jason Docherty,
Weta Workshop Special Make-up and Prosthetics Supervisor

Whenever we might see Dwarves with their sleeves rolled up it was up to our on-set prosthetics team to punch hair into their silicone arms. We got the arms from Weta pre-painted, but we had to hair them. Dwalin always has his forearms showing, but sometimes others had bare arms too. We also had to reinsert the hair when it came out, which it tended to do just with the wear and tear of taking the arms on and off. We had a girl whose responsibility it was just to take care of all those hands on set. She wrangled and prepared them, having around five pairs in circulation, repairing and replacing them if damaged.

Tami Lane, Prosthetics Supervisor

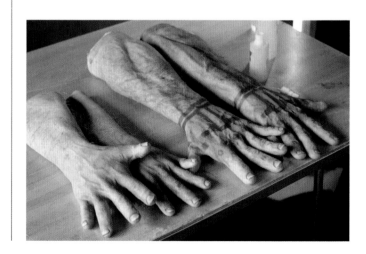

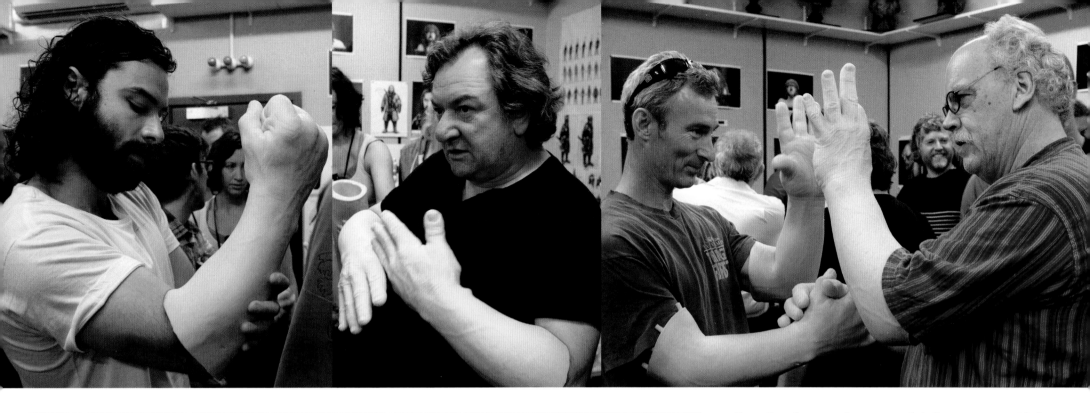

Above: Dwarf cast members react to their first encounters with the silicone hand prosthetics.

My job was to try and make the character of Thorin feel very real, despite the heavy make-up, working my facial muscles, making sure the wig moved like hair, without too much appearance of vanity, something which Thorin has very little of. The biggest challenge was the prosthetic hands. I think hands reveal so much about a character. They are sensitive little beings all of their own, and the enlargement with the silicone hands could be quite restrictive. I wasn't able to put my hands through my hair, or pick up anything with ease. Touching my face or touching another character's face in a tender moment, was always going to be difficult. Hands are also connected to the emotions. The clenched fist and the relaxed shaking fingers – these were things we had to live without.

Richard Armitage, Actor, Thorin

Facing Page, bottom left: Weta Workshop Sculptor Lindsey Crummett sculpts a Dwarf hand in Plasticine. Facing Page, bottom right: Thorin and Dwalin's full silicone arms. Left: Painted and haired mitts hanging ready for use.

Applying Dwarf Make-up and Prosthetics

From left to right: Prosthetics Assistant Kala Harrison and Senior Prosthetic Make-up Artist Valter Casotto with Stephen Hunter as Bombur. Prosthetics Make-up Artist Rachelle O'Donnell with Peter Hambleton as Gloin. Prosthetic Artist Don Brooker with Mark Hadlow as Dori. Additional Make-up Artist Claire Wolburg with Aidan Turner as Kili. Make-up Artist Jennifer Stanfield with Richard Armitage as Thorin.

The process of putting a Dwarf into prosthetics and make-up began each day with a raw silicone appliance provided by Weta Workshop. Our make-up team members preferred to receive them un-painted because we each have our own way of working. We prepared our own pieces, painting them to a certain level in some cases, but often the majority of the painting was done once an appliance was glued onto an actor, making it easier to blend.

As part of the preparation of an appliance we punched the eyebrows, which, depending on the nature of the piece or the experience and skill of the artist, could take between forty minutes and four hours. Back in the old days eyebrows could be glued or pre-knotted on to lace, but the clarity of the cameras being used is so unbelievable that it's possible to see where the hairs grow out of the skin, so we've been hand-punching all our brows. The new high definition cameras are great, but torturous in this way.

Curiously, it turned out that a wig lace was actually easier to hide in a silicone appliance than on real skin. This led Peter King to joke that in future he'd love to have every actor he works with wear prosthetic foreheads just to better hide the edges of his wigs!

To get all our Dwarves on set by 8.30am each day we usually had to start around 5am, with one artist assigned to each Dwarf. When we began this was looking more like 3.30am, but we managed to reduce our make-up times substantially and buy ourselves a little more sleep.

Each Dwarf's make-up began with flattening their hair using hairspray. Then we put on the foam cap cowl and glued on the ears. The next piece to be glued on was usually the facial prosthetic appliance. We call this a T-piece because it is applied to the T-zone across the forehead and down the nose. Probably the most important part of the application involved gluing this down and blending the edges perfectly, because it would be very easy to accidentally create a wrinkle or glue one brow lower than the other. Sometimes this was a challenge. When Graham McTavish (Dwalin) and Adam Brown (Ori) were in the make-up chairs next to each other they liked to laugh and joke around. The Ori make-up was very smooth, with hardly any texture, so it was technically difficult to glue down without a wrinkle, and especially so when he was busting up laughing!

Next the flashing was removed. The flashing is the leftover material around the edges of the prosthetic that is attached when it comes out of the mould. Rather than discard this as soon as it comes out, we kept the flashing attached because we used it to hold the edges flat during application. At this point the application would usually be running about forty minutes.

The next stage involved sealing the edge, blending the paper-thin edges of the prosthetic so that nothing popped off or came unglued, after which we began painting. That step usually took ten to twenty minutes, depending on the complexity of the paint job and whether the character had any cuts or scars or was bloody in that particular scene.

Often we encouraged the actors to take a nap. It's actually much easier for us to appy our prosthetics when we can lay the actors back with relaxed faces and let gravity work in our favour. The hardest part was staying awake ourselves as this tended to be going on at some unholy hour of the morning!

Thorin's make-up usually took an hour to an hour and a quarter up to this point. At between twenty and thirty minutes Kili's was the shortest Dwarf make-up, but most tedious because it was nothing more than a tip to change the shape of his nose. But being so small, it had to be laid down perfectly or it became an obvious problem right in the middle of his face. Because of her experience, Prosthetic Make-up Artist Katy Fray applied both Kili and Ori's prosthetics.

Speed was very important. We had to become quick at our work to avoid insane call times. In most cases we managed to trim two-hour make-up processes down to around an hour and a quarter. Even with a senior artist and an assistant assigned to him, Bombur's was the longest at an hour and a half, which was still very impressive considering we were spending three hours or more on Gimli each day during *The Lord of the Rings*. Bombur took longer because he had so many pieces. In addition to the head cowl with ears, he had a foam neck that gave him big jowls. Bombur's T-piece came all the way down over his cheeks, over his nose and covered his entire face. There was also a silicone chin (silicone more closely resembling skin than foam) and he had a scalp piece that sat under his wig, with a bald spot like a medieval monk.

Above, from left: Senior Prosthetics Artist Justin Ditter, Additional Prosthetics Artist Elka Wardega and Prosthetic Artist Marie Kealy working on John Callen as Oin, Graham McTavish as Dwalin, and Peter Hambleton as Gloin.

Some of the most significant advancements to have occurred since the days of Gimli and *The Lord of the Rings* have been in the kinds of materials that prosthetics can now be made in. Gimli's prosthetics were silicone with a latex backing that had a mechanical bond of flocking. It didn't necessarily move as well as the newer materials. Now we have a way of encapsulating silicone in bald cap material which means it has a glueable and paintable surface. It had been that Gino Acevedo had to prepaint every Gimli prosthetic, but on *The Hobbit* we painted them on the performers. Where Gimli had gelatine eye bag blenders, we didn't have to deal with that on any of our cast, nor did we have to glue latex. The soft encapsulation material is less abrasive so we can use friendlier, stronger glues and consequently we haven't had any of the major skin reactions that John Rhys-Davies suffered during the first trilogy.

Once the prosthetics were finished being applied and painted, our Dwarves went to the hair and straight make-up department where they spent another forty minutes before going to wardrobe to be dressed.

When they returned in costume, which was usually around forty-five minutes later, we'd all go to set where we did maintenance and adjustments. We usually had to make adjustments for the kind of lights they might be using that day, or if there was a giant green screen.

Tami Lane, Prosthetics Supervisor

Above, top to bottom: Make-up Assistant Amy McLennan with Fili. Make-up Artist Flora Moody with Oin. Make-up Assistant Anna de Witt with Nori.
Left, top to bottom: Make-up Artist Cath Macquire with Adam Brown as Ori, Prosthetics Artist Ryk Fortuna with Dori's appliance.

Above, this page from left to right: Ori and Bombur's facial appliances sitting on plaster bucks. Bombur's various separate appliances are discernible by colour. Senior Prosthetics Artist Justin Ditter punches eyebrows by hand into Dwalin's facial appliance. Actor Ken Stott is made up as Balin – note the ruddy complexion. Actor Peter Hambleton as Gloin, being shot against a green screen required the make-up to be even more red as the green bounce-light sucked warmth out of the character's skin tones. Peter also wore brown lenses to reinforce his family resemblance to Gimli.

We were in a constant state of prep on this show. The volume of prosthetics work was so huge that at any time we were preparing dozens of new pieces to be ready for the next day of the shoot. Hero Dwarf facial appliances were only used once, and by the end of principal photography we would have produced and used more than 250 for each main character. Every one of these was painted by hand and had the eyebrows punched one hair at a time with a needle, and they all had to match. It would have been easy for things to gradually drift on a project as long as this one, but we were very diligent about maintaining sameness so that our characters didn't change unintentionally.

Continuity was a really big deal. Our Dwarves were seen in so many different conditions throughout the films. They got into fights, got rained on or ended up in the water, got beaten up, battled Trolls and Goblins. We saw some when they were younger. One day we might be shooting Bag End where they were all clean and groomed and then two days later we were filming a battle, so it was essential that we knew at any moment how they were supposed to look at that point in the story. We took lots of pictures to ensure that we were always maintaining a logical continuity.

We had to make one big change at the very beginning, however. We discovered that the silicone being used to create the prosthetics was doing something weird and totally unexpected when filmed through the new Epic Red cameras. The camera sucked out the reds, so our first make-up tests looked great to the eye but when we saw the rushes the Dwarves all looked yellow. The paint had disappeared. To compensate we had to pump the red up much more than looked reasonable to the eye. We ended up going beyond painting things to look realistic and painting for what we call the invisible eye. Walking around on set all the Dwarves looked sunburnt, but looking through the camera they looked right. For the longest time I was being questioned and had to reassure everyone that while it may look odd to the eye, this is what we had to do to make them appear natural on camera.

We also found that if there was light bouncing off a giant green screen, which there often was, it would subtract even more red, meaning we had to add even more right there on the set. I worked on Thorin and after walking off a green-screen shoot he would look completely burgundy under normal light.

Throughout the day we would tag-team our on-set responsibilities because we also had to prepare our prosthetics for the next day. That involved coming back and punching eye brows or doing any pre-painting that might be necessary while someone else was on set who could alert us if we were needed.

At the end of the day, which could be around 8.30pm when overtime was called, the Dwarves came back and in around twenty minutes their hair, beards and make-up were all off.

Tami Lane, Prosthetics Supervisor

Many of the wigs we're using were made specifically for this project by Peter Owen in England. We did all the wigs together for *King Kong*, *The Lord of the Rings* and *The Lovely Bones*. On *The Hobbit*, Peter Jackson asked specifically that all our doubles, be they large or small scale, be made exactly the same way. In this respect it has been a much bigger project than the trilogy was, because we have had to create a minimum of three wigs for each main character – one for the actor, one for their stunt version and usually one for either a large or small-scale double. Sometimes we've made as many as five, plus as many beards as well. Every character is wigged. Gandalf had five wigs and five beards, each Dwarf had six wigs and eight beards and the hero Elves each had four, so very quickly the count entered the hundreds.

The wigs we used were certainly not cheap. We've used Russian hair, excellent for our purposes, but also expensive. Being from a cold climate it is much finer than hair sourced from warmer locations such as Spain, India or elsewhere in Asia. Polish hair is very good, fine hair, but it isn't available to us in lengths over twelve inches. We have not resorted to using synthetic hair, but we have used some animal hair – yak. We used it on the Dwarves to give us a different, wiry texture. It could be achieved with human hair but would take a lot of work, so we used a mixture of yak and human hair on some of them. Yak hair is by nature very rigid and coarse, but that also meant it didn't move much, so Thorin, with his dark flowing locks, was the only Dwarf not to have any yak in his wig.

Being so dense each Dwarf wig took four weeks to make. All the hair was knotted in with a very fine crochet hook, much of it one hair at a time. Although our Dwarves had eyebrows punched directly into their prosthetics, many of our characters had knotted lace eyebrows too. These were delicate little pieces that it would be very easy to misplace.

We also had to invent things to cope with the numbers we faced, like the hundreds of Dwarf and Elf extras. For instances where extras have worn helmets or hats of some sort we have invented hair nets that go over the head with wefts sewn on. We've made so much weft hair. I bought some but we made miles of it. It's a way of weaving hair in between three strings so it can be sewn on, like ribbons of hair.

Everyone had long hair in *The Hobbit*. Bilbo had the shortest, which was ironic because if you saw him walking down the street you would likely think he had quite long hair.

I think hair is very important in make-up. You can age someone very simply and successfully just by moving their hairline or changing the colour. In my experience a make-up artist with a good understanding of hair and what can be done with it is worth a fortune. Sometimes you don't even need to apply make-up to someone's face and you can tell an entire story with their hair.

Peter King, Make-up and Hair Designer

Above from left to right: Make-up Assistant Natalie Henderson wefting, Make-up Artist Lucy Garguilo blocking a wig, Make-up and Hair Artist Richard Muller prepares a wig.

If you were to analyze someone's hair you would find that it's made up of many different shades. The melanin in hair gives us black, brown, red, orangey-red, yellow and no colour at all, or white. Those are all the colours that provide every natural hair tone you'll find on every person around the world. To create a realistic red wig I would take auburn, some mid tones, light tones and some gold and mix them. It doesn't really work just to dye the whole wig one colour, so I try to construct colour by mixing rather than dying. We will still do some dying, but it is usually just for certain colours that we might want to include in the mix rather than dying an entire wig one colour, because they tend to look very 'wiggy' and unreal that way.

We sometimes include some less natural colours to help nudge a wig a certain way, but always very subtly and in a manner that no one would be able to see unless they inspected the wig a strand at a time. If doing a cool blonde we might use some violet to help create an ashier colour.

Peter King, Make-up and Hair Designer

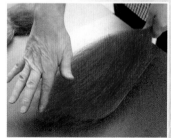 

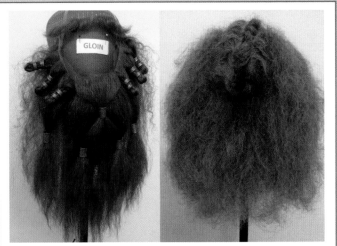

GLOIN

There is less structure to a beard than a regular wig, so it would be easy to stretch them out of shape, and some were quite heavy. It was something that had to be borne in mind when we pinned the beards to blocks after a day's shooting. We took wraps off the cast to accurately understand the shapes of their chins and make blocks to match. Making wraps involved covering a head or chin in film – the same kind that a person might wrap their lunch in each day – and then taping it to keep the shape. The beard or hairline was traced onto the wrap with a permanent pen. Effectively we took a kind of simple mould of the chin or head that informed the shape of the padding of the block upon which the wig or beard would rest when not on an actor, ensuring the shape was preserved.

Given some beards were so heavy, we used an invisible strap to tie them over the heads of our actors and thereby take some of the weight. Glue alone wouldn't be adequate. In a number of instances we only glued around the edges and instead used incredibly strong toupee tape that would take the skin with it if you tried to remove it without alcohol.

Peter King, Make-up and Hair Designer

The thing about yak's hair is that it's thicker. It was a little bit more like straw than actual hair against the face. I didn't find it too bad, though some found it very itchy. I've had a beard for years so that didn't bother me. I think the hairdos were quite extraordinary and very appropriate for the characters. Funnily, that little pony-tail stinger on the back of my head was maybe the only minor issue in that, if I went to lie down on my back to rest for a minute, the wire inside made it somewhat problematic. Lying on one's side wasn't really an option as it pushed the prosthetic on my face out to the side, but an arrangement of cushions meant I could grab those essential forty winks when I needed to. The prosthetics we all had and those hairdos were all appropriate for the characters we were representing. They weren't always comfortable, but they were very important and every one of them was amazing.

John Callen, Actor, Oin

As we approached the end of the main shoot I tallied some of the numbers regarding materials that we've used so far. We've used seven kilometres of toupee tape, which is what we attach beards onto Dwarves with. We've used 500 bottles of spirit gum and then 860 litres of isopropyl alcohol, which is what we use to remove prosthetics. We've used 270 bottles of hair product called Fudge Cement, because we use that on everybody. Another product called The Frizzies, which we use to matt hair down in a way that makes it look worn in and unwashed, is up to tube 400. Even weighing just the hair itself that we have bought, we're up to forty kilograms of yak hair and ten kilograms of human hair. That's a lot of hair.

We block all our wigs and hair pieces to prevent them from losing their shape between uses and so that the lace is laid down flat. I bought 160 polystyrene head blocks, 280 canvas blocks and 160 chin blocks. I recall when we first came to order those canvas blocks I ordered 15. How naïve was I?

Angela Mooar, Key Hair and Make-up Artist

We're under very heavy make-up and there's no getting around that. It's what is necessary to achieve the look we're seeking – we're not playing humans after all. The heat factor has been a major challenge at times. If I get a new home I'll be looking to insulate it with yak hair because it holds the heat like you wouldn't believe! As warm as they were, those wigs were incredible, and the skill that has gone into them is humbling. Maintenance, heat and perspiration were things we dealt with and, thanks to the clever people we work with and a lot of discussion, ways were always being found to alleviate discomfort and smooth the process wherever possible.

Peter Hambleton, Actor, Gloin

THORIN

Leading the Company to the Lonely Mountain is Thorin Oakenshield, heir to the lost throne and the Dwarf upon whose shoulders the hopes of a displaced nation weigh heavily. As a lead character, Thorin had to be someone the audience could believe in and sympathize with, to feel the responsibility and history that hangs on him and understand the loss and grief that drives him to undertake this seemingly foolhardy expedition. Most importantly, they also had to like him, so it was essential that the filmmakers cast an actor in the role with the same charisma and simmering dignity the character commanded.

Fortunately the casting directors found Richard Armitage, an actor with the quiet intensity and thoughtfulness needed for the role and a man in whom both the rest of the cast and the audience could believe.

The first meeting I had with Peter, Fran and Philippa was the casting. I was given a scene to read that was actually a construct – it wasn't from the book. It was at this point that I became really excited by the idea, that the book was going to be the backbone of a much more fleshed out, well-rounded story. The scene they gave me to read was Thorin talking to Balin about who the Dwarves had once been, what they had become, why the Wizard had come to him with the map and the key, but that he didn't feel he had the strength to do this. In one scene, the writers had captured exactly what the character was all about – his dreams, his regrets, his insecurities, and his power.

Throughout the filming process, I was able to bounce my ideas around our forum. Often, ideas would spring from drafts of scenes being 'workshopped', or in progress. As we all grew to know and understand Thorin, the collaboration became easier. The way the character looked was very much in Peter, Fran and Philippa's hands; the way he moved, spoke, and delivered the ideas on the page were mine and Tolkien's. I was inspired very much by a particular pencil sketch of John Howe's, particularly the hands, eyes and nose. I felt they weren't dissimilar to my own. There was also a gentle, pensive attitude in the picture which I hadn't seen in Tolkien. It gave me a useful colour to paint with.

The most exciting part of collaboration though, isn't when one sits down to negotiate for ideas to make it into the script or film, but when they appear in the script at the very moment when they are desired. This happened a lot. This is when I felt we were all in tune. The lines never had to be learned. I suppose Peter, Fran and Philippa were hearing my voice when they wrote a scene – another great compliment – and when imagining that scene, I was in tune with the flavour of neo-classicism that I felt our writers were enjoying: the Dwarf kingdoms felt like the great fallen Roman empires, and the literature and philosophical ideas were in line with Greek tragedy, at times Shakespearean. I felt that it was appropriate to allow myself to wander down that path, after all Thorin was heading for a kind of megalomaniacal insanity, which is a difficult thing to play without embracing that 'full throttle' style of art.

I always imagine characters who are defined by their history. If it's not there then I will inevitably construct a detailed biography. For Thorin this was very easy as Tolkien had given so much material to us through various other sources in his literature, but I still needed to investigate a more domestic biography; 'What do Thorin and Dwalin "chew the fat about"?' or, 'What was Thorin's relationship with his sister Dís like?' I felt that might inform how Fili and Kili would feature in Thorin's life.

The difficulty with Thorin is that he enters the story on the edge of failure, but with everything to win. I remember thinking when I first read the scene for the casting, that here was a character who felt like a dying ember, yet with the energy and hope to reignite into the furnace that once powered this great warrior. But, he has all the potential to fail.

I connect personally with that last sentiment. I was never really sure if I could pull this role off; I felt secretly that many others also felt the same and it's one of the reasons I could never sit down on set (I am a pacer, apparently). I could never rest.

Thorin is the same. He hasn't slept easily in his bed since the Dragon expelled them from Erebor. Thorin's grandfather went mad and his father disappeared a year ago to the day when the Quest begins. The desire for revenge upon Smaug and also on Azog, who beheaded his grandfather, has been bequeathed to him. That's a huge burden to carry, and one that can't be shared.

The glory of returning his people to their homeland is also in the mix, along with the personal revenge on the slaughter of his family. Also, buried deep inside of Thorin is a dormant lust for gold, a lust inherited from the line of Durin, and just as the Dragon who will be woken when the King returns to the Mountain, so too that dormant illness inside of Thorin will awake. He knows this and he fears it.

So really, the 'engine' which brings Thorin to lead his fellow Dwarves to their destiny is fuelled by the past but is 'front wheel' driven, towards their future, their destiny, their prophecy. It's a great place to imagine a character because they are always in flux, pulled towards something, which they fear, springing from a rage-fuelled past.

Richard Armitage, Actor, Thorin

First impressions are often lasting. We make up our minds about people upon first glance, so when you are designing a character for the screen it is vital that you get their look absolutely right for the first shots in which they appear. As a story progresses, half the fun can be in showing how wrong that first impression may have been, but that first look is still something we have to craft so that we impart the message about a character we want them to understand instantly when he walks on screen.

Consequently, we put a lot of thought into Thorin, and his arrival in the movie is built up by the other Dwarves as they await his appearance at Bag End. There is an awe and reverence that surrounds him. He is very strong and slightly scary, but also hypnotic and charismatic. Thorin is the leader, a king among his people and the Dwarf upon whose shoulders the future and hopes of his people rests. We went through a number of iterations before we settled upon his final make-up, which consisted of a thin forehead and nose, wig and ears.

Thorin's nose was Romanesque, which imparted a sense of nobility. His wig was also entirely composed of human hair, without any yak, which we used to add body to some of the other Dwarves. That allowed it to flow and move more romantically. For the same reason, Thorin's beard ended up clipped quite close, to preserve his more refined appearance and not hide the actor under a full face of hair. It was important that people understand and relate to Thorin, so we didn't want to build a wall of hair in front of him that would impede that in any way.

Peter King, Make-up and Hair Designer

Early on in the shaping of Thorin's look, we had some quite extreme prosthetics and elaborate beard designs. I was very pleased with the effect, which was such a transformation. I looked like another being – older, and very much like a Dwarf. As the design began to change through re-sculpting, reshaping, and stripping back, I realized that it was a process that we were going through, to find a point at which Thorin and the actor inside of him were both visible. Of course that feels like a great compliment, although Richard Taylor did tell me fairly near the end of filming that they straightened my nose, which is apparently off centre... I didn't know that!

Richard Armitage, Actor, Thorin

Bilbo has probably never actually sat and had a conversation with a Dwarf before they turn up at his door. He knows they exist, and I think may have an admiration for them – at a distance. When he opens the door to Dwalin, he doesn't know quite where to look, or how to be. He's certainly a bit intimidated. By the time Thorin comes, he's had enough of these bloody Dwarves! But Thorin obviously has a charisma about him, and is respected as the 'leader', so Bilbo responds to that.

He knows Thorin has massive doubts about his involvement, so throughout the story we are seeing them yo-yo to and from each other; Bilbo earning Thorin's respect little by little and also his fury on occasion. It's a classic case of a big (well, about four feet), powerful man learning things from someone who isn't exactly Alpha. Like my relationship with Richard, in fact. Only I'm Thorin in real life.

Martin Freeman, Actor, Bilbo Baggins

What Richard does in the film – playing northern English, speaking in a voice register lower than his own, and playing a noble leader of thirteen – is one of the most committed performances I've ever seen. He chose to stay in character on set, which is only sensible given the transformation he was making. I know he won't mind me saying that Peter saw potential in Richard that hadn't been fully exploited before. Richard was due to appear in another season of *Strike Back* for Sky. He turned down that opportunity to make himself available to *The Hobbit*. His commitment to the films, pulling out of a sure-fire job for the chance of appearing in a project that was 90% likely to go into production, but wasn't 100% green lit at the point of casting him, was an inspiration to all of us. And, I believe it was a much needed boost to the filmmakers' morale during a marathon casting process. Richard really deserves credit for that. He's a hero on screen and in life. Other actors made similar sacrifices, but Richard made this one very early in the casting process.

Amy Hubbard, UK Casting Director

BALIN AND DWALIN

Brothers Balin and Dwalin were Thorin's most trusted companions and deepest confidantes in the preparation to retake Erebor from Smaug. His cousins by blood and brothers in arms, the three Dwarves escaped the sack of their mountain home together and fought at each others' sides during the war with the Orcs. Their resolute commitment to the Quest formed the heart of the Company – Balin, with his confident dignity and thoughtfulness, and Dwalin, with his grim solidity and indomitable bearing.

Dwalin, of all the Dwarves, bears the literal scars of a life of battle and toil. A general and tactician, the tough, war-chewed Dwarf stands with the assured confidence of a man able to take care of himself in any situation. Balin, on the other hand, while no less a warrior, carries himself with the gentle grace of someone who has nothing to prove. Wise and circumspect for a Dwarf, who as a people tend to be inward looking and quick to perceive insult, Balin assumes the role of counsellor and elder to the Company's younger Dwarves. Assuming the mantle of these characters were Ken Stott and Graham McTavish, well-established actors in British film and television, and both with distinctive voices and the great screen presence to carry off such strong roles, even under very heavy prosthetics and costume.

Balin and Dwalin were written as Thorin's closest confidantes, Balin as the Old Warrior advisor and father figure, Dwalin as an equal in all but name, his friend, his advisor, and his sparring partner. Thorin has a relationship with every one of his men, but these two and his sister's sons, Fili and Kili, are particularly close.

Richard Armitage, Actor, Thorin

Balin and Dwalin are classic brothers, gently mocking of one another but able to rely on each other when they need to.

Graham McTavish, Actor, Dwalin

'There's a simplicity and dignity about Balin.'

There's a simplicity and dignity about Balin. His wisdom and reluctance to be drawn into battle are reflected by the fact he isn't armed to the teeth the way some of his travelling companions are.

Ken Stott, Actor, Balin

Bombur defers to Balin. He's been brought up well; to respect his elders and the higher-ups, and Balin is the sort of elder statesman of the group. This Quest means a lot to Bombur personally, so he is very respectful towards him. It's a natural reaction. He's friendly and chats away with the likes of Balin, because I think that Bombur and Bofur's family have a bit of that country, Kiwi and Irish thing going on where they treat everyone the same way, regardless of class or history. But he's respectful and will go with what's expected rather than cause a fuss. When in Rome, play along.

Stephen Hunter, Actor, Bombur

In many ways it was an advantage that the Dwarves were, on the whole, so loosely described in the book. For the films, the first point is always the script. What does it tell us about the character? In this case, Philippa and Fran gave me a great place to start with such a distinctive character. We talked together, and with Peter, about how he fitted in with the others. We felt that Dwalin was a veteran warrior, someone who has seen more than most and has an attitude formed from his experiences. He does not talk except for good reason. He values loyalty, commitment and honesty above everything and has very clear views on who are his friends and who are not.

Some part of who Dwalin became was led by his physicality, and his appearance. A big, tattooed Dwarf with axes strapped to his back and scars on his face is not going to be at the back in a fight. He and Thorin have a very close relationship, forged from childhood and facing enemies together, always at the front of a battle.

Dwalin feels differently about different Dwarves in the Company. Some he knows well, but others, particularly Ori, Nori and Dori, Bifur, Bofur and Bombur are untested and, therefore, to be kept at arm's length until they prove themselves worthy of his trust. Dwalin has a soft spot for Ori, who he quietly admires for being so determined to come on the Quest against the wishes of his family. He protects the naïve young Dwarf in battle, and keeps a watchful eye on him throughout the journey. I think Dwalin admires this youngest, weakest member of the Company who is, nevertheless, willing to risk his life. All of these choices came from long discussion with the other actors, with Peter, and with Fran and Philippa.

Graham McTavish, Actor, Dwalin

'Dwalin, being a war chief, respects courage and fight in a person ...'

I think Peter liked putting Ori and Dwalin together in situations. We were paired up a lot! It was the two opposites – the weak one and the strong one. Dwalin soon came to respect Ori and his blind determination to succeed with the Quest. Ori looked up to Dwalin and wanted to be a warrior like him.

It helped that Graham and I became good friends on the job too!

Adam Brown, Actor, Ori

I really love the strength that comes through in every aspect of Dwalin's look. This is an uncompromising Dwarf. He's another example of a character design that isn't the stereotypical fantasy Dwarf and yet cuts such a powerful, enduring and undeniably Dwarven silhouette. He is so staunch and individual, and of course Graham is such a fine actor that the character oozes presence, making him a joy to watch.

Richard Taylor,
Weta Workshop Design & Special Effects Supervisor

Graham McTavish's Dwalin is such a great second-in-command to Richard Armitage's Thorin. Dwalin isn't a leader like Thorin, but he's that rock-solid sergeant that you know you can depend upon and would follow anywhere. Graham has brought that power to Dwalin, an unrelenting loyalty to Thorin. That confidence in our leader permeates and filters down through the entire Company. It's impossible to tear your eyes away from it when it's working between these two actors. They're incredible.

Mark Hadlow, Actor, Dori

Nori and Dwalin have an interesting relationship. When they first meet in Bag End Dwalin thinks he can bully him, but it doesn't work that way with Nori. They have a disagreement over a chicken that Nori tries to steal off him and from then on, if Dwalin catches Nori's eye, he glares at him. Dwalin, being the war chief, respects courage and fight in a person and Nori won't back down from anyone. He stands up to Dwalin and, if there's a fight, he's a Dwarf who can handle himself, so over the course of the films this mutual respect forms between the two. If there's a fight about to go down, Nori's going to make sure he's next to Dwalin. They're very different, but I think over time Nori comes to look up to him.

Jed Brophy, Actor, Nori

Graham McTavish has a great sense of humour and we get along well, so we had some fun playing the relationship between Dwalin and Bombur. Bombur looks up to Dwalin because he's such a big, fierce, powerful leader, but he's also totally scared of him. There are a couple of funny moments when Dwalin gives Bombur the evils for whatever reason and Bombur is super-intimidated.

Stephen Hunter, Actor, Bombur

'I really love the strength that comes through in every aspect of Dwalin's character.'

I knew this was going to be a physical show, and particularly for Dwalin. The second call I made upon getting the job, after my wife, was to my personal trainer. I spent three months getting into the right physical shape for what lay ahead, and continued that in New Zealand with stunt training and my own regime. I focused on hard cardio work, keeping my heart rate up and doing dynamic exercise that was not all about lifting weights. I needed to have stamina, flexibility, and be injury free. I'm glad to say that, apart from a tweak on my hamstring running across the South Island, I got through it without incident, or passing out!

Graham McTavish, Actor, Dwalin

Dwalin's prosthetics consist of a silicone facial appliance and piece that creates the character's bald scalp. His foam latex head cowl and ears go on first, then the silicone head appliance goes on over the top; the reason being, if we had cast the entire cowl and scalp in silicone it would have weighed three kilos. Most of our silicone faces themselves weigh in the order of 400 grams, which is a lot to carry attached to your face all day along with everything else the Dwarves wear.

Jason Docherty,
Weta Workshop Special Make-up and Prosthetics Supervisor

I think the tattoos on Dwalin's arms are rougher than those on his head because he got them when he was a teenager. As we see by comparing how he looks in the flashback scenes versus his regular appearance, while he already has his arm tattoos, he doesn't get the tattoos on his head until later in life, when he's lost his hair. They're a little more sophisticated, so I think that works.

Tami Lane, Prosthetics Supervisor

Movement Coaching Dwarves

For a painter, getting to work with the very best paints is a joy and it is only going to improve what you paint. In exactly the same way, working as I do in motion coaching, it is a pleasure to work with such incredible actors. While I teach, I also learn from them every day. Through the years, I've come to appreciate how important it is to be connected to your body – it's your vehicle of expression. An actor learns to drive their vehicle like a person learns to drive their car. It's the device they use to express themselves, because emotions affect our entire bodies, even at a cellular level.

The body can be such an effective tool when used with understanding. An exercise we go through is to first establish the blank canvas, which is reached when we identify those unconscious habits, ticks or blocks that we all have. I keep myself a little separate from the actors when I'm working with them. I don't socialize with them outside of work because by maintaining that distance I can be objective with them about their performance and give them honest feedback. I observe them very closely and, going back to the car analogy again, help them fine tune their engine like a mechanic. We look for those blocks or tensions, those habits, and in calling those out we can choose to remove them from the performance if we want to.

We begin with exercises, starting slowly, gaining trust and going back to sitting and breathing. We learn how to breathe again, how to calm the mind and let thoughts dissipate, becoming completely open, receiving energy, but not holding onto it, blocking or guarding. We go from sitting to standing. You can see a lifetime of habits and conditioning in the act of standing up, so we go through the exercise of standing together. I guide them through it, identifying those unconscious controls that will otherwise creep into a performance and together we break them down. We do the same with coming from the floor to a stand, rolling – all in an effort to get to that neutral body.

Once we have explored a range of movement and played, I have a sense of who they are. Often there will be little organic things that happen in these exercises that are beautiful and worth filing away to bring back into the performance later. The point is not coming in with a preconceived notion of who that character is, but of taking them back to nothing, clearing the slate and building the character from there.

One of the key things we have done is explore and establish the movement footprint and parameters for each race in Middle-earth. Dwarves are gut-driven. They lead with their core. It's as if their core is an iron ball.

They have a deep-rooted connection to the ground. They work with their hands. They're tactile and, like old-school Jazz musicians, they have a deep, deep soul. When a Dwarf shakes your hand, it's a real connection that they are making with you. There's no nonsense in their society.

Dwarves carry a shroud of weight about them that is the weight of experience. They ingest the world in an unfiltered way and with great heart, but this means they carry everything they experience. It's not in their nature to shrug things off, so they hold on to grudges and memories. They aren't quick to trust other races.

Dwarves are a proud people. They are short in stature but they feel no need to be tall. Their power comes from rooting themselves down so that everything they do feels as if they are towing an anchor. They're like little tanks. There isn't a flippant move that a Dwarf makes. They don't fling their weapons, but power them through every move, leading from their cores.

Rhythm is something we work with a lot and use to define characters. Every rhythm evokes a feeling and if we can't find a rhythm in a character then it can create a sense of unease, something we have exploited with our Orcs. Among the Dwarves, it begins with an idea, draws back into an intention, expresses in an action as they drive forward, unfolding in four counts, and concludes when they land.

Terry Notary, Movement Coach

Right: Movement Coach Terry Notary works with actors Graham McTavish (top) and Jed Brophy (middle and bottom, wearing oversized Dwarf boots, the increase in size being all the more apparent without the rest of the costume).

'Appreciate how important it is to be connected to your body – it's your vehicle of expression.'

FILI AND KILI

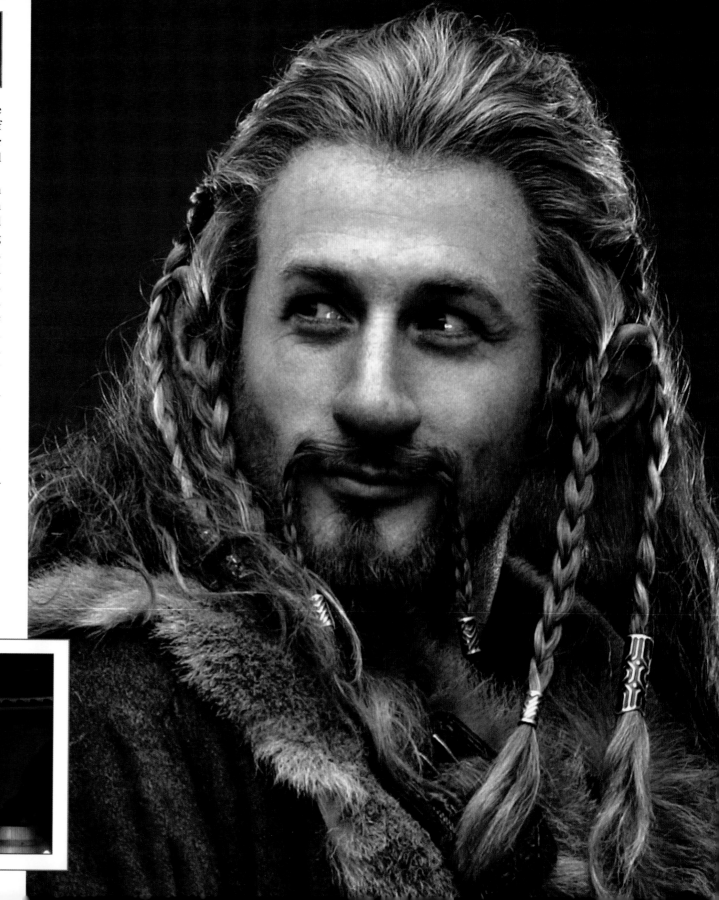

Along with Ori, Fili and Kili are the youngest of the Dwarves in the Company. Brothers in the royal line of Durin and nephews to Thorin, the pair is played in Peter Jackson's adaptation of *The Hobbit* by Dean O'Gorman and Aidan Turner.

Too young to be able to recall the burning and destruction of their people's home in Erebor, Fili and Kili have grown up as princes in exile, nurtured by tales of lost glories and grandeur. Emboldened by their uncle's dreams of reclaiming the Mountain and the treasure and pride of the Dwarves, they join the Quest with a sense of adventure and youthful exuberance, perhaps naïve to the dangers that await them, but nonetheless well prepared as trained fighters and outdoorsmen. Though born to a royal heritage, neither are precious or boastful, but take pleasure in simpler things such as the camaraderie they share with their fellow Dwarves and Bilbo on the Quest, and are never too proud to lend their able hands to any task that might be required of them. If anything, the young Dwarves represent a generation unburdened by the sense of loss that weighs on their elders.

Fili and Kili are Thorin's closest family – Fili, who will inherit the kingdom should Thorin fall, and Kili, the youngest of Thorin's sister Dis's children. With no sons of his own, Fili and Kili are his family. Thorin is tough on Fili, and overly protective of Kili. He sees their hope and their ambition, their youth. It's a great driving force for him, to seek out something to bequeath for their future.

Richard Armitage, Actor, Thorin

Dwarves are small. We're almost cute – there's no getting around that – but it will be interesting to see how our size is received in terms of still being taken seriously and being intimidating. When the camera is in close with us it is easy to forget that we're quite short, but go wide or throw in a human or Elf and suddenly there's the risk it becomes funny. I am curious to see how audiences react to the Dwarves.

On one level, we're funny little guys, but on another, we've won wars and are actually pretty dangerous. In the fight training we've done we're encouraged to be quite aggressive and to make big sweeping moves. We're like pit bull terriers, short but really tough. It should give someone pause to think, 'I'm not going to mess with him.'

Gimli was often played for laughs, which can be done when he's one Dwarf in a cast of different races, but we're an entire party of Dwarves. There's got to be humour and I'm sure they'll take advantage of the size issue to find some, but at the same time it's important that when we're doing our thing it comes across that an army of Dwarves is something to be taken very seriously. Don't laugh at the Dwarves because they will mess you up.

Dean O'Gorman, Actor, Fili

It's tough being a Dwarf in Middle-earth. It's exhausting. They're basically on the run for four months, being chased and captured. With each thing that happens, as a viewer you think, 'Oh man, what's gonna happen to them next?' They get chased around and for all the times they get caught, they're really not wanted anywhere.

Aidan Turner, Actor, Kili

Poor Aidan had to go on tape with us in London so many times as the filmmakers loved him so much. He was up for so many roles and it was just a matter of 'which one?' Aidan is fearless. He came in full of confidence and Peter knew that he wouldn't be intimidated by the epic scale of these movies. No matter how many times actors told me they weren't nervous about auditioning for Peter, within a couple of seconds of being in the room with him I could see they were visibly so: it dawns on them that they are in the presence of an icon. Now that's no good to Peter if you see him as that rather than the director with whom you need to roll up your sleeves and get to work, so actors with Aidan's courage are essential.

Amy Hubbard, UK Casting Director

'I have to wonder after these films come out whether there might not be a sudden rise in braiding and beard decoration?'

Dwalin's relationships with Fili and Kili are typically avuncular. He admires their courage but wants to temper some of their youthful enthusiasm.

Graham McTavish, Actor, Dwalin

Fili and Kili both began with forehead prosthetics, but these were cut back and back because they aged the characters too much. It was important these young Dwarves remain open-faced and easy to relate to, particularly for younger audience members. Their larger noses also became reduced with each make-up test pass, again because the larger noses they began with made them look too old or slightly grotesque.

Such character-filled faces are something we can accept in the older Dwarves because as we age our noses and ears do get larger and as a species we are used to seeing this. Fili and Kili had to be young and handsome, leaving it up to the actors to bring character through their performances.

Peter King, Make-up and Hair Designer

Beards are already in at the moment, but I have to wonder after these films come out whether there might not be a sudden rise in braiding and beard decoration?

Dean O'Gorman, Actor, Fili

Dwarves are a proud and noble people who were at one time very wealthy. They carry jewellery and ornate plaiting in their beards as an expression of their pride and a way of holding on to their lineage. What is so nice about the visual journey we see these characters embark upon is the contrast between how they start and how they end up by the time they are closing in on the Lonely Mountain. They begin looking very ornate and proud, but their journey humbles and batters them and you see this in the gradual disintegration of their beard and hair dos.

But what is interesting is how that is expressed across the whole thirteen, because it isn't the same for each of them. Fili and Kili, for example, represent the next generation and it is telling that they don't have the big ornate, blinged-out beards of their fathers. They have a different attitude and aren't as burdened down by the loss that gnaws at Thorin and Gloin and the other Dwarves who are more obsessed with the gold. They haven't decorated themselves as heavily, like kids who can't see the reason for wearing shoes into a restaurant. They're not holding on to an old grudge. They're freer spirits.

There is an astonishing amount of thought that goes into every decision. Peter, Fran and Philippa all have incredible eyes for detail. The slope of the cut of a piece of costume or a flick of hair – all these details say things about the characters and they are aware of them, so nothing happens according to chance. It is why our show-and-tell sessions with them are so important, because they offer a chance for us to bring our characters in front of the filmmakers and have them react and tweak them before they end up in front of camera.

Peter King, Make-up and Hair Designer

Representing the old guard alongside Balin and Dwalin are brothers Oin and Gloin, distant cousins to Thorin. Hard of hearing Oin and fiery Gloin are loyal retainers, but also self-made Dwarves who value their independence as much as their wealth. Father to Gimli from *The Lord of the Rings*, Gloin is played by Peter Hambleton, while Oin is John Callen, both well-known New Zealand theatre and screen actors.

We were looking for the unique skills that each Dwarf contributed to Thorin's group, with each of us being specialists in some area like a shorter, hairier Ocean's Eleven. We needed simple points of difference for each Dwarf, and these often became jumping off points for character development. The writers had the idea that Gloin might be the Company's finance guy. I thought perhaps he kept records of their accounting, but then the notion that he had actually personally invested in it

was suggested, and I thought that would be great. Now he's not just keeping tabs, but it's actually his money being spent.

I spun ideas around that notion – was Gloin entrepreneurial? There might never be a scene in which we saw him doing accounts or anything like that, but the attitude would come through. It's true, he is very focused on the financial reward that looms at the end of their Quest, that being the treasure, but for me the thing that matters is the particular kind of person he is. What came through was a character who takes things very seriously. He's not boring or a stuffy accountant type – he's actually very fiery and passionate, and while the gold matters, equally important to him is the history and heritage that they are trying to reclaim. Gloin could quote the history of his people line and verse and carries it very close to his heart. What rose from that was the notion that Gloin feels it is his role to share that history with the younger Dwarves who have had less exposure to their heritage.

I am hoping what comes across is that while Gloin is in one way a very buttoned up character, there's a generosity to him that is expressed in other ways. This whole thing is about legacy for him, and restoring what his generation have lost for the next. It's very clear in this script that he has his wife and son at home who he loves above all else and is very proud of them. He wants to reclaim the power, wealth and dignity of the Dwarves for those who have never experienced it.

My sense of Gloin is that he is a good sort. He can be a terrible grump and a bit of a drag at times, but when it comes down to it he is staunch and will stick up for what counts. He is older and not as fit as some of the others, but he gives every bit as good as he gets.

Peter Hambleton, Actor, Gloin

I reread *The Hobbit* when the opportunity for auditions came up, and was reminded how very thinly sketched most of the Dwarves are. They are distinguished primarily by the colour of their hoods and the role that they play within the group. Peter, Fran and Philippa came up with some thoughts for how these personalities might be extrapolated and defined but very generously invited us to offer our own to the creative process, so, in discussion with Philippa I drew up a document with a whole bunch of ideas based around the notion of Oin as a fire-lighter and the uncle of Gimli.

Among the ideas the writing team came up with was the thought that my character might be a bit deaf. That gave me a whole range of things that I could think about. They gave us indicators of status; of history, of occupation, and in my case being that much older than almost everybody else.

What we ended up with was a character comprised of a mixture of suggestions from different people, including the actor playing my on-screen brother Gloin, Peter Hambleton. If we were brothers then there might be some similarities in this aspect and that aspect. He might, for instance, sometimes need to draw things to my attention on account of my deafness, or wake me to the advance of an enemy, or generally keep an eye on me because I'm a little older than the majority of the Company. Those were some of the little touches that help fill out a character, whether they are picked up or not as individual character notes through the films.

It was decided that while Oin was a warrior, he was less that now than a thinking person. He might be an apothecary, which I thought was great. Could I carry with me a bag in which I would keep little samples of things, bottles of potions of various kinds? If anyone was injured or sick Oin would be called upon. It would make sense to have someone like that on a quest of this sort where misadventure was a near certainty. There was also the notion of Oin being an old soothsayer, which some might consider to be a load of rubbish. Gloin references this when he speaks up in Bag End, telling them that, 'Oin has seen the portents and the portents say that it is time.' 'Yes,' says Oin, 'the birds have been seen flying back to Erebor, therefore we must go too.' These things combined and gradually we found we were talking about a character with a purpose. Oin has come from his laboratory where he has a vast store of herbs and minerals that he grinds and mixes into medicines to be the team medic, but he's also up for the punch-up if it comes to that.

During the practice for what would happen when shooting, we found that Balin developed a manner that suggested his character was in fact a bit older than Oin, though in life I am eight years older than Ken Stott, so we repositioned Oin and made him a little more physically active to preserve the distinction, permitting Balin the space to be the senior of the Company. What that meant was that despite being referred to by one of the other characters as an 'Old Dwarf', I found myself up the front in battles when I had anticipated being towards the back observing the melee and perhaps having a less active participation.

Oin's purpose and indeed his priorities become evident when we get deeper into the story and he has to make a choice between the Quest and his calling. It affirms his role in the group as a healer, and is done in a way that isn't soppy, but minutes later he's back in the fray and giving it all he's got.

John Callen, Actor, Oin

Dwarves fight and bicker among themselves loudly over everything and anything, and everyone has an opinion they want to voice on any decision being made, but when it comes to it, they look after and depend upon each other. No one else will, after all. They have to present a united front and loyalty and honour are very important to them.

There are big hearts beating inside these little people. We've all got our own particular flavour of being ornery little bastards, but it's because Dwarves do everything so wholeheartedly. Whether we see it on camera or not, I know Gloin misses his family dearly. For him this Quest is about passing things on, and indeed we see a literal passing of things between the generations in our trilogy and *The Lord of the Rings*. Gimli carries Gloin's axe, or perhaps it's the other way around? Right there is an example of Gloin's passion for heritage that will endure beyond his presence on the screen.

Peter Hambleton, Actor, Gloin

There is a story that Balin tells about the loss of our treasure. Our treasure is not just something that has a monetary or materialistic value. It is our heritage. We have lost that. Fili, Kili and some of the younger Dwarves are going along for a rich boy's adventure, but I think that Oin knows what the importance of it is before they even go. His investment in this Quest is as an older man wanting to regain that heritage.

That said, I think he and his brother have a few bob in it.

John Callen, Actor, Oin

With the help of the experts, John and I had it confirmed that in all likelihood Gloin and Oin could have been around to witness the loss of the Lonely Mountain to Smaug. We decided that while Thorin, Balin and Dwalin experienced the attack first hand, we might have been elsewhere, perhaps on business, but we came home to witness the aftermath. It is very real to us and raw, and it burns us as much as it does our cousins, even if we weren't there to see it personally when the Dragon came.

The homelessness that resulted saw us fall back upon what we were good at and had been doing – trading. That's likely where Gloin and Oin's money comes from. I can imagine Gloin in the role of negotiator, making trades with other cultures and being well travelled. He's not a Dwarf who finds it hard to make a living so I don't think he has had to go without comforts since, but the loss of his home and heritage still gnaws at him.

Peter Hambleton, Actor, Gloin

They spark off each other at first, but I believe Dori respects Gloin's vigilance when it comes to money. Gloin is all over the Company's finances and very mindful of any misuse, which appeals to Dori's fastidious nature. He approves and admires Gloin's accountancy. In some ways there is a certain similarity in their situations; Gloin and Oin, and Dori, Nori and Ori.

Mark Hadlow, Actor, Dori

I don't normally wear lenses but I did for a short film a number of years ago, so I wasn't in unfamiliar territory wearing brown ones for Gloin. I have blue eyes and we wanted to make the connection with Gimli whose are brown. The application of eye drops helped alleviate issues associated with being in dusty, windy or hot environments, or if we were in a set with a lot of plant material. We had a wonderful lens technician, William Perriam, a qualified optician with particular expertise in contacts, so I was in good hands at all times. We were able to dispense with them in shots that weren't close enough to discern my eye colour, but when we needed them William would pop them in and out for me. It was easier that way than me doing it myself, particularly with the hands. I hope the brown eyes sing out.

Peter Hambleton, Actor, Gloin

One of the things I do in life is read talking books, and one I recall reading a couple of years ago was called *Deaf Sentence*, written by David Lodge. Lodge was himself a university lecturer who was losing his hearing, and in the book he relays the astute observation that if someone has full sight and goes blind, everyone regards it as terribly tragic, but if you're going deaf people think it's incredibly funny. It's an interesting observation, and it is for the most part very true. We make light of it in these movies, but the truth of it is it is very isolating and Oin is sometimes isolated. Gloin feels he has to watch out for him, so in a way it helps show their affection as brothers.

John Callen, Actor, Oin

'Our treasure is not just something that has a monetary or materialistic value. It is our heritage.'

'When Thorin does things that aren't in their best interests, it is deeply troubling to Gloin and difficult for him to process.'

Oin and Gloin are there for each other when it counts. John Callen and I talked about how we might play their relationship and while it was appropriate that Gloin look after Oin on account of his hearing problem, we didn't want their interaction to become dominated by the notion of a fussy younger brother looking after a doddery older one. That's not who these two are. Gloin does look out for Oin, but more in the sense of naturally gravitating to his brother's side when the chips are down and they need to have each other's backs. If they spend too much time together, like many brothers, they tend to fight.

Gloin and Oin are also cousins to the royal line. They're high ranking, but a few steps sideways of the throne. Gloin is upper middle management and very proud of his status. He has a deep reverence for Thorin and takes everything he says very seriously. When Thorin does things that aren't in their best interests, it is deeply troubling to Gloin and difficult for him to process.

Peter Hambleton, Actor, Gloin

Gloin and Gimli are as different as my father and I am. I spent a lot of time watching *The Lord of the Rings* and absorbing as much as I could, but it would have been wrong to treat Gloin or any of the Dwarves of Thorin's Company as literal retreads of Gimli, and fortunately no one wanted to do that. There are clearly signalled connections between the father and son, eyes and hair colour among them, but both are unique individuals.

Peter Hambleton, Actor, Gloin

In my research in to what an apothecary did, I discovered that they assumed the role of midwife. Peter Hambleton and I shared a little joke when I suggested Oin was probably there delivering the child at the birth of Gimli. He said, 'Yes John, that would explain a lot because you probably dropped him.'

John Callen, Actor, Oin

Left: John Rhys-Davies played Gimli, son of Gloin in The Lord of the Rings, *introducing the world to Peter Jackson's interpretation of J.R.R. Tolkien's Dwarves.*

DIGITAL DWARVES

On a project like *The Hobbit*, it's our responsibility at Weta Digital to provide anything and everything that has to be created or replaced digitally. As much as possible is shot live in-camera, but given the size, scope and subject matter of these movies, there's a huge computer-generated component. What can be photographed only ends up being part of the picture Peter wants to create on the screen, so we do the rest. Sets may need to be extended to convey the true scope of an environment, environmental or magical effects may need to be applied to scenes, characters may need to be augmented or extended, performances enhanced beyond what could be done live, or there may be entirely digital characters and creatures that need to be created from scratch.

For various reasons, such as a character needing to do something that they couldn't accomplish practically or in order to control the performance in a certain way, we have created digital versions of all the characters in the movies. We have digital versions of all the Dwarves because you never know when they'll be required to do something that can't be achieved with an actor in that kind of physical situation.

Most of the time these doubles are not required to sustain a close-up, but we have found that it's easier conceptually to build to the highest level because then we have a real benchmark for everyone involved to understand. We can be confident that the model will work out no matter what is asked of it. It's much harder to go back and build from scratch if later we find we need a close-up of a character and what we had didn't hold up.

Joe Letteri, Weta Digital Senior Visual Effects Supervisor

We have made digital doubles in the past, including for *The Lord of the Rings*, but on that project they were more or less generic. They looked like a character, but used a common facial system. None was specific to a character's performance in the same way they are now. We have done full scans and turntables of every character and captured their individual facial facts – getting them to sit in a chair and go through a hundred poses so that we know what their facial characteristics are and how they move. This information is reflected in their digital doubles, so they don't just look like their namesakes; they act like them too, and with good reason. We've had a few full-frame digital doubles, particularly in scenes involving significant action.

Eric Saindon, Weta Digital Visual Effects Supervisor

Above: James Ogle scans a head cast of actor Jed Brophy, reference that will form the basis for a digital version of his character Nori. Below: The unposed fully digital double of Balin.

We have used performance capture a lot to populate scenes. If we need a whole lot of Orcs, or perhaps if we have wide shots of the Dwarves in the Stone Giant sequence, for example, where they're up on the ledge, then we'll use digital versions with movement provided by performance capture. It ensures we get the right physicality in our characters despite not being able to film a shot like that on a stage or location. If our characters are teetering on a huge, moving slab of rock then there is no such location to be filmed practically, so performance capture is a great tool by which we can bring the actors' performances into an otherwise entirely digital shot or environment and have it be in keeping with their live action work.

We capture specific actions for each of the characters for each scene when we're doing these sessions, but while we're there we also gather alternate takes and generic motion so that we are building a library of material to draw upon later.

Joe Letteri, Weta Digital Senior Visual Effects Supervisor

SCALE COMPOSITES

The idea of doing scale composites was pioneered in *The Lord of the Rings*. Forced perspective is an old trick to give an illusion of different scales in our characters. We would film Elijah Wood as Frodo and Sir Ian McKellen as Gandalf in the same pass, but cheat Elijah to hobbit scale by positioning him further from camera to make him look smaller. By doing it on multiple passes and using different scales, we got it to work quite well all those years ago.

We've had to extend the concept and find ways to achieve it in stereo, because *The Hobbit* was filmed in 3D. Some of the one-camera perspective tricks that we may have been able to get away with in the past don't work any more, because now we have two cameras. We've had to either do multiple stereo shoots at different levels and blend them together or basically re-track and re-scale everything by taking elements off of the original play and scaling them up and re-tracking them in the proper dimensions. Most of this work has been the province of our compositing department, which handles both the 3D and 2D manipulation of photographed images. As far as the scale issues regarding stereo in anything we generate digitally, that's

relatively straightforward because we can simply make the Dwarves and hobbits be there, their physical real-world scale. Digital doubles can be any size we need them to be so we just build them to proper scale to begin with.

In some cases Peter has been shooting two different scales on two different sets at the exact same time. We have used what we call a slave-cam. It's a motion-control rig that is driven by the camera that is shooting the primary scene. It scales the camera's movements up or down and applies them to the second camera filming on an adjacent green screen so that they match perfectly. For example, for a scene in Bag End we have filmed our full-sized hero Dwarf actors on the set, but treated them as if they were smaller so that Gandalf, who was being shot at the same time against a green screen next door, towered over them at his appropriate size. We shot a motion-controlled rig that moved exactly the same way as the camera on the set. The move was scaled to be one-third smaller on Gandalf's camera, meaning the movement appeared proportionally correct to the wizard's size because he was a normal-sized human being. We had markers along the set with tennis balls

that were at Dwarf-scale size so Sir Ian knew where his eye line needed to be directed at specific points in the shot and where he had dialogue with Dwarf characters. This was all pre-choreographed and then the two were shot together with Peter directing them simultaneously. It required some set up but allowed for very fluid directing.

We've been working to integrate all these techniques into the live-action filmmaking process, rather than coming at the end of the process after everything is shot and trying to figure out how we're going to make it work. Now we're there at the beginning and trying to figure out how to integrate it while Peter's shooting.

Joe Letteri, Weta Digital Senior Visual Effects Supervisor

We have made a point of really separating Bifur, Bofur and Bombur from the rest of the Dwarves. Our family isn't necessarily related to the rest. We're a little bit rougher around the edges, aesthetically.

James Nesbitt, Actor, Bofur

Bifur, Bofur and Bombur are the only Dwarves not linked to Thorin by heritage. Being of a different clan and class, they represent the average working Dwarf; warriors, craftsmen, musicians and friends, defined by their simple tastes and lighter manners, except perhaps poor Bifur. Played by William Kircher, he suffers the lingering effects of a rather pronounced and unmistakable war injury.

The optimistic trio are led by James Nesbitt's Bofur, with Stephen Hunter as Bombur beneath a mountain of mass-adding prosthetics and costume.

Bofur is protective of his family. He looks after Bifur because someone has to. Bifur's an idiot with an axe in his head – it's like having a very sophisticated chimpanzee in the family. He's always trying to interpret or apologize for Bifur's lack of grace and lack of communication. He also has to look after Bombur because he's just so huge, but he looks after Bilbo a great deal in the film too. I think he's the first Dwarf that really thinks, 'Actually, we should give this guy a chance.' I think he understands other people's plights. What I like about him the most is that he has a good soul, which is not what one would think of the Dwarves because they tend to just believe in themselves and their own business. Bofur is perhaps a less common Dwarf because he can appreciate other people's issues.

James Nesbitt, Actor, Bofur

Bombur doesn't say much, so he's essentially a visual character. As we were looking for ways to define him his size obviously played a big part. We had a prosthetic design from Weta Workshop with that big strangler beard, his bald spot and chin. That all helped say something about this character and gave us somewhere to start. I looked for things to add as we went along and kept discovering new things about him.

One of the big questions was, 'Why is he actually along on the Quest?' He trips over, he eats a lot, stuff keeps happening to him, so why is he with the group? It turns out he's actually quite a fierce fighter. I was enjoying the fight training and so it felt like a good fit to have Bombur actually be a bit of a weapon. There are some awesome comical moments, but he's actually useful and he proves himself in a fight.

I wanted to flesh out other parts of Bombur's history and personality too, though with a cast this big there's only so much that makes it on screen. A lot of the back story stuff would just be too complicated to portray without explanation, and there isn't time for that.

Something we do see is that Bombur loves to cook and loves to eat. He's passionate about food, which was easy to play because I like food too! If he has to go hungry he gets grumpy, but essentially he's a silent type of character, so what we learn about Bombur is mostly what we see him express physically.

Stephen Hunter, Actor, Bombur

For a nanosecond upon seeing Bifur's design for the first time I was a little shocked and concerned, but only for an instant. We were all sat in a room together, the full Dwarf cast, and Peter unveiled our character designs, one at a time. I saw the axe in Bifur's head and reacted, but then almost immediately my mind started racing ahead and I was thinking, 'Wait a minute, if there are going to be thirteen Dwarves and one of them has an axe in his head, I want to be that guy because he's got something that is immediately unique.' It was a genius idea and became the source of so much that we would later build around his character.

I spent some time researching those kinds of head injuries and what effects they can have on survivors. Working with the writers, the notion of him only speaking in Dwarvish came about. That's Khuzdul, and Bifur speaking it established itself as one of his defining characteristics.

We had a scholar in England, David Salo, working on the language and creating phrases for me, and dialogue coaching to get the pronunciation correct. It's almost like Germanic or Arabic, but quite guttural and hard sounding. I had a long list of phrases that were translated for me, but we also came up with things that were sent off as requests. The scripts didn't necessarily contain much Khuzdul, but the films are full of it. It's peppered throughout so it can be heard as Bifur is busy doing things.

William Kircher, Actor, Bifur

'Gelekh d'ashrud bark.
Time to swing an axe.'

Bifur is an old warrior. We never really defined exactly when he received his head injury, but in my own imagined back story I thought he might have got it when the Orcs took the mines. We're a displaced people so our history is a story of loss. Like a grudge, I imagined that he had carried it ever since, and in everything he does he's always hoping to cross paths again with the Orc that gave him the axe in his head.

In the meantime he has been a bit of a lost soul. When we first meet Bifur he has been gathered up and dragged along on this quest by Bofur and Bombur, who are his cousins. They were probably worried about him, out there fending for himself. They bring him along, but he was a bit bewildered and didn't really know what's going on to begin with. That changed as we got into the story and it's part of the arc that I've so enjoyed playing, that we see Bifur find himself and a sense of purpose and focus along the way. That's true of much of the Company. We started off in Bag End as the dirty baker's dozen, which is what we called ourselves, and we really were, but the Quest changes each of us and turns us into something else. Bifur is drawn out and he becomes more than he was. He's not a leader exactly, but certainly he's the first one into a fight, or to jump up and get into action.

What a great thing it has been for an actor like me to be able to be part of such a long-running project and be able to live in a character and develop him as much as we have been able to on these films.

William Kircher, Actor, Bifur

'Nê ikrid ûdar!
Never trust a wizard!'

'Each of these Dwarves took shape individually, but with Peter very cognizant of how they would work as a group.'

I knew very little about this project when we first started talking about it except that it was a Peter Jackson film based on *The Hobbit*, which in itself is enough to convince anyone. There were no scripts; there was no understanding of what we would look like. When I met Peter in London, he touched briefly on the fact that there would be this extraordinary look, there would be prosthetics and all sorts of things involved, but I didn't really know anything. The book doesn't go into great detail about each of the individual Dwarves or describe them, so I had no idea what to expect. When I got to New Zealand and we started going through the process of the first fittings for prosthetics and costume, I realized it was going to be slightly more intense and detailed and complex than I had imagined.

We went through many different looks in terms of prosthetics. When the first round of prosthetics were tested, everyone agreed that the look was too harsh. Through rehearsal at that stage we had decided that Bofur was an optimistic, friendly character that an audience could side with. The character didn't come across that way with the first prosthetic design, but we went through a refining process and eventually found a look with more of me coming through. Bofur had my voice, but it was important to also see more of my face than the first prosthetic permitted because the filmmakers had cast people in response to how they felt about us. If that is covered then we've been lost. The later prosthetics were softer and less obscuring so they worked much better in that way.

James Nesbitt, Actor, Bofur

James Nesbitt brought a jovial cheekiness to the character and too much prosthetic build up on his face would only hinder expression of those qualities. In the end he retained a small forehead appliance and nose, but it was much reduced.

It all highlights the importance of the experimentation phase when it comes to make-up. We went through a few iterations and by the end had found the perfect quirky mix of prosthetics, the actor's natural charm and looks, hat, beard and hair that created this memorable and original character.

Each of these Dwarves took shape individually, but with Peter very cognizant of how they would work as a group. It was critical that they all be distinct, and yet function as an ensemble, complementing each other when brought together, which they did in the end. I can remember the day we brought them all together as a full assemblage of thirteen for the first time. It was great.

Peter King, Make-up and Hair Designer

Jimmy Nesbitt's reading for Bofur I'll never forget. He came in with a newspaper rolled up under his arm and did his Bofur audition: it was 'broadcast quality' and I just knew the filmmakers would love it. Normally we do two or three reads, maybe more, but Jimmy just arrived, whipped up the stairs to our casting room, nailed it in one, and shot off again to street level with his newspaper lodged in his armpit for the entire exercise. When he came back to meet Peter they didn't feel they needed to hear the read again – it was all there in that first read. He had prepped it in case, as he didn't quite believe me or his agent! No newspaper that time.

Amy Hubbard, UK Casting Director

As with everything and everyone on the project, there was a development period for Bifur's make-up. I loved the concept art for Bifur's look, but the first make-up test we did didn't really reflect what was so great about the design. His nose was too long, the axe too big and it just didn't look right. I remember going up to Philippa Boyens and pressing the tip of my nose back in and saying, 'I think we need to do this.' Fortunately that's the wonder and joy of this filmmaking process, because things evolve, so he got it in the end. Everyone learned and responded as they went along, so by the time we got into it Bifur was looking fantastic, the spitting image of that great concept art that I so loved, with the mad old rocker hairstyle.

William Kircher, Actor, Bifur

Bifur's hair kept changing all the way up till the last minute. We called him Elizabeth because of his dark hair with the shock of white that reminded me of Elizabeth Taylor. Like a number of the Dwarves with bigger hair, including Balin, Oin and Gloin, it's quite wiry. I have to say, the notion of embedding an axe in his head was pure Peter Jackson genius. It's a mad idea, really, but the look and individuality of the character that resulted is fantastic.

Peter King, Make-up and Hair Designer

I think Bofur is the most optimistic of the bunch. He enjoys the adventure rather than thinks of it as a quest. I don't think he has the emotional draw towards Erebor that drives Thorin and the rest; I think he's probably just gone out there on an adventure. I think he's there to keep morale up. He doesn't take things as seriously as the rest of them.

That's not to say he isn't serious when he needs to be. What should be a given about Dwarves is that they are fierce and they can fight, but if I was to send just two Dwarves to fight for me, of course one would be Thorin, but the other one I would choose would be Bofur. While Thorin might have all the gilded, beautiful weaponry and a lifetime of training in battle, Bofur has the ability to pick up anything near him and smash it over someone's head. He's rough and ready.

James Nesbitt, Actor, Bofur

A lot of the relationships we had as characters were based on our relationships within the group of actors. Jimmy Nesbitt and I got close – Bombur hangs off Bofur. He looks up to him because he's older, wiser, more experienced, but also someone who can be relied upon as a friend, which was us.

Bombur is quite a naïve character. Family is important to Dwarves, so he follows Bofur and looks to him for direction. That's the reason he has come along, I think, but over the course of this journey Bombur has times of clarity and comes to understand what this is about.

It's also about finding a home. The idea of a proper home is very appealing because these guys are displaced. We're chasing this big dream, but we don't really know what it looks like. Bombur never saw the Lonely Mountain. Bofur has a better understanding of that than Bombur when we set out.

Bombur's a bit green to begin with and he doesn't comprehend exactly what he's got himself into, but he's strong and assured, so when it comes to it he's in there with the rest of them and can fight if he needs to.

Stephen Hunter, Actor, Bombur

'Bombur's a bit green to begin with and he doesn't comprehend exactly what he's got himself into, but he's strong and assured, so when it comes to it he's in there with the rest of them and can fight if he needs to.'

DWARF DOUBLES AND SUPPORT CREWS

On such a demanding project, no individual could do their job unsupported, and this is true as much for the lead cast as anyone else. As all involved came to appreciate, characters often found their voices in the form of choirs rather than solos. This was especially true of the Dwarves, with the main cast members each leading a group of performers who contributed their particular skills and physicality to that character.

Given how physical the act of playing Dwarves was, involving heavy costumes and prosthetics and bouts of sustained exertion and sometimes risk, each Dwarf had a stunt double. Furthermore, in order to achieve the height trickery that would convincingly portray each Dwarf as being around four to four-and-a-half feet tall, scale doubles were also employed, matching performances at three-quarters the scale.

Additionally there were the many other doubles and technical support crew, each contributing unique skills to help form the characters that audiences would come to love.

Dori isn't just one guy playing a character. He's a team of people who contribute to the character. There's a Team Dori. We have a president who is Jamie-Leigh MacIntosh – so good, so professional and with a take no prisoners attitude. Team Dori's secretary is Don Brooker and I'm the facade, but we're all members of Team Dori. I don't forget that. Jeremy Hollis did my stunt work and little Amy Brighton, who was so diligent about getting everything right, was our scale double Dori. All contributed to the character. The doubles studied me very well because I can see it in their performances. The only issue with Jeremy is that he is something like thirty years younger than me (so from that perspective I hate him).

There are others too. Richard Thurston looked after all our weapons and stuff, and Kate Trafford was Team Dori's dresser. It is very important for people to appreciate that a character like Dori is more than one person. I had three different make-up artists, beginning with the fabulous Sarah Rubano, then Ryk Fortuna, and finally Don Brooker. You can develop quite a strong relationship with your make-up artist when you're in the chair every day. Don has been unbelievable; he has been my mentor throughout this.

Attention to detail is what Dori is all about, and that fastidiousness is something every member of the team has taken to heart and made part of their work as well as the character's personality. Audiences owe the wonderful character that Dori is to the whole of the team. That is the message to take from this.

Mark Hadlow, Actor, Dori

One of my most treasured mementos from the shoot is the jacket given to me by my stunt double, Ike Hamon. It's like a US college jacket with *The Hobbit* logo, T.O. and the number '13' on the right sleeve. Thirteen was Oin's character number on call sheets. On the left sleeve it says Team Oin, and the names Callen, Hamon and Wilhoit, the three of us who all played Oin. Callie Wilhoit was the scale-double Oin and Ike had these jackets made for the three of us to wear. We were Team Oin and it truly speaks to the collaborative approach adopted for these characters.

Before we started shooting and were just in the training phase, we had dinner as a group. The three of us talked about who this character was. I let them know all the things that Peter, Fran and particularly Philippa and I had talked about.

We had many situations in the shoot where one group had to replicate what had been done by another, so, for example, the scale doubles had to match what we had filmed as actors in a different shot, or sometimes the reverse, and the scale doubles or stunties would have to match us. A number of times we were in the same situation, doing the same things, but my stunt double was doing things far more physically than I am capable of. Someone like Jed Brophy, who is a very fit guy, can do tremendous things for his age, but I'm older and my background is really as a stage performer.

There was one day when Peter told us, 'You're running along here. You're going up there and every step you take you are smashing an enemy character left, right and back.' I simply didn't have the physical strength to get up that ramp and do it in the way that he wanted. We tried it several times and then had Ike come in for a go at it, and he came in swinging my weapon around his head like I wouldn't even have had the nerve to try. He took off and dealt with those baddies magnificently, *bang*, got the shot. It was an instance in which you truly appreciate that the character is more physically capable than the actor, and that's why we have our stunt team counterparts. They're playing the same character and we work together closely to match our performances, but there are limits to our respective abilities.

Another day we had the scale doubles playing their parts. Callie was playing Oin in a battle on Second Unit. The direction to her was to really give this enemy a good seeing to and she went absolutely nuts on him. It was brilliant. There was I, looking at what she'd been doing and I was expected to match her for the close-ups. This is a woman who, well I doubt she's even thirty, and I'm sixty-five, trying to match the physicality and energy that she put into it. It was exhausting that day!

We all developed a great affection for one another as performers. Each of us ended up with a deal of respect for the talent and the work of the other two.

John Callen, Actor, Oin

Left: Dwarf doubles encounter local wildlife between takes in a remote and rugged corner of New Zealand's South Island.

Scale doubles casting was new to us. We have worked in the New Zealand film industry long enough to know the kind of people that are out there for traditional casting, but the large- and small-scale doubles that were required to pull off some of the Dwarf height trickery put us in uncharted territory.

We issued nationwide public casting calls, looking for very tall and very short people, which led to some hilarious lines outside the various venues. Many people responded. They had photographs taken and brief interviews during which we ascertained availability, fitness and general attitude. Out of this process we found a group of thirty who we brought to Wellington and put through what we called scale-double boot camp, with stunt training, performance training involving improv acting, and horse riding. All the while we were assessing how they gelled as a group and what each one was capable of, culminating in a filmed audition and interview at the end, which was submitted and the selections made. It was important that we gave them time to bond as a group.

The number one priority was making sure we had the right heights cast in our doubles to work in proportion to one another and replicate our full-size Dwarf actors relative to one another. If the actors playing Bofur and Bombur, for example, were a certain height in relation to each other, then were their scale-double counterparts similarly proportioned in relation to each other and the rest of the Dwarves? So, our candidates had to hit the heights in order to be eligible for consideration, but then also have the personality, ability et cetera.

The group we ended up with was made up of such great people. It was very rewarding to watch their development. They came from incredibly diverse backgrounds and some made huge changes to their lives, uprooting families, to be part of this project. We had a chef, policeman, nurse, full-time mother, gas fitter, and a boat builder. Sophie Gannon was at school and was our youngest. Callie Wilhoit was an opera singer and music teacher. Leroy Cross, our gas fitter, would go back to work at his trade whenever filming would break. I'm sure he missed the catered lunches!

Paul Randall, who was a tall scale double for many of our characters during *The Lord of the Rings*, was the only full-time tall scale double hired for *The Hobbit*. The others we brought in as needed for shorter stints. We have a tall file which ranges from 6'5" through to 7'. If you were only about 6'7" or 6'8" you were a bit of a shrimp! We weren't just looking for height either. Overall mass was important because being too slim doesn't work when being scaled. That's one of the reasons why Tall Paul, as we called Paul Randall, was so good. He's broad shouldered and strongly built, so he works perfectly as a scaled-up regular-proportioned person. The very tall women are usually the hardest to find.

Miranda Rivers, New Zealand Casting Director

From my perspective, I think it's important that all the crew is recognized for their phenomenal contributions to the success of these films and these characters. That includes all the weapon makers, costume makers, prosthetics teams and everyone. As actors, our talents are certainly what bring these characters to life and we all enjoy recognition for our part, but we've been able to do that because of what we've been given by this crew, so my appreciation for them is endless.

Mark Hadlow, Actor, Dori

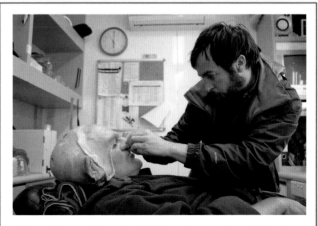

Above: Human Actor Mark Hadlow is transformed into the Dwarf Dori by Prosthetics Artist Don Brooker.

Rounding out the Company of thirteen huddled in Bilbo's kitchen on the eve of their Quest's commencement was the brotherly trio of Ori, Dori and Nori, three Dwarves divided by a common parentage, or at least some portion of common parentage. Played by English actor Adam Brown and New Zealanders Mark Hadlow and Jed Brophy, each of the delightfully distinct and argumentative Dwarves has joined for unique reasons. Nori had to leave town for unspecified reasons that likely have to do with his tendency to live outside the law. Thorin's expedition offers a convenient and potentially profitable escape, while his coddled younger brother Ori sees an opportunity to experience the wide world and be part of a true adventure. As the eldest, Dori feels it is his duty to protect his siblings, even if they aren't receptive to his unique style of nurturing.

'The three of us have the same mother but possibly different fathers.'

Adam Brown came in with a fully formed characterization that Peter, Fran and Philippa alighted on right away.

Amy Hubbard, UK Casting Director

I'm told the writers decided they needed a character like Ori after seeing my original audition for Bilbo! So although I'm not a Bilbo (is anyone other than Martin?!), I think it's fair to say the character of Ori was written specifically for me. From my perspective, this was a perfect way to develop a character...

In *The Fellowship of the Ring* Gandalf picks the Dwarves' record of their misfortunes in Moria from the hands of a corpse. The inference is that this was probably Ori lying there,

because in the books Gimli recognizes his handwriting. Early discussions about that led us to looking at Ori as the scribe of the group. As a result Ori's role within Thorin's Company became very different from the average axe-wielding Dwarf! Peter, Fran and Philippa wanted to push his sensitive side. He was the new recruit – naïve, young and innocent. We looked at images of young World War Two recruits for inspiration.

Peter is a huge *Dad's Army* fan (as am I) and I think there is a little bit of the character of Pike in Ori. He's sensitive about his food and mothered by his brother Dori, but oddly brave and determined to prove himself.

Adam Brown, Actor, Ori

Peter, Fran and Philippa had a dilemma. In the book of *The Hobbit* there are thirteen Dwarves in the Company of Thorin, but only four or five have anything to do or say. That would have been boring for the actors playing those parts and for the audience, so it was a pleasant surprise meeting with the writers and finding out how much work they had invested in establishing how the various Dwarf families differ who make up the group.

Our brotherhood – Dori, Nori and Ori – hasn't been living as a family. That was one surprise for me. Nori has been living rough because he's a kleptomaniac. He likes to steal things. He can't really help himself. If something's shiny and has a little bit of value to it, he finds it in his pocket. So, he hasn't been living with his two brothers and in fact he doesn't know much about his younger brother Ori at all. He's irritated by his older brother because Dori's like the mother hen and Nori doesn't like to be told what to do.

Peter, Fran and Philippa also came up with the idea that the three of us have the same mother but possibly different fathers. I'm not sure whether that's because we were wildly different looking as people or just a little bit of humour. They do have that kind of sense of humour!

This was the initial back story that we were presented with, but it was fairly broad and a lot of it was left for us to flesh out in terms of how we played the characters.

Nori has travelled a bit more than his brothers. I made the decision that he's already met Elves and that he has possibly traded with them. He's already met Orcs and Wargs. He hasn't fought Wargs before, but he certainly knows what they are, having lived rough.

So Nori has a bit more worldliness. That being said, he doesn't know a lot of the history of the Dwarves. He hasn't been that concerned with this, or with their pride as a culture. As a bit of a nomad, he's a product of them having lost their homeland and their hold on the crown, but it hasn't been on his mind. He's been living day to day. Consequently, he's very, very reticent to follow Thorin as King right away. He's quite happy going on the journey because there are lots of things he can pick up on the way. He isn't scared of it because he's been living this way most of his life, and, of course, there's lots of gold!

From that broad background we were given licence to be able to create a world within a world. We were given licence to make these characters our own.

Jed Brophy, Actor, Nori

Dori's two younger brothers are the most important things in his life. Family is everything. Even though Nori is a complete pain in the behind, thief, vagabond, rapscallion etc, Dori adores him and he is deeply protective of Ori. He worries for both of them all the time. None of the Dwarves would admit to it, but they're all vulnerable and need each other. Trying to look after his brothers is very stressful for Dori. There he is in the middle, trying to contain Nori, but bolster Ori and make sure he's alright.

We became very close as actors too. Jed Brophy has been a friend of mine for years, but Adam Brown became very close as well. Coming into each new scene in rehearsals, we'd discuss what we were doing as a group rather than individually. We called ourselves the Gloris – Ori, Dori and Nori. Adam brought a wonderful innocence and vulnerability to Ori, while Jed was a delightful tearaway.

The fussiness and eccentricities make it difficult for Dori to function sometimes. His attention to detail and finesse are as much a burden as an asset, but there's no questioning his loyalty where family is concerned. That is fierce.

All our characters have been taken from essentially interchangeable rhyming names in the book and turned into fully rounded individuals with stories and hopes and arcs. Some people may say, 'Oh no, this is not like the book,' but I say 'Good!' What's been added is a richness that I think will ultimately be so much more fulfilling to watch play out as a film series and ultimately, in my opinion, be its success.

Mark Hadlow, Actor, Dori

'As an actor there's nothing better than being given that freedom to improvise. It implies that Peter placed great trust in us as an ensemble.'

Nori is without doubt my favourite Dwarf, but then at Weta Workshop we have a great affection for Jed Brophy because we have worked with him on so many occasions. Jed is one of New Zealand's great actors. He throws himself with such enthusiasm and gusto into every role he plays, and has such a great attitude. I had the opportunity to catch up with him socially a year and a half into the shoot and he was just as energized, dynamic and thrilled by this opportunity as the day he started, and his grace is one of his great qualities. Jed has always been there to support us – any test, trial or public appearance of a character required, we have always been able to count on him to be there alongside us.

And I love his character design. It's a bold one. We took a risk with an extreme look, but I feel it works and clearly establishes something iconic for Nori, so there is no risk he will ever be mistaken for another Dwarf. He's a character that marches to his own beat, and that comes across as soon as you see him. And it's fun.

Richard Taylor,
Weta Workshop Design & Special Effects Supervisor

Nori is dodgy, but he's also very loyal. The writers came up with the notion that we fight within our family groups, and ours especially. I love that. There's always something going on with Dori telling Ori what to do and Nori getting in the middle of it, but when an outside force threatens we become very, very loyal and extremely determined. I think it's true for the Dwarves as a whole but especially for our family. It's part of the Dwarven genetic code. They might bicker constantly amongst themselves, but they'll present a united front if threatened.

Something else that Peter, Fran and Philippa did for us was give us great leeway. Quite often we would be in a scene where the focus was on Thorin and Balin, or Bilbo and Gandalf, but we're in the background doing things unscripted. Directing us, Peter did a great thing. He'd say, 'You deal with where you are in the room.' He'd let us come up with things to do in a scene that made sense for our characters, the way we imagined them, and as an actor there's nothing better than being given that freedom to improvise. It implies that Peter placed great trust in us as an ensemble.

So, my thinking was, Nori's first reaction on entering a space is to look for the exit. I don't know if the audience will pick up on that, but for me it was something to do that came straight from the character. Nori's first thought was, 'Is there something I can steal here?' and secondly, 'Where's the back door?' If there isn't a back door then, 'Where's the window?' That's the life I think Nori has been used to. He's not comfortable indoors, but he's probably quite comfortable in caves because that's where he's spent many a night.

Jed Brophy, Actor, Nori

Ori's view of the Quest changes over the course of the journey. Initially he just wanted to be part of an adventure and to escape his mothering brother, but he comes to appreciate the importance of the Quest at a larger level. Yet I think he soon realizes the importance of Erebor and of reclaiming his people's homeland.

Adam Brown, Actor, Ori

Adam is a joy to watch in his role of Ori. I find myself suppressing a giggle whenever I see him wander by in make-up. He's such an endearing character.

**Richard Taylor,
Weta Workshop Design & Special Effects Supervisor**

Bombur and Ori share a connection. I remember our very first day on set when we walked into Bag End. Adam Brown and I were looking at each other, waiting for someone to tap us on the shoulder and tell us it was just a big joke because we were the two out of all the cast who had the lightest working history. This was a really big thing for us both! Ori and Bombur, a bit like Adam and me, are both naïve and a little unprepared for what's coming, but they rise to the challenge of the journey.

Stephen Hunter, Actor, Bombur

When we began, I'm not sure Dori really wanted to go on the Quest. Thorin and his family are a bit removed from the rest of the Dwarves because they're of the old guard – they lived in Erebor. Our family is the next generation and we're not royalty. We've been out in the real world making a living and just coping. Thorin is removed from that. He's of a different time and he wants that back, but he's unproven. I think Dori had grave doubts about Thorin, and he certainly had an issue with Bilbo's seemingly pointless inclusion, but he also doubted the whole point of the Quest. It was Ori's enthusiasm for the adventure that I think compelled him to do it. He went along with it out of obligation to begin with, but in retrospect he's probably delighted that he did.

I've been imagining Dori's life outside of this Quest and I think Dori bakes. I imagine him cooking at home, but also probably owning a restaurant in a village. Ori waits on tables and does the dishes. Dori supervises and acts the Maitre D'. There's probably some long-suffering Dwarf chef who puts up with all Dori's fussing and micro-management. It's a wonderful place and people book months in advance to get a table. I can imagine that Nori turns up from time to time to scavenge a free meal or hide and catch an earful from his brother.

Mark Hadlow, Actor, Dori

As the uptight members of our respective families, Dori and Gloin spark off one another. We see that happening in Bag End and Mark Hadlow and I had some fun playing being pissy at each other. This sort of thing usually isn't scripted, but it's the kind of thing we like to lay in as texture that plays in the background.

Dori's brother Nori, for example, is almost as different from Gloin as a Dwarf could be and they start out very suspicious of each other, but whether it's a case of opposites attracting or whatever (him being a thief, they both have an appreciation of the value of things), they come to respect and learn from one another. Nori isn't much younger than Gloin, but he's been living outside of society so he's detached from Dwarf culture. Jed and I talked about how Gloin might take it upon himself to share some of that with him and educate Nori.

Peter Hambleton, Actor, Gloin

As a fastidious character, Dori had to have a fastidious hairdo. It really didn't change at all from one of the first drawings that was done, and Mark Hadlow loved it when he saw it.

Dori is Mr Fussy. He's Mr Doom and Gloom, and definitely of the glass half empty rather than half full variety. He's the one who says a plan isn't going to work or that it's going to rain, in that northern English accent of his. But he is also caring and his attitude is often motivated by protective, brotherly concern for Ori, or in direct reaction to his other brother, Nori, who is a bit of an imp. He's a mother hen who will complain about something forever but always do the right thing, and he's certainly brave when it comes down to it.

Peter King, Make-up and Hair Designer

On my first day, when I saw the wig and the hair piece I demanded to know who had done this. I think it was a bit scary for Jaime Leigh McIntosh and Rick Findlater in the make-up department, but they consented and led me through to her, and I couldn't thank her enough. The design drawings were wonderful, but they established a tremendously high level of expectation. How do you replicate that? She did a marvellous job, and not only did she reproduce what was drawn, but she understood so well how to manipulate and construct it that she also knew exactly how it should fall apart as the journey goes on and we all come to pieces.

Mark Hadlow, Actor, Dori

Poor Ori. His brother cuts his hair and by all appearances uses a pudding bowl over his head to cut around. From our perspective as his make-up team, there were practical reasons for some of the choices made with Ori's hairstyle as well as aesthetic. We had to have some dangly bits to hide the cowl he wears, but we also wanted to have the bowl shape, so we tried cutting and cutting some more. In the end I cut around the front but hadn't done the back when Peter, Fran and Philippa saw and loved it, so he has a straggly bit at the back which looks like either Dori doesn't care what it looks like from the back or perhaps Ori got away from him before he could finish the job. There are some little decorative plaits, but he's not allowed any jewellery yet because he's too young.

Originally Ori had a little more facial hair, but it was too heavy. Peter really liked the idea that Ori has little more than bum-fluff around his chin. He's a Dwarf that, at least so far, is struggling to grow a beard, which also helps tell us that he's young. To achieve this fine fluff look, we laid on tiny strips of mohair. Anything else made him seem too old or sophisticated.

Nori, meanwhile, is an example of a Dwarf with such an elaborate hairstyle that we used a different wig when his hair was distressed and coming out of its do. The girls who styled Nori's wig into its elaborate shape have it down to a science.

I love that Peter chooses things like this. I think he enjoys throwing challenges at us sometimes. I recall that when he chose this design he looked at me and smiled.

Peter King, Make-up and Hair Designer

If you're going to live outside of society and be judged, you might as well look good doing it. Nori has pride, like all Dwarves. It's what gives him the sense of who he is. He does things his own way, which is a very Dwarven trait.

I have to admit that I was a bit scared of the hair at first. I was worried about how Nori could believably keep it looking that good. And of course the answer is he doesn't. It goes, and that's a way we show what the Dwarves are going through.

One thing we haven't explicitly defined in these films is, who does the hair? Is it Ori? Is Ori the hairdresser? Maybe Dori's the hairdresser? We haven't yet seen the guys all sitting around a campfire pimping themselves up. That might be one scene I'd love to have seen – the Dwarves all doing their hair and plaiting their beards. That might have been interesting to see, but the movies are so full there was never really a space to put it in there.

Jed Brophy, Actor, Nori

DWARF ACCENTS AND LANGUAGE

Supervising Dialect Coach Roisin Carty, Sarah Shippobotham and I were responsible, as dialect coaches, for looking after everyone who speaks in the films. If anyone utters a line, we're there. We help with accents and dialect work, but also speaking in other languages. We support actors on set with their script work and even perform lines off-camera in lieu of another performer being there to speak the off-lines. If the script contains lines directly out of the books, then we're on hand to help ensure the wording is accurate.

When vocal placement and linguistic choices are made with a character, the character itself evolves. Some of our characters came with somewhat predetermined traits as a result of their prior appearance in *The Lord of the Rings* or connection to characters established in those films such as family members. This has a bearing on what kind of accent a character might have. Equally, an actor also brings something with them, so in the case of some of the Dwarves who were unencumbered by previous associations an actor's own ideas or native accent may strongly influence what develops. Roisin Carty and the creative team (Peter Jackson, Fran Walsh and Philippa Boyens) looked at the qualities the actor brought to their audition and the qualities they encapsulated for the character to see what might fit. Actors like Ken Stott, Richard Armitage or James Nesbitt all brought a clear creative offering with them regarding their character that Peter, Fran and Philippa responded too. In those cases we have stuck close to home with those actors.

Leith McPherson, Dialect Coach

There were so many Dwarves that I was asked to divide them up, accent-wise, to help distinguish them. If they all sounded like Gimli it would be difficult for the audience to follow who was speaking. Visually they were all so distinct, so it made sense that each one would be similarly unique in vocal character.

The creative team and I began by dividing them into family groups, with a key individual in each group who established the lead that family would follow.

Richard Armitage's native accent is northern English, a dialect well suited to a regal line of Dwarves: drawing on British history for inspiration, the royal families were northern and would have spoken with regional accents. At the same time, the qualities of a northern English accent match the kind of characterisation Richard was wanting to explore: qualities of nobility, strength, groundedness, command and

industriousness. So for Thorin we preserved Richard's own accent but worked with him to make it less broad and, in turn, helped teach features of it to Fili and Kili, though their accents would be described better as RP with a northern flavour. Dean and Aidan have Kiwi and Irish accents, respectively, so it's high praise indeed of their talent and the work we did with them that they were able to adapt so well.

Gloin had to sound like his son Gimli, played by John Rhys-Davies in *The Lord of the Rings* with a Scottish accent, so it only made sense that Gloin and his brother Oin follow in kind. Brothers Balin and Dwalin would also have Scottish accents, a choice made easier by Ken Stott being Scottish and Graham McTavish being from a Scottish family.

In choosing what kind of Scottish accent our Dwarves would favour, we wanted to avoid anything too urban or modern. We used Ken Stott as a native-speaking model for the Scottish-sounding Dwarves and he recorded passages that we distributed for everyone's reference.

Graham was very familiar with the Glasgow accent, which we initially thought would be too urban. However, his characterization lent itself to a more roughly spoken accent, so in a sense a hint of Glasgow in Dwalin's accent wasn't

inappropriate. The only issue to be mindful of was clarity, which was an important note for every accent in the films. American audiences in particular could have some difficulty understanding a strong Glasgow accent because it's not one they are usually exposed to. There would be little point in using an accent that made a character unintelligible to sections of the audience or be so strong as to be distracting.

Roisin Carty, Supervising Dialect Coach

Peter Hambleton and I were told to adopt Scottish accents because we were cousins of Balin and Dwalin, who are of the royal line, and to be in keeping with Gimli's accent. Why might different branches of the family have different accents? In discussion with the writers we theorized that our accents were a product of where we might have gone to trade. The Dwarves travelled far and wide trading their gems and toys and expert crafts. Thorin, being in direct line to the throne, had a different accent to some of us, and some of the others followed him.

John Callen, Actor, Oin

'We theorized that our accents were a product of where we might have gone to trade.'

Unless they are speaking in Khuzdul, their own native and secret tongue, whenever we hear Dwarves talking in the films they are actually speaking in what is a second language to them: Mannish, or English to us. As a dispersed culture they have grown up travelling, bartering and dealing with various races of men across Middle-earth. In doing business with them it would be fair to assume they might have taken on the accents of those cultures they have mixed with, which could explain the diversity of their accents and, in some cases, similarities to other races.

Roisin Carty, Supervising Dialect Coach

Accents are something I enjoy and over thirty years have developed some facility with. There are many research tools available to familiarize oneself with an appropriate accent for a character, where in the mouth various sounds and shapes are formed. We had the support of the most amazing dialect coaches on The Hobbit and could draw upon the expert knowledge of those who know how Dwarven phrases should be pronounced.

In Gloin's case, it was a Scottish accent that was chosen, and I had the benefit of a CD of Ken Stott, who is Scottish, reading some of the script. I listen to Scottish songs and in the privacy of my own trailer would sing them from time to time.

Peter Hambleton, Actor, Gloin

Among the sometimes amusing and also frazzling aspects of dialect coaching is offline reading, where we provide lines for actors who are responding to an out-of-shot character without that actor being present. I've had to be three or four different characters in one scene, delivering lines in three distinct Scottish accents, for example, so that it is clear to the actor being filmed that at this point I am being Balin, but now Dwalin, and next Oin.

Leith McPherson, Dialect Coach

The most varied group was Dori, Ori and Nori. Each of these characters had their own distinct vocal qualities and dialects.

Adam Brown had an astonishing audition that clearly just wowed everybody and brought him into this world. He went for an accent that was a bit of a blend of west country English mixed with a standard British. Philippa in particular really wanted to maintain what she saw in the audition process, so this became part of Ori's character, but that mightn't necessarily fit Dori and Nori.

The notion came up in preproduction that because Dwarves live so much longer than humans, these brothers could have been born decades apart and raised in very unique situations. Their bloodline connection mightn't be matched by their life experiences or upbringings, so the vocal character of each might well be distinct. That storyline isn't scripted, but hopefully is something that intrigues and adds texture.

Leith McPherson, Dialect Coach

The first thing we were given the chance to think about for our characters was our accents. With a lot of what we've developed for Middle-earth's various accents in both trilogies, the origin is in something from the British Isles. There are English bases, there's Scottish and there's Irish, there's a slight hint of Welsh. In *The Lord of the Rings* Gimli's accent was John Rhys-Davies' Welsh Scotsman mix, but Dwarves don't all sound like that. They're a very mixed bunch, as were we.

Mark Hadlow was determined to play Ronnie Barker's Mr Arkwright from *Open All Hours*, which was a great fit for Dori, but it wasn't right for Nori. I didn't want to give him the Yorkshire accent so I thought, being slightly dodgy lends itself to a London boy – no offence to Londoners!

Jed Brophy, Actor, Nori

Even though we come from the same place, we didn't want our accents to be all the same. It's funny when we're all in a scene together because I have to be so conscious not to slip and start letting bits of Adam and Jed's accents creep in. Yorkshire suits Dori. It's something about his proud middle-class Dwarvishness, but with a bit of earth and reality. We're not suggesting that Dori is from Yorkshire, or Nori is from London, or that Ori is from Berkshire (although Adam is), but adopting these accents gives a grounding, and it immediately tells an audience something about their status and perhaps background. In the case of our group, it says they're a bit egalitarian or plebeian, and Jed's dodgy.

Mark Hadlow, Actor, Dori

Peter, Fran and Philippa just loved Mark's accent for Dori. Character-wise, Dori is the mother of the troop, so it worked for the character to have that quality and the accent fit so well. It was part of the creation of his character and to remove it would have been to lose something important.

Likewise, Adam Brown's native Berkshire accent, tempered by having lived in London for several years, was perfect for Ori.

Roisin Carty, Supervising Dialect Coach

Dori and his brothers' accents are an example of something that I think we glimpse every now and again – a window into different parts of Middle-earth that we glance through, even if we never walk into that room. It's the feeling that if you look beneath the surface there is a richness that invites deeper exploration. To me as an enthusiast of Tolkien's world and the film adaptation, it's one of the most compelling, interesting and sumptuous things. I'm an acoustic person, focused on how I receive the world through sound, but every day on set we were surrounded by these amazing sets full of texture and detail. I like to think that this world is as vocally dense as it is visually. That has been our passion as coaches. Tolkien had such a passion for his fictional languages that he created Middle-earth as a means to express them, so there is the pressure and expectation to honour that by paying deep attention to the vocal depth of the films.

Leith McPherson, Dialect Coach

James Nesbitt has a non-urban Northern Irish accent, so we decided to base Bofur's family group on Northern Irish. Unlike all the other Dwarves of the Company, they aren't related to Thorin, not being from Durin's line, so the difference in accent worked to help reinforce that these Dwarves come from a different line and class.

Even though Bombur said very little and Bifur spoke in Khuzdul, we conducted accent sessions with all three of them in which Jimmy would model his accent for the others. It helped Stephen Hunter because Bombur does have some lines in the film and, as Bifur, William Kircher thought it was important to get a feel for the accent as being a part of his character, whether he spoke or not. It speaks to the kind of commitment to these roles that all the cast shared. William wanted to be able to make grunts or intonations that would be appropriate to his Dwarf family's native accent.

Roisin Carty, Supervising Dialect Coach

Anyone who has read *The Hobbit* will have a very fixed idea of how a character or place-name should be pronounced and many will have lived with that pronunciation for years!

For example, I was told that Peter (among many others) was attached to pronouncing Smaug as 'Smorg'. Strictly speaking, following Tolkien's pronunciation guide in the appendix of *The Lord of the Rings*, the vowel should be the one found in the word 'house' (otherwise Tolkien would have written Smóg). Thankfully, and in credit to his desire to honour the source material, Peter was happy to oblige!

Tolkien is very detailed in his writing concerning the correct pronunciation of vowels in all the languages in his books. When he writes the letter O it represents the sound in the word 'fall', which is 'aw'. Oin and Gloin, for example, should be pronounced with two syllables AW-een and GLAW-een. But, when you have thirteen rowdy Dwarves shouting at each other across a dinner table or across a field as they are chased by Wargs, all in their prosthetics, running about, sweating, the last thing that they're going to think about is the correct

pronunciation of an unusual-sounding name. It was simply more natural for them to run the syllables together and say Oin as you might say 'join'.

We could have put our foot down and insisted, but in this case we let it go. It could be surmised that the Dwarves are saying their names in the context of speaking accented Mannish speech, whereas when speaking in Dwarvish they might adopt a different pronunciation. Their own language is, after all, a secret one, so perhaps their names are said differently when spoken within earshot of other species? There will always be debate on some of these topics. During *The Lord of the Rings* there was endless discussion around the correct pronunciation of the word palantír.

Roisin Carty, Supervising Dialect Coach

Khuzdul is the secret language of the Dwarves. Very few know it outside the Dwarves themselves. Gandalf didn't seem to know it, and he knew just about everything. Aragorn understood enough of it to reprimand Gimli when he insulted the Elves in *The Fellowship of the Ring*, but to most it is virtually unknown and the Dwarves guard it.

Tolkien himself wrote down so little of Khuzdul in his works and letters, instead referring to it as a secret language. In contrast with the Elvish languages, so explicitly laid out by the professor, Khuzdul is very scant. David Salo, who was the Tolkien language expert on *The Lord of the Rings*, provided all our translations on *The Hobbit*. He had to respond to the requests from the Production for many translations and expressions, extrapolating and interpreting Tolkien's intentions for a language of which very few examples exist in his writing.

Leith McPherson, Dialect Coach

Tolkien is quoted as having said that the languages came first and the stories we all know and love were somewhere for him to place them, rather than the reverse. Clearly Tolkien had a great passion for language, so we have done our best to honour that.

David Salo expanded upon what little existed for us as need arose, using the same rules of grammar and pronunciation that Tolkien employed. When it came to pronouncing Khuzdul, we followed what had been established when Gimli spoke it in the previous films. Dwarves are quite curt in their speech – the language sounds sharp and it has heavy consonants. We needed to make it phonetically distinct from the Elvish languages and Black Speech or Orcish, and it had to sound very foreign to Western ears. Elvish sounds foreign but also familiar, and phonetically it has hints of Celtic and Italian in it, so it isn't too far removed from things that we've heard before. But Dwarvish had to use very foreign phonetics. The TH, for example, is almost spat out. Thorin would be pronounced 'Torin' with a very heavy T if spoken in Khuzdul.

Initially we had a lot of translations for battle cries and asides to each other prepared, but as we were filming we began to realize that it wasn't necessarily appropriate for the Dwarves to be screaming their secret language all the time. Muttering to each other in Dwarvish in the company of Elves, hobbits or other races didn't always seem right, so while we started out with a lot of it, gradually the amount of Khuzdul being spoken was reduced. It was an example of an instance when we had a plan going in but found that we were naturally led down a different path during filming.

Roisin Carty, Supervising Dialect Coach

We have encouraged the actors to think of Khuzdul as a private language and to guard its use closely. It may not be secret, but it is private, and none has embraced this more so than William Kircher, whose character Bifur speaks only in Khuzdul in *The Hobbit: An Unexpected Journey*. He has taken ownership of it. Literally every day William would come to us and ask for phrases that related to what Bifur was doing or thinking in that scene. He carried an internal monologue in Dwarvish relevant to every scene even if he didn't have any dialogue. That commitment to the integrity of the character and language was exciting and infectious.

Leith McPherson, Dialect Coach

'Imrid amrad ursul!
Die a death of flames!'

'Ikhf' id-ursu khazâd!
Feel the fire of the Dwarves!'

YOUNG THORIN, BALIN AND DWALIN

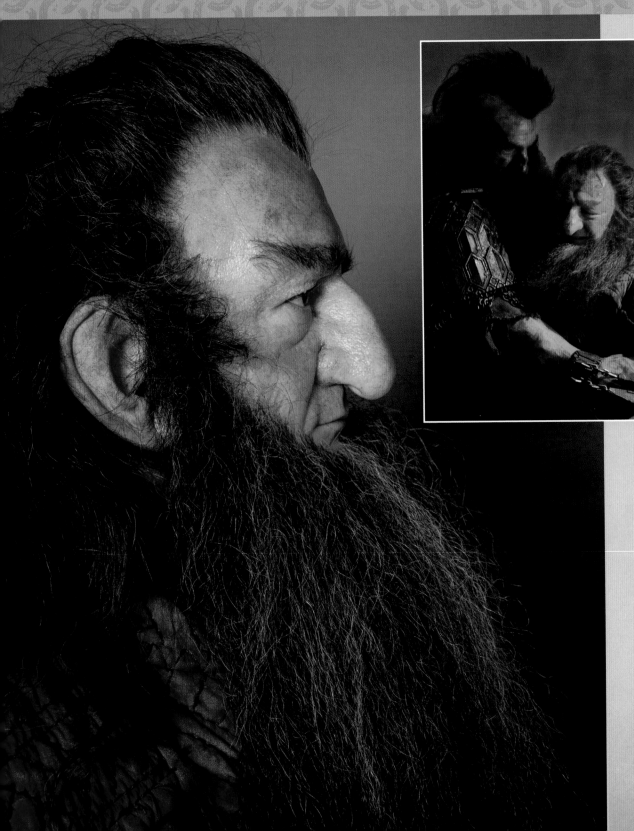

Thorin's history is shared with audiences via flashbacks in which they witness the legendary glory and wealth of the Dwarves in their prime, meet Thorin's father and grandfather, and witness firsthand the sack of Erebor by the Dragon Smaug. Glimpsing the travails of the Dwarf exiles in the years that follow, sharing in the defeat at Azanulbizar and seeing the humility of princes shoeing horses to scratch their living, the audience should gain an insight into the palpable sense of loss and displacement that drives the Quest. It is important that they understand what it is that compels the film's heroes to risk everything in pursuit, not of treasure, but of stolen dignity and pride, of destinies unfulfilled and futures unwritten.

Actors Richard Armitage, Ken Stott and Graham McTavish stepped into fresh make-up and costumes to play younger versions of their world-worn characters in earlier days, scribing the early strokes of the arcs their Dwarves would chart through the three films.

'When he breaks the limb of the tree to ward off the pale Orc, he becomes Thorin Oakenshield and his future legend is born.'

Young Balin was depicted with a moustache in some of the early artwork, but that was a hangover from the days in which older Balin was going to have a moustache as well. Once older Balin lost his moustache it made little sense to keep it on his younger self too, as the beard with no moustache became Balin's iconic look. To see this young, dark-bearded Dwarf with a moustache would probably have confused audiences and I doubt many would have recognized that it was still Balin they were looking at.

He had a new forehead with some of the wrinkles taken out, longer hair and a smaller nose, but otherwise Balin is as we have come to know him in the rest of the movie.

Peter King, Make-up and Hair Designer

One of the most important aspects of portraying a younger Thorin, as we see him in the flashback scenes, was the chance to show him as a young warrior, seeing his potential to become a great warrior, which has yet to be fulfilled. He is fitter and faster than older Thorin, but he is less precise. At the battle of Azanulbizar, he transitions from youth to man. He is almost defeated by Azog, a far superior fighter. We see young Thorin fighting at speed, but really flailing around compared to the indomitable Azog, but then when he breaks the limb of the tree to ward off the pale Orc, he becomes Thorin Oakenshield and his future legend is born.

We witness young Thorin observing the rift between the Wood-elves and his family, his grandfather's madness, his grandfather's slaughter, and his father's helplessness. We also see young Thorin at work at the anvil: 'The hammer will keep the arms strong until they can wield sharper tools again' was a great mantra for preparing Thorin. That we see these earlier wars, his survival, his perseverance, will hopefully arouse some empathy for a character who, without knowing these things about him, may seem greedy, power hungry and bad tempered. He has carried these burdens alone and led his people west to the Ered Luin. His arms are now certainly strong enough to wield sharper tools. His potential to fulfil his warrior destiny lies in the Mountain. When we know all of these things about Thorin's life, I hope we might forgive him a little for his failings, and what befalls him later on.

Richard Armitage, Actor, Thorin

Thorin had a handful of young looks. We created a look for him at his youngest, at home in Erebor with Thror, with short hair and more jewellery to signify his noble birth. His hair lacked any grey, though it had the same texture, dark and rich. He was a young prince at this time with an empire and fortune to inherit.

As Thorin's story unfolds he loses everything and becomes a practical man. His hair grew out and became wilder. We lost the beard jewellery. Fighting the Orcs outside Moria, Thorin's pretensions have all gone and he is a fighting man. The idea was that we made successive changes as his story unfolded, but that they wouldn't be so noticeable as to be jarring to the audience. We couldn't make him so different that it might require telling the audience who he is.

The big challenge for us came in the fact that Thorin's history wasn't shot in sequence. There had been talk of shooting it in a way that would permit us to clip back the beard between shoots and then let Richard regrow it over Christmas, but it didn't work out that way, so we had to work out systems for putting in little bits of facial hair to make it longer when we needed it, and likewise his wig.

Peter King, Make-up and Hair Designer

We had experimented with how far to push the differences between old and young versions of characters. In Dwalin's case the main difference was giving young Dwalin a Mohawk hairstyle. We thought about losing the scar that runs down the side of his face, dropping his tattoo and straightening his broken nose. When we showed this to Peter and Fran they both agreed that the broken nose was iconic to Dwalin and we needed to keep it, and really, so was his scar. Without them he didn't look like Dwalin – he looked like Dwalin's lost brother, so we ended up keeping them all.

We did lose the tattoo on his scalp and there was talk about losing the tattoos on his arms as well, but Fran was right when she said we needed to be able to recognize him and that the arm tattoos are part of what makes him so distinct.

It's a perfect example of how you can rationalize these kinds of differences in your head but in the end it has to work on screen in a second without explanation. When we tested them, the result was too far from Dwalin as we knew him. We changed his hair and lost the tattoo on his head, and that was enough.

Tami Lane, Prosthetics Supervisor

THROR

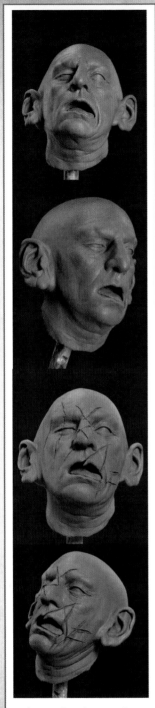

Above: Thror's severed head as a raw Plasticine sculpt by Weta Workshop sculptor Brigitte Wuest with scars added by sculptor and designer Greg Tozer, based on designer Paul Tobin's concepts.

The personification of the ancient might and majesty of the Dwarves, Thror is Thorin's grandfather and King Under the Mountain in the age when the wealth of Erebor's Dwarves is at its peak. Proud and avaricious, the ancient Dwarf guards his vast treasure as jealously as the Dragon that will come to take it from him, and in his disdain for others we glimpse the seeds of an enmity that will later haunt Thorin.

Played by Jeffrey Thomas, Thror was conceived upon his stone throne by the designers as a man-mountain, the shadow of the Lonely Mountain made of flesh and hair, immovable and stubborn as rock.

Sadly for Thror, though he escaped the burning of his home, his end would come at the East-gate of Moria, when Azog would cut off his head and carve into it his sigil, thereby earning the title The Defiler.

Thror has blue contact lenses that tie him to Thorin and Thrain. Richard Armitage and Mike Mizrahi both have ice-blue eyes, while Jeffrey Thomas also has blue eyes but they're very dark and look black. There is a ring of blue around his left eye which is very cool, but we requested the opportunity to try Thror with light-blue lenses in order to tie him to his son and grandson and reinforce the family connection. It also served to age him as well as give him a hint of the crazy eye, which fits considering his obsession with the gold.

As it was scripted, Azog beheads Thror and carves his name into the old Dwarf's head in the Black Speech, so a head was made for that shot. We have a few beheadings in these movies. It's pretty violent stuff.

Tami Lane, Prosthetics Supervisor

We had pictures of the make-up the actor wore on set which we followed and matched for his decapitated head. The sculpt of the head also had scars where Azog had carved the skin, so we looked at various gruesome references and came up with something suitably disturbing in our paint job on the cuts.

Dordi Moen, Weta Workshop Prosthetics Painting Team Leader

THRAIN

The haunted son of Thror and father of the young Prince Thorin, it falls to Thrain to recapture past glories when his father is killed, but Thrain's attempts prove vain and when he is lost it is up to Thorin to take up the mantle. Prior to this, however, we witness Thrain at the Lonely Mountain standing by his father's side, and later fighting next to him at Azanulbizar, resplendent in shining crimson armour. In order to appear distinct from the many other Dwarves in the films Thrain needed to have strong iconic features that would set him apart. His red armour and robes, a bold brow and nose tattoo, together with the loss of an eye, all helped define him visually. He was also one of the only Dwarves to sport a black and white beard and fall of hair, other than Bifur.

There was dialogue for a little while concerning when exactly Thrain might lose his eye and whether it might make sense for this to happen in a specific scene and perhaps be used to drive home a story point. My understanding is this notion and the idea of his eye patch were dropped for the sake of expediency. Not everything has to be explained!

Daniel Falconer, Weta Workshop Designer

There was a day when we were filming Thrain with his Dwarf followers at the Front Gate of Erebor and the Dragon was going to burst through. Peter suggested it would be great if the Dwarves were doing the entire scene in Khuzdul so we prepared in case that was how it ended up playing out. When it came time to film we found that it was being shot from behind, but even though the actors' mouths couldn't be seen the actors insisted on continuing to perform it in Dwarvish because it felt right and gave the action the right rhythm and texture.

It is very gratifying and thrilling for us as dialect coaches to see people embracing the linguistics because they feel it enhances their connection to their characters in those moments.

Leith McPherson, Dialect Coach

Dwarf Miners, Merchants and Blacksmiths

Thirteen main Dwarves and Thorin's family were certainly work enough to keep multiple departments very busy during the films' production, but in addition to them were the innumerable other Dwarves audiences would glimpse as the history of the race was told, among them miners, courtiers, merchants, soldiers, workers and even women and children. Dozens and dozens of extras were found, wigged, bearded (yes, even the women) and the varied and striking culture of the Dwarves took form.

One thing I've noticed is how into it the extras are on *The Hobbit*. The poor Dwarf extras have been put through a lot, especially by our department, having hair stuck to them everywhere that's going into their mouths or tickling up their noses. It's not nice, but they don't moan. They just good-naturedly do what they've got to do.

Angela Mooar, Key Hair and Make-up Artist

We sat down one afternoon with all the designs and started experimenting with Dwarven women's wigs. I liked the idea that they expressed themselves with their hairstyles just as elaborately and beautifully as the Dwarf men would with their beards. Peter liked everything we had done, so that was a very successful and well spent afternoon.

We did a lot of research into the facial hair on our women. Historically there have been societies of bearded ladies and we found reference material both contemporary and Victorian, but I felt strongly that if we had beards on our Dwarf women, they had to be soft and feminine. We used mostly Polish hair because it is very fine, and some mohair.

We also had Dwarf children for a scene in which they are fleeing the attack on Erebor. We used mohair for their wigs to get the right texture. They were actually small people playing youngsters, which was a practical decision based on the amount of time we would require to film with them and the difficulty we would have had in sticking hair onto small children or babies.

Peter King, Make-up and Hair Designer

Above: Dwarf Extra Rebekah Hart is fitted with a prosthetic nose and wig by (from left) Key Hair and Make-up artist Angela Mooar, Make-up and Hair Designer Peter King and Senior Prosthetics Technician Katy Fray.

When we have had scenes involving lots of Dwarf extras, be they traders, miners or soldiers, we often reused prosthetics made for other characters in addition to those specifically created for these characters. It helped give us the variety we needed. Some of our featured hobbits had a particularly lumpy prosthetic nose that worked as well for Dwarves as it did for a hobbit. We used those quite a bit for generic Dwarves. We'd add and subtract warts to keep them looking distinct.

We also had a large number of prosthetic moulds left over from when we were developing the prosthetics for the hero Dwarves. We pulled casts out of those moulds for the sake of diversity amongst our generic Dwarves.

Tami Lane, Prosthetics Supervisor

Many of the earlier concepts for the hero Dwarves had larger noses and heavier make-up, which was reduced as they developed. It was important to see the actor through the make-up so it makes sense that they were reduced, but those early make-up tests were somewhere we could go for our extras.

Katy Fray, Senior Prosthetics Technician

Our Dwarf miners came together very quickly. By this time everyone had found their groove and we knew what was wanted so we just went ahead and did it, so their hair, beards and make-up came together very smoothly.

Peter King, Make-up and Hair Designer

An opportunity for some spontaneous creativity that came our way was the tattoos. We didn't have a design, but embracing the Dwarf aesthetic we came up with something that I thought looked really great.

Tami Lane, Prosthetics Supervisor

Michael Asquith, Greg Tozer and I were briefed to sculpt some prosthetic noses to be used on the Dwarf miners. We were told to go extreme, adding bulbous, whiskey soaked tips, twists, warts and really deep textures. I was very pleased with how they turned out. They looked fantastic.

Gary Hunt, Weta Workshop Sculptor

In my opinion some of the background Dwarves have been the most dramatic and therefore the most fun. It's such a treat to be able to make bold character statements with the look of certain characters and, more than any other of the humanoid races, Dwarves lend themselves so well to bold statements.

Richard Taylor,
Weta Workshop Design & Special Effects Supervisor

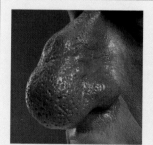
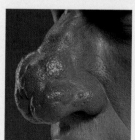
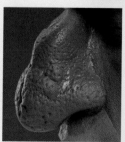

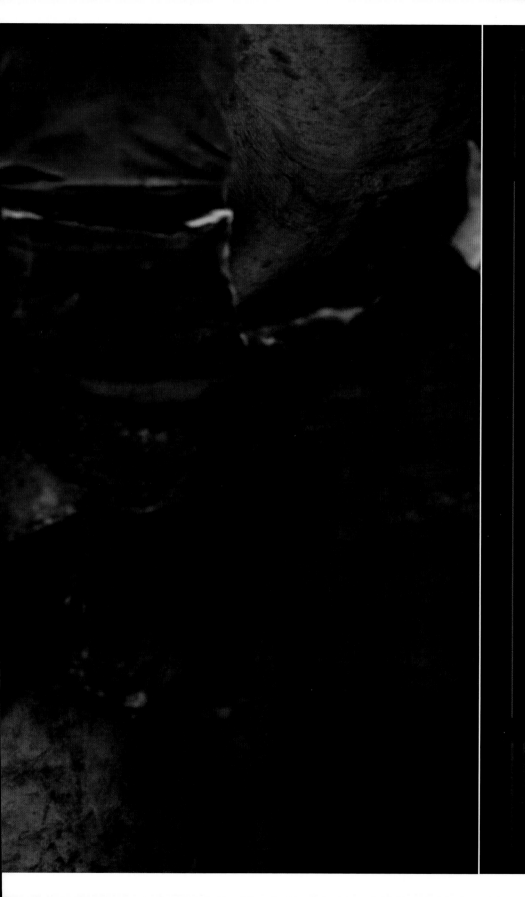

OF TROLLS

' TROLLS WILL EAT ANYTHING, BUT DWARF IS FABULOUS BECAUSE OF THEIR TEXTURE AND THAT VERY PARTICULAR TASTE. '

- Mark Hadlow, Actor, Dori and Bert the Troll

CONCERNING TROLLS

The first obstacle on the Company of Thorin's journey east comes in the form of three monstrous Trolls, along with a somewhat unwelcome opportunity for Bilbo to prove his worth to his sceptical travelling companions. What follows doesn't quite go as planned for anyone involved, but some improvisation and the timely return of the Wizard sees disaster averted.

A slightly different breed of Troll than those seen previously, the three marauders of the Trollshaw Forest are more human in features and manner, in keeping with the characterizations in Tolkien's book. William, Bert and Tom have been ransacking their way around the countryside of the region, raiding farms and stealing livestock when they come upon the Dwarves' ponies. They finish up no less hungry a good deal less dangerous when dawn's rays freeze them into rock, stony relics for Frodo's party to shelter under half a century later.

Our Trolls have been a lot of fun. We were constrained in as much as they had to find themselves in the same positions, turned to stone, as we briefly saw them in *The Fellowship of the Ring*, but Peter was keen to not be limited by that, so there has been room to develop them as individual and distinct characters.

They're big ogre-like creatures that survive by pillaging and ransacking. They're dangerous, but also stupid and comedic, so part of the fun has been in bringing out their personalities. One drools and talks in odd ways. We've got a lazy eye so you're never sure which way he's looking. These are things that help convey personality, but without making them less frightening or dangerous. If anything, being so stupid and so big presents its own danger, never mind their nasty disposition.

Joe Letteri, Weta Digital Senior Visual Effects Supervisor

Even in this fantasy world of Middle-earth, everything is grounded in reality. I'll never forget what Peter said to us in the first meeting we had for *The Lord of the Rings*. He said that every weapon had to seem like it could have come out of an archaeological excavation here in our own world and be a real, functioning sword. It had to look as though it belonged to a time and a culture and not just be something dreamed up for a fantasy film. That attitude is everywhere in these films and applies equally to the creatures, from Trolls down to Goblins and everything else. They have to live in this reality and that means we must push things as far as they can go before falling into total fantasy or something cartoonish.

**Gino Acevedo,
Weta Digital Textures Supervisor/Creative Art Director**

Above: Troll character designs modelled in ZBrush by Weta Workshop Designer Andrew Baker.

Building Trolls

These Trolls are a different breed to the Cave-troll the Fellowship encountered in Moria, or even the Trolls we saw in Mordor. As per their brief appearance in *The Fellowship of the Ring*, they're a bit more human in appearance, especially in the face, though unmistakably Trolls when you see their whole bodies. Another different characteristic is that they turn to stone at the brush of sunlight. They're a little fleshier than the Cave-troll, without quite as much heavy lumpiness on their backs but with softer bellies. As part of their slightly more human features, their eyes have white sclera, which also helps the audience accept them as talking creatures.

Troll flesh is loosely based on something elephant-like: scaly and coarse. As a result our Trolls tend to be tougher on their backs than they are on their fronts, where they are actually quite fleshy. Their backs are covered in nasty looking bumps and moles that don't look healthy. They haven't showered and in places they're a little oily, with lots of build-up in the logical places where dirt would cake as they move about.

Their claws are long and dirty. They have some hair; at one

The stereo 3D aspect added a dimension of complication to what we've done with the Trolls. Getting them to interact perfectly in stereo was its own challenge. Traditionally in 2D movies there is a certain amount that can be faked or cheated, but in 3D everything has to be perfect or it doesn't work. The Trolls are three huge creatures in a fairly small space, surrounded by and interacting with trees as they move about. There were lots of things for them to brush up against or affect,

and we had Dwarves running about, stabbing and slashing, as well as big smashes and crashes through trees – it was a big battle. Bofur almost got wish-boned and Bilbo was being flung about with Troll-snot flying everywhere.

But the stereo aspect also gave us some wonderful opportunities as well. We have spent a lot of time making sure we maximized its capabilities to really put the viewer in the scene, and there was a lot of fore- and background material

that helped establish a sense of place. We were in a forest, so we were looking through leaves and seeing deep into the forest behind the scene. There was a lot of foreground, background and back-background depth.

Jeff Capogreco, Weta Digital Digital Effects Supervisor

CAPTURING TROLLS

Motion capture, whereby live performers' movements are digitally captured and translated into reference data to drive digital models, is a technology being used throughout *The Hobbit*. For the Trolls, it permitted actors William Kircher, Peter Hambleton and Mark Hadlow to set aside their usual roles as Dwarves Bifur, Gloin and Dori and adopt the personalities of the three brutish marauders Tom, William and Bert, respectively.

The actors worked with movement coach Terry Notary and director Peter Jackson to workshop their characters, coming up with a group dynamic and specific movement styles that would distinguish each of the Trolls from his peers. Personalities that had been sketched in the script began emerging and a comedic trio of bumbling, but nonetheless very dangerous, monsters evolved.

Our slave motion control camera system enabled Peter and the camera operator to see as a composite in real time what the motion-captured Troll actors were doing while they were filming the live-action set. The Dwarf actors, however, couldn't see this when they were performing so they had to imagine where the Trolls were and what they were doing for the most part. It's quite a difficult thing for an actor working in a scene with a fully digital creature, not having something real to perform against. However, they got used to it and once they understood the process it worked very well, but it's still a difficult thing to do. Actors like Ian McKellen have been doing this for a long time and have become very good at it.

Eric Saindon, Weta Digital Visual Effects Supervisor

The Trolls had to come together very quickly. We played fo a day in the motion capture suits, developing ideas for thei performances and then the guys went on set and shot for three days. Building a character is a bit like building a house. You lay a foundation first, but when you're in a situation in which you need to get it figured out in a day, it was more like putting rooms in first and then building the foundation underneath We tried things and examined them on the monitor, which instantly translated what the actors were doing on to crude versions of the digital Trolls. They weren't fully rendered lacking moving faces, but the fingers moved and for what we were doing they were great. They captured subtle little shift and emotions perceptible when a character inflates or falls and we could see the chests moving with intakes of breath, so there was enough for us to work with. We could look at these in real time and assess what we were doing, plucking those littl moments of magic that we found to begin with, and building on them.

Then I removed the screen and allowed the actors to jus feel their performances without checking themselves in the monitor, because there is the risk that you can start self directing to the point where you tighten up and don't let the accidents happen. Pulling back from mistakes is a reflex, but i means you don't get the chance to go beyond the mistake and find something really good, so we started with the monitor bu then set it aside and allowed the characters to develop more organically with each other.

The three characters had to complement each other, being of the same gene pool, but with their own personality and rhythm. Trolls are huge, so the actors had to find a way to carry themselves that conveyed the appropriate sense of weight Sudden movements would destroy the illusion of mass, so we imagined moving as if through thick space where the ai was denser. It's not slow motion, but it's heavy. Every action would have momentum so there's a degree of swing and reel to everything, and nothing could be flippant. It helped to imagine that the world around was smaller. It was challenging, but i was about feeling rather than acting out the weight. It's almos a dance, or like being on a big ship, moving through thick oil o pulling yourself through quicksand or gravel. It helps to have imagery like that in mind because the right imagery inform the right feeling better than words.

Terry Notary, Movement Coach

I wanted to play a Troll the minute I read the script. I actually asked to audition for the opportunity. It's very different to playing a Dwarf, but such fun. They're huge and powerful creatures, but blundering, ugly, stupid and mean.

The four days we spent being Trolls were some of the most enjoyable. Peter Hambleton, Mark Hadlow and I were a sort of comic threesome, like the Three Stooges. Mark did some brilliant stuff, slapping me around. We had great fun workshopping them with movement coach Terry Notary. Andy Serkis also came by. Andy is peerless as far as experience goes in this kind of work and offered some very insightful suggestions, such as thinking about old wounds, which led to me having weights tied to my limbs so they dragged and required effort to move.

William Kircher, Actor, Bifur and Tom the Troll

As actors we provided the personality for each Troll character upon which the digital artists would expand. Our movement and habitation of each one was recorded in the motion capture studio. They took our performances and applied them, dressed and finessed them into these giant, monstrous characters.

It was a very fun sequence to film that marked the first moment of jeopardy for the Dwarves. How they deal with it is a test and it almost goes rather badly for them. One of the great things about Peter as a director is his understanding and control of this story. He knows what matters and how to be sure he honours the source material with integrity while also not being completely slave to it. He had this sequence scripted, knew precisely what he wanted to cover and how he intended to cut it, but was also open to discovering the nuances that help bring things to life. There's room inside his plan for actors to offer suggestions, and he'll gladly accept a good idea if it serves his intent for the scene. There was some delightful material concerning the recipe for the Dwarf stew that was a product of that fresh, organic process.

Peter Hambleton, Actor, Gloin and William the Troll

To get the right level of interactivity for the Dwarf actors on the live set we put stunt people in armour to stand in for the Trolls. They had helmets and padding as if they were going out motorcycle racing. This was all so that the actors could go nuts hitting the Trolls' legs (actually our padded stunties) but not actually take them out. It was their job to get hit as if they were Troll legs and be digitally replaced later.

Glenn Boswell, Stunt Co-ordinator

Facing Page: Actors Mark Hadlow and William Kircher (back) in

Even though our modellers are not animators, we like to see what the actors were doing when their performances were captured because there's information there that we can use. Our team members are preparing the facial set-up for the animators, so they need to see how the actor moves and all the subtleties and expression they bring to the character because that has to be built in to the character for the animators to use.

Marco Revelant, Weta Digital Models Supervisor

Trolls are huge, so we ended up taking the actors' performances and slowing them down even more to convey the appropriate feeling of great mass. They could end up looking over-animated if we didn't get their pace just right, so the animators finessed the motion capture performance to help it fit the physicality of the Trolls at their true scale. Building upon what the actors' had done, they also pushed the Trolls' facial performances a little further as well, given they have such large, heavy featured faces.

Jeff Capogreco, Weta Digital Digital Effects Supervisor

It is interesting to me as a language enthusiast that the Trolls are the only characters in the book who are in fact written in dialect. It is very clear what Tolkien intended in this instance. It is a kind of London Cockney-inspired energy.

Leith McPherson, Dialect Coach

The nice thing about the Trolls is that while they are Cockney, they're not modern gangster Cockney, but more of the Bill Sykes variety. They speak an old-fashioned Cockney which is colourful and energetic.

Roisin Carty, Supervising Dialect Coach

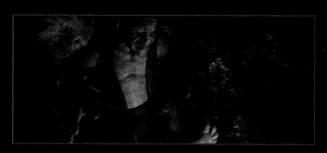

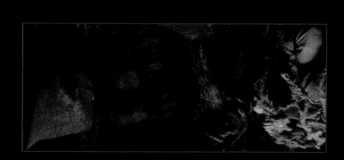

WILLIAM

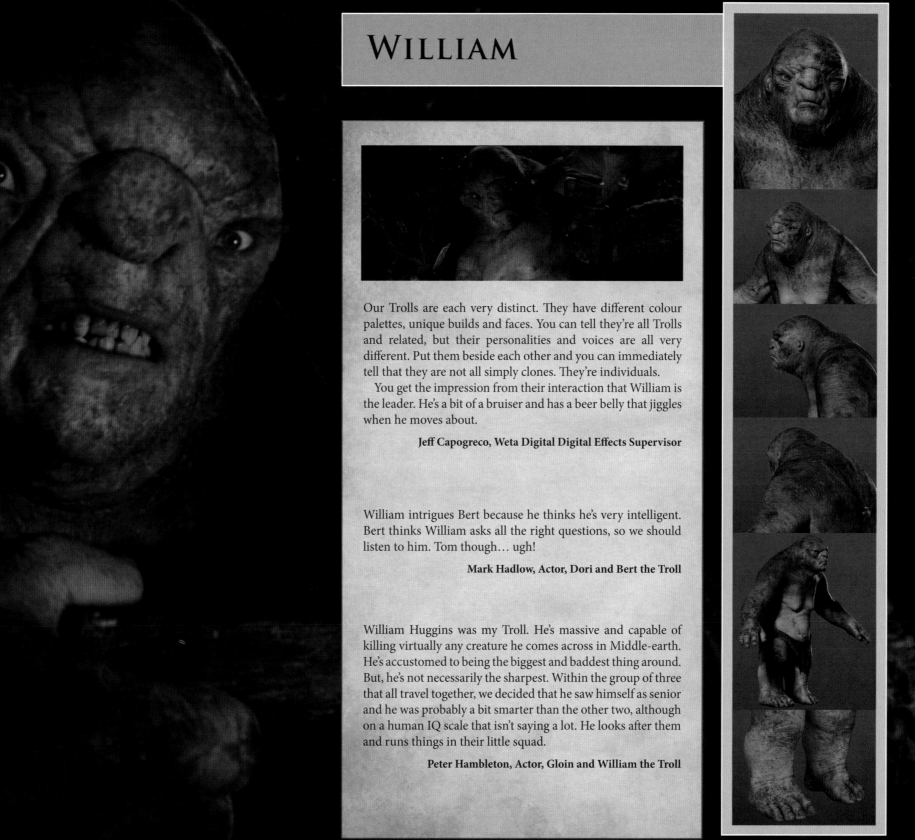

Our Trolls are each very distinct. They have different colour palettes, unique builds and faces. You can tell they're all Trolls and related, but their personalities and voices are all very different. Put them beside each other and you can immediately tell that they are not all simply clones. They're individuals.

You get the impression from their interaction that William is the leader. He's a bit of a bruiser and has a beer belly that jiggles when he moves about.

Jeff Capogreco, Weta Digital Digital Effects Supervisor

William intrigues Bert because he thinks he's very intelligent. Bert thinks William asks all the right questions, so we should listen to him. Tom though… ugh!

Mark Hadlow, Actor, Dori and Bert the Troll

William Huggins was my Troll. He's massive and capable of killing virtually any creature he comes across in Middle-earth. He's accustomed to being the biggest and baddest thing around. But, he's not necessarily the sharpest. Within the group of three that all travel together, we decided that he saw himself as senior and he was probably a bit smarter than the other two, although on a human IQ scale that isn't saying a lot. He looks after them and runs things in their little squad.

Peter Hambleton, Actor, Gloin and William the Troll

TOM

When the three Trolls were described to us I was immediately drawn to Tom, because he's such a great juxtaposition of things. He's skinny for a Troll. When you think of one you think burly and gruff and heavy, but he's this wheedling character who gets hit by his brothers. They're not nice guys. He's at the bottom of the pecking order in this trio but he's still horrible. He delights in the thought of ripping someone into bits.

William Kircher, Actor, Bifur and Tom the Troll

Tom is the comic relief of the group. He's the gawkiest with long hair and a bit of a beard, almost Willy Nelson-like in a Trollish way. He wears straps on his outfit that resemble suspenders. We've done something fun that is quite subtle but which people should be able to catch and that's give him a lazy eye that drifts off when he is trying to focus on something. He has a little Marty Feldman thing going on.

Jeff Capogreco, Weta Digital Digital Effects Supervisor

Bert doesn't think too much of Tom. He suffers him with pain. Tom has special needs and Bert just can't be bothered with him. I think if he could, he'd quite like to cook Tom. He wouldn't eat him, just cook him.

Mark Hadlow, Actor, Dori and Bert the Troll

'Bert just can't be bothered with him. I thin[k]
he could, he'd quite like to cook Tom.'

It turns out that Tom is snotty, which we play up for all kinds of pretty disgusting humour. His nose is constantly running and it gets everywhere.

William Kircher, Actor, Bifur and Tom the Troll

Troll snot – it's a favourite topic of conversation. Too stringy? Too thin? Too chunky or just right?

Tom has a cold, and in the course of reaching for his handkerchief he discovers Bilbo, completely by accident. Bilbo is reaching for Tom's knife in the hopes of cutting free the ponies and proving he's got what it takes to the doubtful Dwarves; only Tom goes to sneeze and grabs for his handkerchief. He ends up grabbing Bilbo and sneezing all over him. Imagine bucket-loads of snot all over poor Martin Freeman. He gets tangled in this repulsive goop and it's very funny... unless you're Bilbo.

We had a guy in the effects department who was devoted full time to snot detail. He would put giant stringy boogers all over *The Hobbit*. He was the Troll snot guy, and there was plenty of Troll snot to be done. Tom has it caked under his nose. It's one of his defining features. He even ends up sneezing in the stew that Bert is working on, which Bert of course ends up tasting and proclaiming as great. We'll have done our jobs if audiences are crawling under their seats at that point.

Jeff Capogreco, Weta Digital Digital Effects Supervisor

BERT

Bert is the chef. Once again, like Dori, there's a connection with my character and food – how odd? Bert makes all the Trolls' food and he's very proud of the quality he brings to what is basically pretty crummy fare. He can pluck a herb and throw it in his broth, 'I'm just looking for a little bit of class to put into this stew.' That's Bert.

They're silly old Trolls, these three. All they want to do is eat, and Dwarves actually add the piquancy to a stew that is wonderful because they have this pheromone that is released when they're slaughtered. You put that in the stew and it's wonderful. It adds a whole new and exciting component to the dish. Trolls will eat anything, but Dwarf is fabulous because of their texture and that very particular taste.

There's the most wonderful moment in the film where Dori, with his bolas, whacks Bert between the legs. Peter thought this was fabulous. He said it's the best moment of self-abuse in the film, my character Bert being assailed in the unmentionables by my character Dori. And bless him, he's kept it in. I'm so glad. It's wonderful, it really is.

Mark Hadlow, Actor, Dori and Bert the Troll

Bert is draped in a big apron which folds and crinkles nicely when he moves. As well as being the cook of the crew he is the shortest of the three Trolls, which helps make him recognizable. He also has a dead eye which is really quite gross.

Jeff Capogreco, Weta Digital Digital Effects Supervisor

'Dwarves actually add the piquancy to a stew that is wonderful because they have this pheromone that is released when they're slaughtered.'

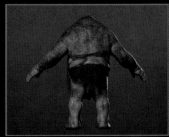

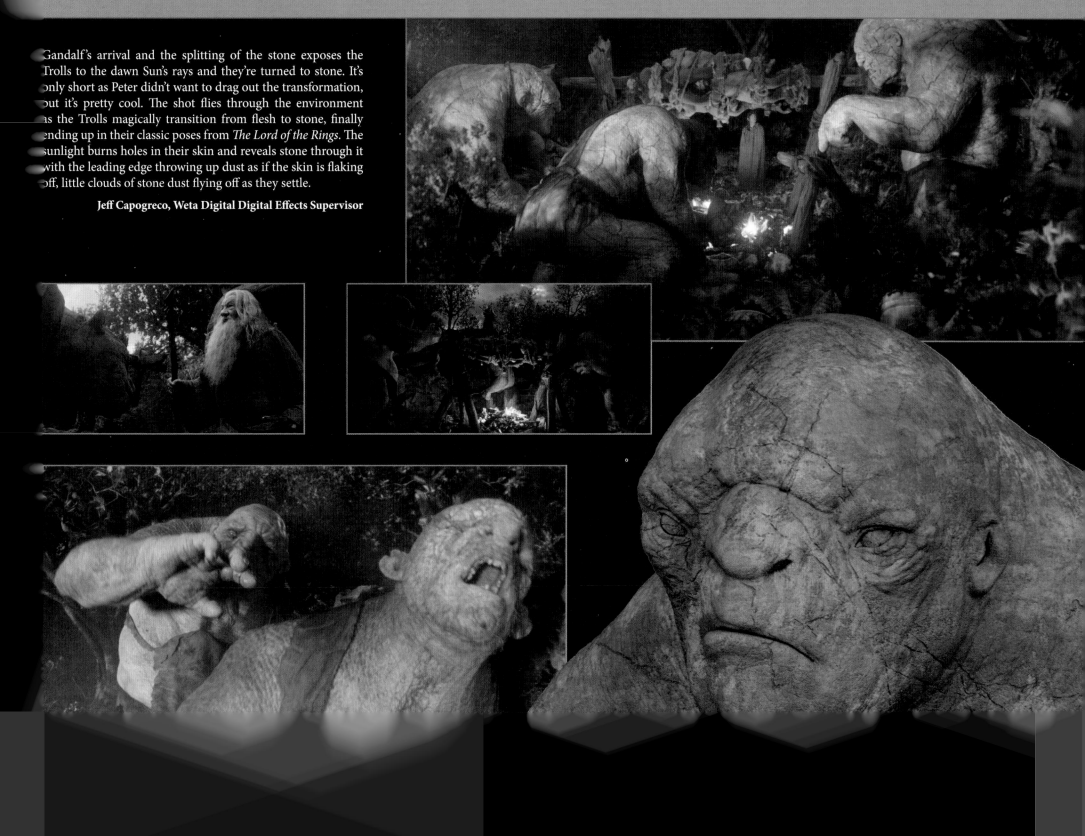

Gandalf's arrival and the splitting of the stone exposes the Trolls to the dawn Sun's rays and they're turned to stone. It's only short as Peter didn't want to drag out the transformation, but it's pretty cool. The shot flies through the environment as the Trolls magically transition from flesh to stone, finally ending up in their classic poses from *The Lord of the Rings*. The sunlight burns holes in their skin and reveals stone through it with the leading edge throwing up dust as if the skin is flaking off, little clouds of stone dust flying off as they settle.

Jeff Capogreco, Weta Digital Digital Effects Supervisor

OF ELVES

'*ELVES HAVE THIS INNATE BEAUTY, THE KIND POSSESSED BY A PERSON WHO IS UNAWARE OF HOW BEAUTIFUL THEY ARE.*'

- Terry Notary, Movement Coach

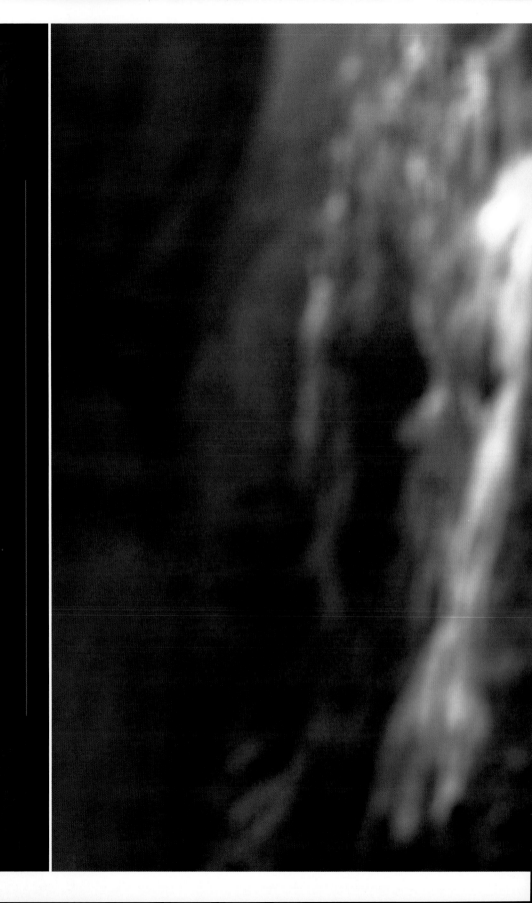

CONCERNING ELVES

Against tthe better judgement of the Dwarves, who harbour a deep mistrust of Elves, Gandalf leads the Company to the sanctuary of Rivendell. Protected by the might and magic of the Elves, the haven offers a chance for the Dwarves and Bilbo to catch their breath while the Wizard takes council with their host, Lord Elrond. In spite of the Elven hospitality, Thorin and his party are uncomfortable and keen to leave as quickly as possible. Thorin avails himself of Elrond's deep rune lore, but resents the Elf Lord's reservations about the nature of their quest.

Elves are a long-lived people, untouched by disease or the mortality of men. Only grief or injury can destroy them, though experience has seen many withdraw from the world and take shelter in their protected realms, eschewing the agendas and petty business of the younger races. Elven sight is keen, their movements purposeful and their manner tempered, but when moved to act in wrath any Elf is a force to be reckoned with, their actions directed by centuries of training and garnered wisdom.

ELVISH LANGUAGE AND ACCENTS

While working on *The Lord of the Rings* I became particularly interested and involved in teaching the Elvish languages. Returning to New Zealand a decade on and getting translations from David Salo again felt like coming home.

We were very lucky to have eight weeks of preparation time before we began shooting. The accents for many of the characters were chosen to provide continuity with the world established in the previous films and therefore were chosen from within the British Isles. They were intended to seem familiar without being immediately identifiable with a particular region, or too distracting. Every accent choice was made to serve the character and to tell the story. The actors had dialect sessions every day, to begin with, and as their confidence grew this became every other day. The aim was to prepare them to such a degree that on set they would need little or no coaching and could handle any script changes thrown at them!

When we teach English accents the actor generally has access to references (whether their own or from other native speakers) to the accent in question, as was the case with the hobbits and Dwarves, but it is a very different experience learning to speak an invented language. In this case the Dialect Coaches had to provide the model.

Dialect Coaches Leith McPherson and Sarah Shippobotham joined me on *The Hobbit*. They hadn't worked on the previous films, so, to prepare, I spent some time every day teaching them Elvish, Dwarvish and Black Speech. This was particularly important with the Elvish languages as Tolkien left detailed and specific instructions on the pronunciation – the consonant and vowel sounds as well as the stress patterns. I broke down all the phrases so that Leith and Sarah could understand the syntax as well: commands versus requests versus negative statements, the plural forms of words, first versus third person singular etc – a veritable masterclass in Elvish! This was always accompanied by drilling phrases – listening and repeating – one of the methods used with the actors to achieve fluency in the various Tolkien-invented languages.

Throughout prep and the shooting of all the films, when new phrases were required in Elvish, David Salo would send me the translation and I would record it as a model for Leith, Sarah

are the models for the Elvish tongues, which are Sindarin and Quenya, respectively. Tolkien is quite explicit in stating that the invention of these languages was the foundation and the stories were made to provide a context for them to exist within.

Each Elvish language has its own character. Quenya could also be called 'Elf-latin'. It is mainly used for spells or invocations. Radagast speaks a Quenya spell in Rhosgobel:

Cementari celvamelde, Si a hlare omaquettar, Lerya laman naiquentallo, na coilerya envinyanta.

Roisin Carty, Supervising Dialect Coach

Sylvester McCoy loved Quenya. Galadriel also spoke it. It is such a beautiful shift acoustically, when characters begin speaking in one of the Elvish tongues.

Leith McPherson, Dialect Coach

While Quenya has its roots in Finnish, Sindarin is based on the phonetics of Welsh. It is used in everyday speech – greetings, sharing information and in songs.

Nae nin gwistant ifanneth, mal U-eichia I Chiril Lorien

'It is such a beautiful shift acoustically, when characters begin speaking in one of the Elvish tongues.'

The two languages are quite distinct. I think they could be equated to shifting between speaking French and Latin. There is definitely a connection between them, but when speaking Quenya there is a formality. It's a more magical kind of Elvish expression and is mostly used for invocations in the films. In Shakespearean terms the two languages could be likened to the difference between prose and verse, or musically, from speech to song. Quenya evokes a feeling of passionate connection to the energy of the world in which these characters are living. It comes out of those heightened moments where someone is pleading to the Valar to help them in whatever task they are trying to achieve at that moment, so it has a different quality to it and a different rhythm. In contrast to Quenya, Sindarin has more the flavour of the common language of communication for the Elves, beautiful, but also practical.

Leith McPherson, Dialect Coach

The starting point with speaking either Elvish language is to think of it sounding beautiful. Anyone speaking it has to be very precise, very fluid. It's lyrical, musical, and should sound like someone singing. Apparently when Elves speak you're meant to hear bells ringing.

Elvish wasn't new to most of those who spoke it this time. Elrond, Galadriel and Gandalf had all spoken it in *The Lord of the Rings*. We have found that in teaching Elvish lines some actors preferred just to work by listening and repeating the sounds, while some want to know what each word means, which would influence their intonation. Because Elvish has a different word order to English a person might naturally want to stress a word that they think is the subject at the beginning of the phrase. With a literal translation they might instead find that the subject is two-thirds of the way through and that can change the rhythm of the phrase. Literal translations can be very helpful. Sir Ian McKellen always liked to know exactly what he was saying.

When the Elves spoke lines in English their accent was Standard English and well enunciated, with a delicacy of articulation (foregoing any sounds which might be perceived as modern or slovenly). It's important to feel the power of the Elves. They are ancient. Elrond, in particular, is a lord and very wise. He thinks before speaking so his speech is measured.

One thing that kept us on our toes was the tendency for the pronunciation of names to drift on set. We can coach someone to pronounce a name a certain way and they'll know it, but once on set amid countless people of varying accents and nationalities, all of whom have their own habitual way of saying that name, it's easy for someone to be affected and slip into saying it a different way. Sometimes all we can do is make sure the mouth movements are correct and get it right later in the additional dialogue recording sessions.

Roisin Carty, Supervising Dialect Coach

'In a film with so much digital content, the fact
t they have focused and given so much attention to
performance is, I think, is awesome.'

When people begin the first day of Elf training it's funny because, almost always, they're of the mindset that they need to stand straight, tighten up and pull in that belly. In fact, it's the opposite. It's really about undoing everything. For someone playing an Elf, it's about stripping back everything and starting again from neutral.

You have to soften the body, beginning in a relaxed, aligned state. We do a lot of Alexander Technique work, breathing in to the side ribs, lengthening through the torso and drawing into the core, but not tightening anything on the outside. The front body softens and widens through the shoulders, lengthening through the neck and letting the neck fall forward and then again coming to a stand. We did a lot of sitting and standing with the Elves because it's all about ease and grace and form without being aware of oneself. As soon as someone pulls into a pose, it's horrible.

Elves have this innate beauty, the kind possessed by a person who is unaware of how beautiful they are. They have a kind of sixth sense that permits them to see everything all around them at once. They listen with their backs, drawing in and becoming completely centred and neutral in their bodies. So, when they look at something, they don't look to discover it, but instead look with a knowing, as if they know what they will see. You might think that knowingness would remove you emotionally, but it doesn't. You actually become more emotionally involved because you're listening and feeling even more and you're allowing yourself to be open and to feel everything. You're opening up your fear centre and releasing the neck, which as human beings we tense if we don't feel comfortable. Becoming an Elf, a person draws in, allowing themselves to feel.

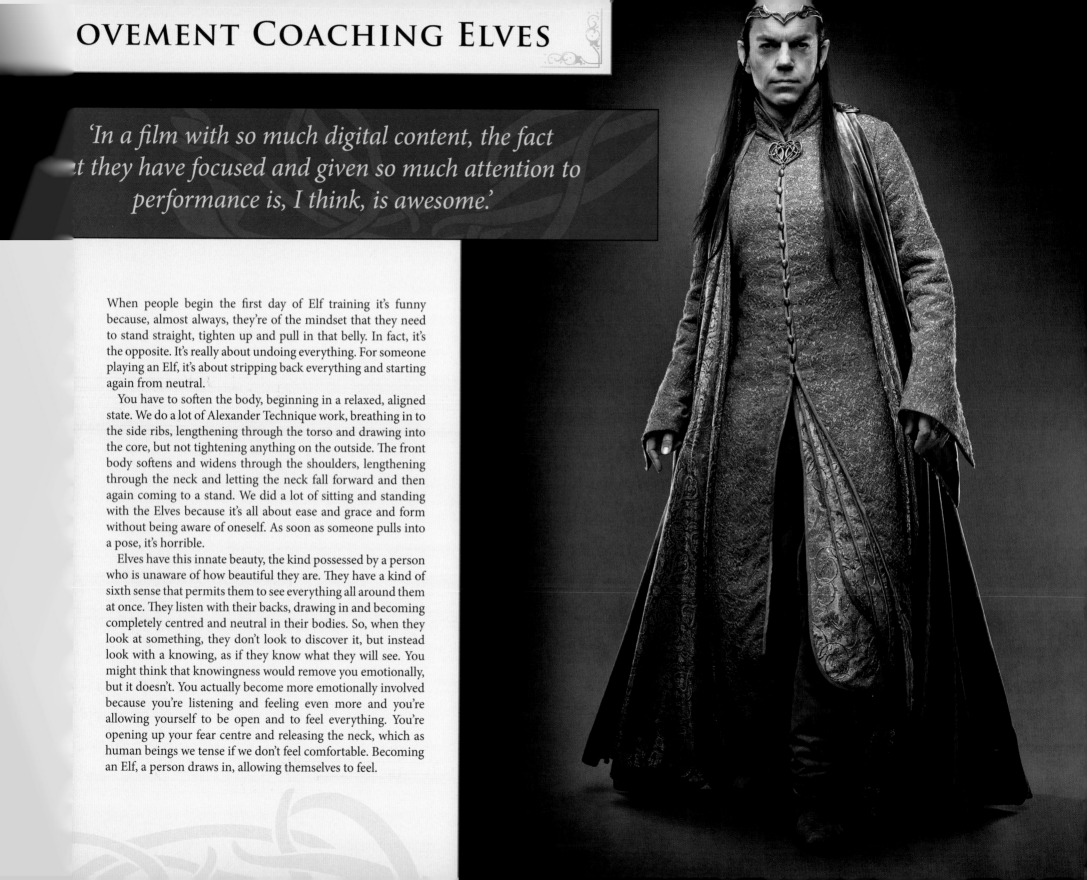

For an Elf, everything has fluidity and a sense of connection and harmony with nature. Their thoughts and actions are seamless, so there's not a sequence of thought, decision, initiation and action but rather the thought and the action are one and are in time with each other. They draw in and project out.

Imagine a five-year-old sitting on a beach, looking out at the ocean, perfect, relaxed, content and just listening – that is the perfect Elf. The best Elf actors on this show are those who can allow themselves to be completely neutral in their faces, trusting those emotions to well up in just their eyes and know that is enough for us as an audience to understand what they are feeling.

We do a lot of exercises in which I ask the actors to show me what they are feeling without showing me, by just feeling it and seeing what happens to the body, focusing on the emotion rather than the expression of that emotion. There is the tendency to want to tense up in the neck, but opening and letting that all pour out through the eyes – that is the magic of the Elves. When that is captured, it's beautiful.

While I acknowledge what was done in *The Lord of the Rings*, we aren't basing the performances in these movies on trying to replicate what was done in them. I didn't research the trilogy and try to copy how an Elf might have moved. Instead, we wipe the slate clean and build from the ground up with our characters. Sometimes people come to a movement coach on day one and say, 'Show me how I am supposed to move.' That is the opposite to the approach we take. If I were to tell the actors, 'This is how you're going to move,' then I would have a bunch of people trying to mimic me. Each Elf has their own personality. For an actor, it's much more refreshing and satisfying to know they are creating their character, it's coming from them, and it's coming out of them, it's something we have built instead of copied.

I offer images for them to work with that may help them find the right state. Elves have an internal core that is soft and flexible. They're beings of nature, of the wind. They move from their back, as if propelled by a wind, but then settling as a breeze pushes them from the front till they're held by these two energies, lifting them. If an actor has an image in their head then they will feel it and we will see it rather than if they are trying to emulate someone else's performance.

Terry Notary, Movement Coach

Elves are graceful and elegant in the way they move. I think Hugo sets a good standard for that. He floats around and holds himself very regally. Peter Jackson's often saying, 'Smooth it.' When I walked down, he was hassling me for looking like some sort of cowboy. I think I was really swaggering too much. Elves: regal, graceful.

Bret McKenzie, Actor, Lindir

Credit must be given to Terry Notary for the way the Elves move in this film. Terry is an incredibly talented man. He has found a way for each of us to move that characterizes not just our species but also our individual characters, so we each move in our own way.

It's about putting the body back into its most natural state, like a tree, relaxed and sensitive. The image of seaweed in the water comes to mind; a balloon floating on a string. Terry's insightful direction is so helpful. I might have days in which I have a lot of lines or things on my mind, but something Terry has said to me will occur to me and put me right back where I need to be. I might see him on set and he'll change the way he's standing in a way that I can understand and take on and apply to my work.

In a film with so much digital content, the fact that they have focused and given so much attention to performance is, I think, awesome. As an actor I am so grateful for that and I think it is part of what makes these films so special. Creating these worlds and all of the stuff that makes this film mind-blowing works only because at the centre of it there is heart and authenticity. There is something very real to it, and that is something as subtle and essential as the way in which we move.

Lee Pace, Actor, Thranduil

ELROND

Elrond is Lord of the Elves of Rivendell and he's about 3,000 years old. He has one of the three Elven rings, Vilya. He is half-man, half-Elf. His full name is Elrond Half-elven. He's one of the older souls in Middle-earth and therefore has vast experience and wisdom.

Hugo Weaving, Actor, Elrond

Elrond has nurtured Rivendell as a haven of knowledge and beauty, protected by Elvish magic from the touch of time or corruption. Standing as the Last Homely House before civilized lands give way to the wild, his home offers welcome and an opportunity to share insight for all fair peoples of Middle-earth. This welcome is met with distrust by the Dwarves, whose age-old enmity with the Elves discolours their gratitude, even if Elrond himself is responsible for no past wrongs.

Wise as he is, Elrond harbours misgivings concerning Thorin's purpose and voicing these concerns does little to endear him to the Dwarf. As one of the White Council, Elrond is ever concerned with the broader scheme of events and watchful for the signs of change in the world that may signal the return of their ancient enemy, Sauron.

For me as a fan of the first films now working on this trilogy, it was incredibly exciting to witness characters like Elrond, Legolas and Galadriel re-emerging. There were scenes and characters and days at which point I felt like I had stepped into *The Lord of the Rings* and was working in Middle-earth. This sensation was strongest with the Elves.

It might be twelve years on, but Hugo Weaving stepped straight back into Elrond. We were there as dialect coaches to help remind them and rebuild their confidence with speaking Elvish, but I was delighted to see how quickly that familiarity re-emerged. Those languages bring realism to the world, which is very important in helping us to believe in it.

Leith McPherson, Dialect Coach

The Dwarves have a map and it can't quite be deciphered. Gandalf knows who might be able to, which is why he leads the Company to Rivendell. The map has certain symbols on it, which can only be read by the light of a certain moon. Elrond reads the map for them and deciphers what the moon runes say, which can then help them go and get into the Mountain. That's his primary function in the film and it's certainly his primary function in the book.

The Hobbit is an innocent story, a more childlike narrative: a group of Dwarves and a hobbit going in search of their treasure. Within the book Elrond reads the map for them and says, 'Here, you guys, have a good trip,' but in the world of the film there are certain broader political undercurrents and that's where Gandalf, Elrond, Galadriel and Saruman play their roles, illuminating the politics and machinations beneath the journey of the Dwarves and what's going on in the bigger picture.

Hugo Weaving, Actor, Elrond

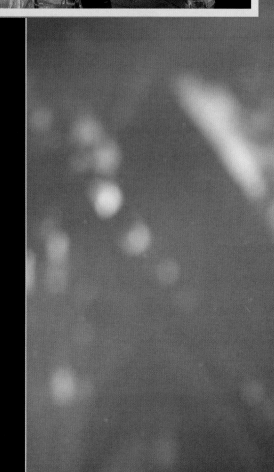

LINDIR

Bret McKenzie, whose brief appearance at the Council of Elrond in *The Fellowship of the Ring* captured so much attention and saw him get a line in *The Return of the King*, is back again for *The Hobbit*. This time he gets a name, Lindir the Elf. He's a big deal now, he gets his own ears rather than generic ear tips.

Tami Lane, Prosthetics Supervisor

When *The Fellowship of the Ring* came out the fans liked my Elf performance at the Council of Elrond. They gave me the name Figwit, "Frodo is great... who is that?" and started a website. This was pretty early on in the world of websites. The internet was just taking off at this point. It's such a short moment that they had to take screen grabs and draw big red circles around me with arrows pointing to which Elf because otherwise you wouldn't notice; but Figwit became this cult Elf character that people connected to, sort of as a joke. It was a ridiculous idea: being in the movie for two seconds, yet I've got a website. It was a funny situation. The filmmakers asked me back to be in *The Return of the King* as a tribute to this Figwit phenomenon and I think, again, for *The Hobbit*, it's a similar nod to the bizarre cult Elf status I had from the first film. So, thanks very much to the creators of the Figwit website.

Bret McKenzie, Actor, Lindir

The way I see it, Lindir is Elrond's personal assistant, so anything Elrond doesn't want to do, he throws on to me. When all the Dwarves come to stay with Gandalf at Rivendell, I'm the guy there looking after them and dealing with their terrible behavioural problems.

Bret McKenzie, Actor, Lindir

As Key Hair and Make-up Artist I was going to be doing make-ups along with the rest of our team, but the volume of work involved in just coordinating the needs and workflow of our department on a project this large has meant I haven't had the chance to do very much make-up work.

One that I did get to work on was Lindir, Bret McKenzie's Elf in Rivendell. It was great to have Bret come back in after all those years since *The Lord of the Rings*. While we meet so many new characters that expand the world of Middle-earth, seeing familiar faces again reminds us we're in the same world and as crew it was great to see old friends again. He suits the Elf character too.

Angela Mooar, Key Hair and Make-up Artist

Poor Bret McKenzie. He was thrown some Elvish at lunchtime one day. He was making such a good impression on the set that Philippa decided to throw him a scene in Sindarin at lunchtime and have him shoot it that afternoon. That's what we call the deep end, but he did it and did really well with it. That was a tough call!

Leith McPherson, Dialect Coach

The tricky part with Elvish is taking these words and remembering what they mean in English, then trying to put that meaning back on these phonetic sounds and giving them life. That's the challenge. Hugo Weaving is really good at that. He mastered it.

Bret McKenzie, Actor, Lindir

GALADRIEL

'There are fissures in the spirit of Middle-earth. Something terrible is coming. I think what is noble and heroic about Gandalf and Galadriel is they are prepared, together, to look that in the eye.'

Even among the wise of Middle-earth, the Lady Galadriel of Lothlórien is held in reverence and her words carry great weight. One of the oldest beings in the world, Galadriel has seen the mighty rise and fall, lands change shape and powers shift. Bearer of the Elven Ring of Power, Nenya, she possesses knowledge and enchantments unknown even to the Wizards and by her magic is the realm of Lórien kept safe from evil influence or intrusion.

When the White Council convenes to debate what the alarming appearance of a Morgul blade portends, the radiant Galadriel speaks with the authority of countless centuries and her gentle words carry the weight of peerless experience as an enemy of the re-emerging darkness.

Of all the Wise, she is perhaps Gandalf the Grey's strongest supporter and confidante, calling him by the Sindarin name, Mithrandir.

Reprising the role and donning her prosthetic ear tips once again is Cate Blanchett, who played Galadriel in *The Lord of the Rings*, bringing her stately elegance and majesty to the character and creating another link between the film trilogies.

When I got word that Galadriel would be in a small section of *The Hobbit* I was over the moon. It's an amazing thing to be able to return to something that was begun twelve years ago. I think Peter has such an extraordinary sense of the sublimely beautiful and the grotesque and the way that he combines those two things is utterly unique.

Having had the memory of making *The Lord of the Rings*, I would hazard a guess that *The Hobbit* is going to have a very particular resonance, a prescience of what is to come. The audience knows what is going to come: the fracturing of the White Council, the fact that Gandalf and Galadriel sense that something's wrong. It's Europe of the 1930s. They can feel war is coming but everyone is saying, 'The world is at peace.' There are things afoot. There are fissures in the spirit of Middle-earth. Something terrible is coming.

I think what is noble and heroic about Gandalf and Galadriel is they are prepared, together, to look that in the eye. That's what makes Gandalf the most wonderful hero for this decade. He has the courage to move into the darkness that no one else is prepared to go into, against popular opinion, to save the earth. I find that very noble and very brave.

Cate Blanchett, Actress, Galadriel

It's interesting the way Peter has shot the Elves. Normally he is shooting at forty-eight frames, but he shot us at fifty-four to sixty frames to give an otherworldly quality.

Because the Elves are shot at a higher rate, it slows down the delivery of dialogue on screen, so it has been important when doing the additional dialogue recording that we do later to find buoyancy in it, even though I have to match the sync of the voice, so that it doesn't sound like I'm speaking through treacle.

Cate Blanchett, Actress, Galadriel

Galadriel's speech comes through at a slightly slower tempo. There's a dream-like quality to the way she speaks, partly as a result of that process. So it's slow, measured and thoughtful, all qualities that support the magical and timeless nature of her character, placing her just slightly outside our reality.

Roisin Carty, Supervising Dialect Coach

Their effect was very subtle, but Galadriel actually wore contact lenses. Rather than completely recolour them, her lenses were designed to lighten and enhance Cate Blanchett's own pale blue eyes, making them feel even more remarkable and beautiful, but still based within her natural colour range.

Peter King, Make-up and Hair Designer

All our Elves have straight hair with one exception. Galadriel is special and she is the only Elf to have a delicate wave in her hair. Indeed, Galadriel's hair is very special. The same wig that she wore in *The Lord of the Rings* was used again for *The Hobbit* and there is a story to go with it.

Years ago Peter Owen and I were offered the opportunity to purchase this astonishing bolt of long blonde hair that came out of somewhere in Russia. It had been found somewhere, though we will never know where exactly. For all we know it could have been a hundred years old by the time it got to us. Hair comes to us in strange ways sometimes. In some places it is grown and cut for money as long hair of certain types can be very valuable. Sometimes it has been kept in an attic for years by a family member or found in an old suitcase. Hair doesn't rot, so we've had people bring in hair from a great-grandparent that is over a century old. Sometimes they are long braids from a child's first haircut and a person will come forward and ask, 'Can you use this?' carrying a lock of hair that is like spun gold.

We jumped on this hair when we saw it, even though at the time we had no specific use for it, knowing that one day there would be a time when we would need it; but years went by and we never felt that we had the right opportunity to do justice to the hair. It was forty inches long, which is practically unheard of and especially in that colour. For more than ten years this amazing, long pale blonde hair sat safely in a drawer, waiting for the perfect opportunity to be used. When Galadriel came along on *The Lord of the Rings*, it was clear that this was the character that that hair had been waiting for, and we created a beautiful wig from it. Now it will be preserved and kept as a sacred artefact from these films for ever, having been worn by one of the most famous and wonderful actresses of our age in a series of films that made history. It's amazing to think it probably began its journey on a humble person living deep in Russia somewhere, and possibly even generations ago. I hope they'd be happy with how we have honoured them.

Peter King, Make-up and Hair Designer

Peter King pulled out the wig and it was like seeing a creature emerge. To put on that wig felt somehow timeless. The whole thing felt timeless.

Cate Blanchett, Actress, Galadriel

'For more than ten years this amazing, long pale blonde hair sat safely in a drawer, just waiting for the perfect opportunity to be used.'

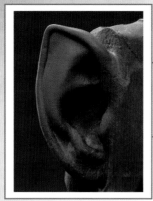

ELVEN EARS

Elves have delicately pointed ears in Peter Jackson's Middle-earth, so we created ear tip prosthetics for our entire Elf cast to wear. The technique we employed was exactly the same as we used a decade ago on *The Lord of the Rings* – creating small prosthetic appliances that glued to the top half of the actor or extra's ears.

For returning cast members such as Hugo Weaving and Cate Blanchett we discussed reusing the ear tips we made for them for *The Lord of the Rings* as we still had all those moulds, but it's surprising how much a person's ears change over time. We have also refined our mould-making processes since then, so we elected to recast and sculpt new ear tips for everyone.

The finished prosthetic tips themselves were all made as gelatine appliances, essentially the same material people bake with. We use a gel-filled silicone for our Dwarf prosthetics because of how beautifully it moves and replicates skin, but for the ears it made more sense to stick with gelatine. We needed to run between 300 and 400 ears a week and two people could turn out close to a hundred pairs a day using gelatine. It is also very friendly to use in application. Gelatine can be blended into skin seamlessly with a little witch hazel or warm water.

All of our lead Elves had specific prosthetics sculpted over positives cast from their own ears and tinted to match their skin tones as a base for the make-up, which was applied by their make-up artist. We created generic ears that were used on all the mid- and background Elves, stunt Elves and supporting characters.

Our generic ear tips were all based on one standard ear core with variations on the length and shape of the point. For extras on *Rings* we had created very simple little miniature tips that glued onto the very top edge on the ear, adding a tiny point, but this time our extras had the same kind of larger prosthetic ear tips worn by the leads. Once glued on, they covered the entire top half of the ear, from where the top rim meets the head, back and down as far as where the curled edge of the ear begins to turn into a lobe.

Jason Docherty, Weta Workshop Prosthetics Team Leader

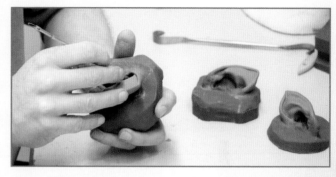

Above: Weta Workshop Sculptor Gary Hunt sculpts Elven ear tip prosthetics in Plasticine.

OF STONE GIANTS

' WE HAD TO FIGURE OUT
WHAT WAS MOUNTAIN AND
WHAT WAS GIANT. '

- R Christopher White, Weta Digital Visual Effects Supervisor

CONCERNING GIANTS

Attempting to cross the Misty Mountains the Company is caught in a storm and finds itself in the middle of an elemental battle between Giants made of stone that tear themselves free of the mountainside. The Giants were a new race of creatures unlike almost anything else seen before. The closest analogue might be the Ents, but even they were composed of living, albeit plant, matter, whereas the Giants, as Peter Jackson interpreted them from Tolkien's suggestive prose, seemed to be entirely elemental. They were also on a scale unlike any other humanoid creatures in the films.

Even among Tolkien enthusiasts and scholars, there is some debate as to exactly what the Stone Giants are and how they fit into the world lore he developed in his writings. Some have suggested they might be metaphorical or perhaps a variety of very large Troll.

As played in *The Hobbit: An Unexpected Journey* they emerge from the mountainsides as personifications of the peaks, infused with ancient and powerful magic beyond the ken of mortals and linked to the power of the storm that rages around them. They are composed of rock entirely, rather than flesh of any kind and as they battle their forms disintegrate, reverting to rubble, with the suggestion being that in a subsequent storm they might reform to do battle again.

BUILDING STONE GIANTS

The scene in which the Stone Giants appeared was very dark and full of rain and lightning. While these creatures aren't human and have their own silhouette, it was important that the audience understand what they were looking at in the brief flashes and glimpses that they got.

We had begun with very different designs, with heads in the middle of their chests, which weren't as human-like as those we ended up with in the movie. While we could go some way from the classical proportions, there was a limit we reached, after which the Giants became too abstract for people to recognize and follow in the action. We had to retain certain key points so that people could see where their heads were, their hands, their faces, and understand what they were doing in each shot.

Marco Revelant, Weta Digital Models Supervisor

Profiles were very important with the Stone Giants because with lightning flashes behind them we seldom saw more than a general shape. They were also part of their environment, so we had figure out what was mountain and what was Giant. We had massive rocks grinding against each other and chunks falling away.

In the end our decisions were dictated by what we were seeing in the context of each shot. It all had to be readable in an instant on the screen. The question was, 'How much do we see and is it enough to convey what needs to be told?' Looking at these creatures in isolation and under bright, flat lighting conditions is misleading. What mattered was how they looked in their shots and whether they functioned in telling the story.

R Christopher White, Weta Digital Visual Effects Supervisor

We had a lot of discussion in the beginning about how the rocks were staying together. Some of the artists suggested that there were vines or roots that could contain the rocks, but it was a weird idea that never really worked so we moved away from that and just went with pure rocks. The Giants as seen in the film are composed of elements that we are saying are not compressible or elastic. They are rock, and elastic rock would look weird, so instead we imagined that these are stones grinding against each other. So, how would that look? We thought there would probably be a lot of dust and crumbling stone when they moved.

Marco Revelant, Weta Digital Models Supervisor

We found that the crumbling stone actually helped us with conveying a sense of scale, because you'd see all these little rocks falling away in the distance. The Dwarves were so small and they were against this mountain. There was this vast thing, well over a hundred metres tall, that was made out of rocks and moving, but it was hard to judge the scale of it. Falling rocks and little clumps of greenery on the Giants really helped us convey how big they were in relation to the heroes.

R Christopher White, Weta Digital Visual Effects Supervisor

Building the layers of a Stone Giant effects shot:

1: The bare bone composite including matte painting, CG mountains, CG giant, FX rocks, dirt and dust debris coming off the giant, CG Dwarves and Bilbo.

2: Cloud layers separate the Giant from the background mountains and mist around him helps convey his true scale.

3: Illuminated by lightning, a layer of atmosphere gives the impression of illuminated air between the viewer and Giant.

4: Diffusion is applied based on distance, further defining the planes of the image.

5: Deep, mid and foreground rain elements are added.

Above: The final frame with night time grade applied.

OF GOBLINS

'*FROM THE LOOK OF THEM YOU GET THE FEELING THEY HAVE BEEN CUT OFF AND FESTERING IN THEIR OWN VERY SHALLOW GENE POOL FOR QUITE SOME TIME.*'

- Richard Taylor,
Weta Workshop Design & Special Effects Supervisor

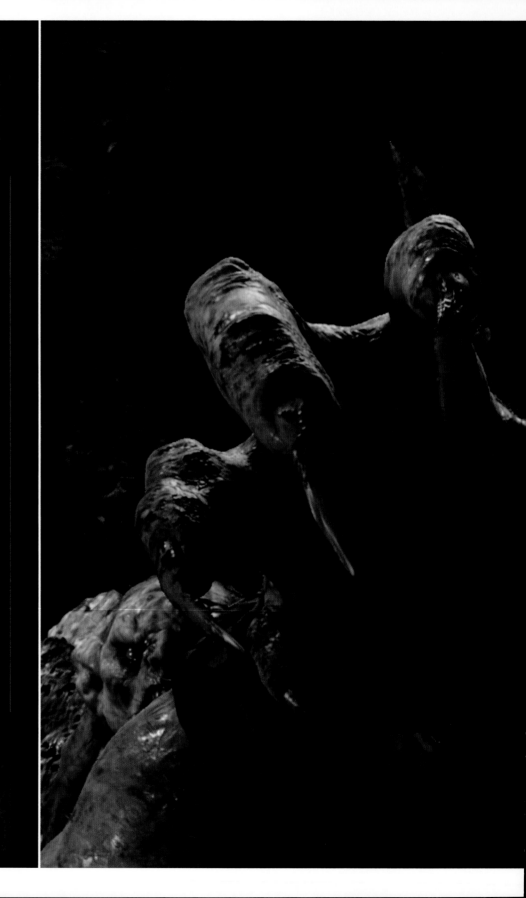

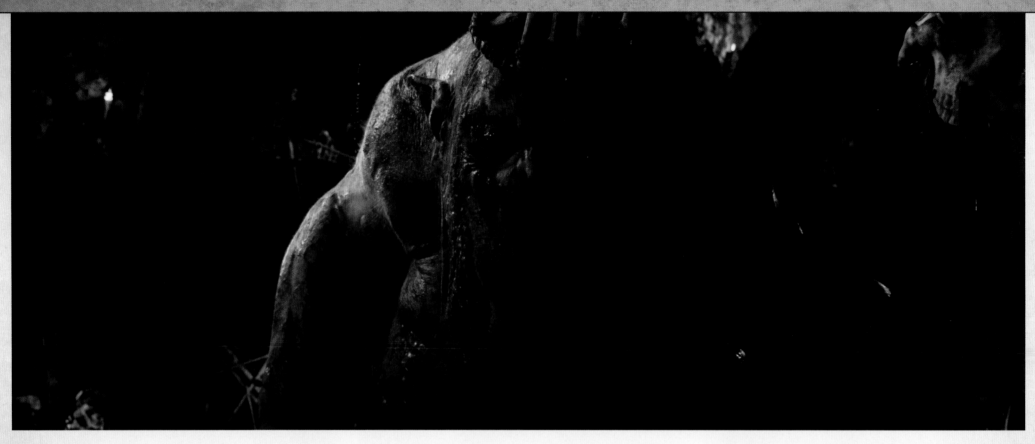

The Company of Thorin takes shelter in what appears to be a welcomingly hospitable cave after their close escape from the storm and Stone Giant battle outside. But seldom are such places unclaimed, and their relief is cut short when the Goblin residents spring their trap. Thrown down a slick shaft and snapped in a cruel trap, the Dwarves are trussed and bound in quick order and marched to an audience with the self-proclaimed monarch of the mountain deeps, the Goblin King.

Distant kin to the Orcs, this inbred population of cave dwellers exist in a precarious state, perched in rickety, high-density accommodation over a yawning chasm and subject to the wildly swaying whims of their bloated leader. Stricken by painful diseases, the Goblins find rare delight in the mistreatment of their guests, but a special kind of fear-fuelled malevolence is unleashed when they recognize the legendary sword Orcrist, whose reputation among Orc kind is rivalled only by that of the blade's mate, Glamdring.

The Goblins went through quite a design process before settling where they finally did. Peter wanted to be sure that they had an unforgettable screen personality and not be a retread of any of the Orcish varieties we had seen before. They're related to the other Orc breeds, but distinct, and from the look of them you get the feeling they have been cut off and festering in their own very shallow gene pool for quite some time. They had to be something new and original. There are similarities to the small Orcs seen in Moria in *The Lord of the Rings*, whom we often referred to as Goblins within Weta at the time, but these new, true Goblins have developed in a novel and disturbing direction. They are very asymmetrical, with bodies that are afflicted by all kinds of disfiguring ailments and rotting diseases, clearly uncomfortable. There's no question they have their own memorable look, which is exactly what Peter set out to achieve.

Richard Taylor,
Weta Workshop Design & Special Effects Supervisor

The Goblins are like a captive audience to the antics of the Goblin King and to his pretensions of grandeur. They're his faithful little underlings, completely terrified of him on the one hand because at any moment he might take one of them and rip them in half, but then attracted to him as the brightest light in their dismal existence. They're like moths around a candle, desperate to get as close as possible but bound to get burned. They have to play up their adoration for him too, because none of them wants to be the one caught not being appropriately enthusiastic or attentive. He has no thought for them at all. They're there for his benefit and he gives no thought to their lives. He even stands on them.

Terry Notary, Movement Coach

GOBLIN ACCENTS

The only Goblin with specific scripted lines was really the Goblin King, but his minions were all chattering away in the background all the time, and we chose to record them in English rather than a variety of Black Speech. They're actually a very chatty species.

Leith McPherson, Dialect Coach

There was the idea at one stage of creating an original Goblin language. The thought was that when they are in the tunnels there would be a constant background chatter of some kind of Goblin language to help convey the unique flavour of their world. In the end it really didn't seem necessary, so they ended up speaking English.

Roisin Carty, Supervising Dialect Coach

Casting Barry Humphries as the Goblin King was an act of creative genius, but it also meant granting free range for him to do what he does best. He is just such an extraordinary vocal performer and such an amazing comedian. Barry can swing from an English to Australian accent at the turn of a sharp phrase and he is very good at it, but just occasionally that was coming through in his performance when the Goblin King was swinging wildly in moods. I recall at one moment thinking, as someone who lives in Sydney, 'Oh great, so there's one character in Middle-earth who sounds Australian and he's the ugliest, most loathsome of them all?'

Fortunately for Australians everywhere, as Barry was recording his additional dialogue work he favoured more of a British base in his speech, and consequently that was what was applied to the rest of his gang as well.

Leith McPherson, Dialect Coach

DIGITAL CHALLENGES

Inset, above: Weta Digital Visual Effects Supervisor Eric Saindon on set with Director Peter Jackson. The complexity of the project demanded that Weta Digital had a supervisor on the live-action set at all times.

For the Goblin Town sequences, the hero cast was filmed on an elaborate set designed and built by the 3 Foot 7 Art Department. Goblin performers were also filmed and motion captured in the scene, providing invaluable reference for the final digital Goblins, but also necessitating their replacement. The successful blending of physical and digital realms, especially in 3D, presents all manner of technical challenges for the teams involved, but which they have become adept at resolving.

We have a visual effects supervisor assigned to both the second and main shooting units (main, in my case) and it's our role to keep abreast of everything that relates to Weta Digital's work on the show, so that means we're there to keep an eye on how things are being handled in the live-action shoot and how that will affect our future effects work. It's a lot of working under pressure and knowing what the best answer to any question about effects is, because the right answer on the spot can make a huge difference to us down the road.

Part of this responsibility involves the capture of information that we'll need later as well, and we have a number of ways of doing this. The mysterious grey and chrome balls, that anyone who watches behind-the-scenes imagery will recognize as something the digital effects guys seem to carry around with them on a set, are part of that set of information-gathering tools. The grey one captures colour. It's 50% grey, so any colour difference that we see on it tells us what colour the lighting on the set is. The chrome ball captures light locations and intensity. We can unwrap the spherical image and it tells us where to place all the lights in our digital recreation of the scene. That's critical when you're working with 3D. Looking at a 2D image on a plate, you never know where the lights might be, so using that we can recreate what was built on set and integrate our creatures and lighting into the scene very accurately.

We also do HDR images, which stands for High Dynamic Range. We take a 360-degree dome reading all around with all the lights in the scene, at low and high exposures, thereby getting the full lighting range from the scene. It's essentially the same idea as the chrome ball, but a step higher.

Another information-gathering method that we used a great deal on *The Hobbit* was scanning, whereby we position a microwave-like box in the middle of the set and it rotates around with a little laser, reading the colour and geometry of everything. We can then very accurately rebuild the same set digitally and position our creatures and set extensions.

With 3D, it's all about being pinpoint accurate. We could fudge things with 2D, which we did a lot on *The Lord of the Rings*: 'Doesn't quite work? Stick a tussock in front of it.' We can't do that anymore. It just doesn't work in 3D.

Eric Saindon, Weta Digital Visual Effects Supervisor

The 3D presentation certainly forces us to raise the bar in terms of accurately placing objects in our digital spaces. We have our paint department that specializes in removing characters from plates and reconstructing those plates, but when this is being done in stereo then we have to reconstruct everything at precise depths or the illusion is blown.

R Christopher White, Weta Digital Visual Effects Supervisor

At 48 frames per second we're essentially seeing twice as much detail. That has been tough. Back in the day, the make-up department could hide a lace beard or hairline in the fuzz of the film grain, but not any more. Now they have to pay extra special attention to details like that and it's the same case with us in the digital world too.

Gino Acevedo,
Weta Digital Textures Supervisor/Creative Art Director

Our compositing department had to be much more accurate and true to physical space than we've had to be in the past. As we learned on previous 3D movies we have worked on, compositing had been thought of as a 2D operation – the layering of 2D elements, but that no longer works. It's not enough to just know in what order elements are layered. Now we need to know where each element exists in space. We need to know the exact depth. We have a technique whereby every pixel element has a value that represents where it exists as a point in space, so all of our compositing is now done in 3D, a big change to the way it has been in the past.

As far as 3D rendering goes, we're rendering the same thing as seen through two cameras. There's more work involved but conceptually it's simple because it's the same as if you were shooting with two cameras on a stage.

In addition to 3D, we are also working at a higher frame rate on these movies. *The Hobbit* has been filmed, and is being projected in some theatres, at 48 frames per second, where the norm has been 24. This has doubled the amount of material we have to work on because we're shooting double the number of frames. Fortunately it hasn't affected anything for us as far as the core technique is concerned. Everything we have to do within one of those frames is the same, regardless of how many there are, but now we just have a lot more to do.

Joe Letteri, Weta Digital Senior Visual Effects Supervisor

Capturing Goblins

Goblin performers were motion captured live on the set with the Dwarves. Even though we might completely replace them with the final digital creature, having something that has been shot with performers on set can be very beneficial because it helps us with lighting and seeing how the characters are integrated into the environment. Also, their physical interactions with the set, other characters and props are all there in-camera.

R Christopher White, Weta Digital Visual Effects Supervisor

The motion capture performances for the Goblins involved a lot of running around. The Goblin Town set was a jumble of platforms and it presented quite a challenge to choreograph and get things to work on such uneven and precarious geography. Attention to detail was very important. We had stunt performers holding green-screen pads strategically placed around the set and green-screen sticks for the Dwarf actors to use to hit them with so that the impacts would register against something, providing the necessary recoil or bounce of the weapon so it would look like they were really hitting physical Goblins. The stunt guys would, of course, be replaced later with digital Goblins getting sliced or bashed up.

We had guys getting thrown or having to jump off the set as the action unfolded. Half a dozen Dwarves running through a shot attacking Goblins meant a couple of Goblins for each Dwarf and very quickly we would have thirty people running around in that shot on elevated platforms, all fighting. It was very involved and a lot of it had to be carefully choreographed.

We also had the hangar, as we called it, a warehouse near the airport, which we set up for rehearsing. We tried to keep our stuff broad so that it could be adapted or changed on set. We would make up action scenarios and design them in such a way that they could be put together in various combinations. Any action by one of the performers could be taken and put anywhere as needed, so Peter could move things around to his taste and we didn't need to choreograph a whole new action each time. Peter gave us a lot of creative licence, which was great.

Glenn Boswell, Stunt Co-ordinator

MOVEMENT COACHING GOBLINS

Each race moves with its own characteristic rhythm. We look for rhythms in people's movements unconsciously and once we find them we feel more comfortable with a person. We worked with our Orcs and Goblins to create a three- or five-count that would feel disjointed – five steps forward, two steps back – advance, retreat, step, flinch. When a Dwarf moves there is a rhythm that comes with his breathing: one, two, three, four. But with the Orcs and Goblins we created a sense of uneasiness in the observer by breaking their movement so that they don't have a sense of being able to breathe with them as we watch them move. The Goblins are like seagulls walking on the sand: tap, tap, tap, stop. They live from point to point and can only remember a point behind them. Everything is immediate and they are trapped in the now. I imagined a crumpled piece of aluminium foil, weightless, without foundation, angular and sharp, uncomfortable and constricted or tight. They're like little balls of electricity.

Fear pervades and provides the only structures to their society, so they are constantly looking over their shoulders. There are no rules, only threat, so they sneak around and attack from the back. They are cowardly and have no sense of pride or loyalty, like vermin at the bottom of everything – exhausting to play but hugely fun.

Terry Notary, Movement Coach

Above: Movement Coach Terry Notary provides direction to Stuntman Shane Rangi, who performs motion capture as a Goblin on the fully dressed Goblin Town set.

BUILDING GOBLINS

Above: Weta Workshop Sculptor Steven Saunders sculpts a Goblin design maquette in Plasticine.

We began our work by taking the design lead established by Weta Workshop, extrapolating the intent behind the conceptual designs to build our basic Goblin from them, with Peter's direction. The benefit of a digital creature is that they can be pushed further than could ever be achieved with someone in make-up.

Marco Revelant, Weta Digital Models Supervisor

With CG we can exploit really unique proportions that wouldn't be possible if we had to rely solely on using creature suited performers. A mask can look fantastic, but sometimes once it's on a performer's head, just from the way it moves and the fact it fills out in a certain way, you can tell there's somebody in there and the illusion can be lost. Digital technology allows us to not just build on top of an actor's shape, but push into it, so features can be deeper and arms can be very thin and elongated in a way that would be impossible to do the practical way. So it made total sense to go digital with the Goblins.

**Gino Acevedo,
Weta Digital Textures Supervisor/Creative Art Director**

The Goblins have very long arm proportions with very short legs relative to their torsos. We had to do some retargeting with the motion capture to accomplish this, but it's something that you don't see very often so it was worth the effort.

Marco Revelant, Weta Digital Models Supervisor

Once we had the basic Goblin design working, we could explore the range of what could be done with it and build diversity into our ranks, because we had an entire Goblin cavern to populate. We started with one basic concept but then extrapolated upon it to make bigger versions, fatter versions, smaller Goblins or all kinds of other variations. We could build a diverse population but still maintain the feeling of commonality throughout, so it was clear they all come from the same gene pool, with varied body types and personalities.

Joe Letteri, Weta Digital Senior Visual Effects Supervisor

I assigned different Goblins to different artists in our modelling department to build. Each one has their own style, so you would see a slightly different approach being brought to each Goblin. That all helps create the diversity that we want in our Goblins, and we had between twelve and fourteen different Goblins in all.

Marco Revelant, Weta Digital Models Supervisor

In addition, we have new software that allows us to import multiple characters and make blends between them to generate many more. We spent some time figuring out how to make the most out of what we had and this tool allowed our artists to pick and choose features. It's actually a lot of fun building Goblins from these multiple inputs – a little bit more of this nose, a little bit more of this head, et cetera.

Marco Revelant, Weta Digital Models Supervisor

We can blend between different eyes, different jaws, different ears and other features, creating novel characters based on a combination of features from our existing builds. The real beauty and genius of the software is that the rigging, which we depend upon to animate those features, comes along for the ride. That is incredibly valuable because it effectively saves us having to build all these individual Goblin variants from scratch. We built twelve key characters and then extracted our hordes from these, blending features so no two were the same.

James Jacobs, Weta Digital Digital Creature Supervisor

Above: Examples of Goblin skin diseases created by Weta Workshop's prosthetic department.

Whatever we build as modellers has to go to the Creatures department and be rigged and eventually animated, so it is very important that we understand the anatomy and that it is believable. Even if we have created something with, for example, a very weirdly proportioned scapula and shoulder construction, we have to understand that human shoulders have evolved to a point where they are probably the closest thing to perfection already. When we distort it, we have to be sure what we are doing will still function. I sometimes have to rein in my guys from going too crazy. We can mess with proportions, but we have to be sure to keep the underlying system valid or the creature will never work. We must be careful not to create too much definition, which is so easy to do when you are designing a new creature. It has to live within the bounds of the reality that we unconsciously understand as an audience. There are certain principles or laws which we have to respect.

Marco Revelant, Weta Digital Models Supervisor

In the Creatures department we try to build mechanically. If it works mechanically then those basic tenets will apply to different characters. Once it's there and has been tested and finessed then we can re-purpose it and warp it to fit other characters with a similar body type. That can help us populate entire scenes with hundreds of subtly different characters.

James Jacobs, Weta Digital Digital Creature Supervisor

We have shots in which we have a dozen Goblins within the frame, up close, so having the ability to create such variation in their ranks is great. We will be able to build more variation with textures as well. The Goblins have these tattered things they wear, and a little hair too, both of which also give us opportunities for even more variation.

R Christopher White, Weta Digital Visual Effects Supervisor

The Goblins are covered in skin diseases, which gives us great scope to play with textures. They have lots of boils and scars and nasty rashes in places you don't want to look.

**Gino Acevedo,
Weta Digital Textures Supervisor/Creative Art Director**

All those lesions and sores do little to improve the disposition of the average Goblin. It affects their behaviour. When we were motion capturing and animating them we imagined they were uncomfortable and contorted in a constant state of pain. It's no wonder they're so angry. We've added the occasional impulsive scratch, especially when something isn't going their way. Terry Notary coached all the Goblin motion capture performers on how to behave and in turn those traits have transferred across into and influenced the animation.

David Clayton, Weta Digital Animation Supervisor

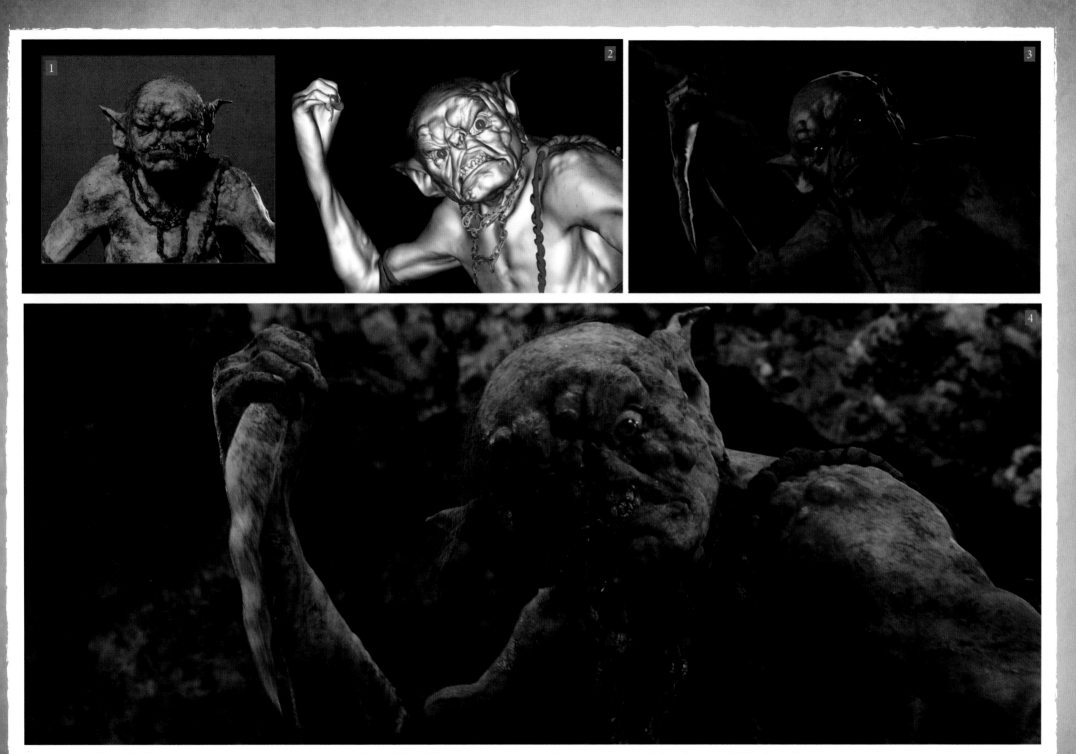

The steps of a digital Goblin shot: 1: Shader turnaround of character (Hero Goblin 12). 2: Pre-vis template. 3: Simulation pass for cloth and hair. 4: Goblin in final shot.

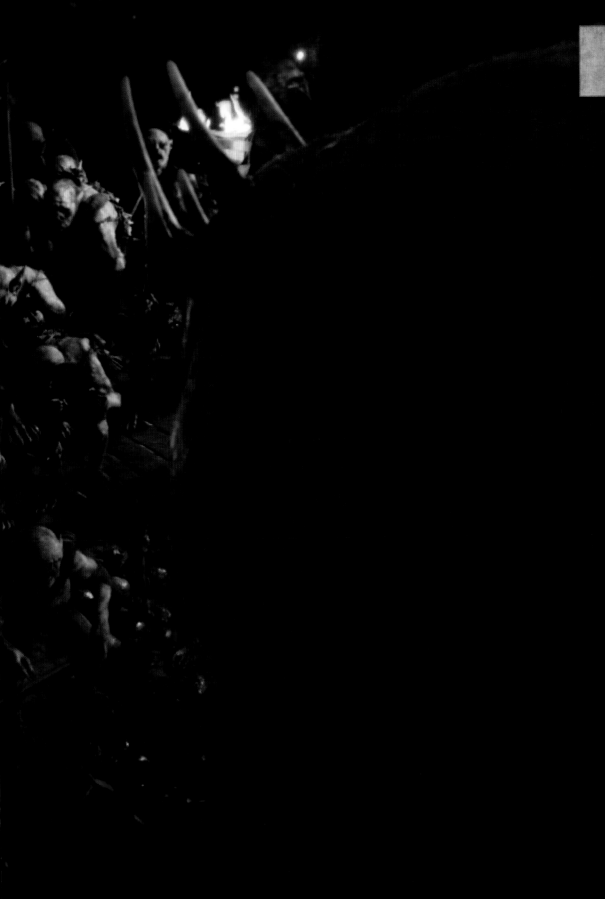

THE GOBLIN HORDE

The Goblins are essentially pack creatures but there's no synergy there. There's conflict within the crowd. It comes across in the final shots. There are Goblins shoving each other aside to be the first to get to the Dwarves. They're running and jumping over other Goblins. They're so bloodthirsty, and even once they have the Dwarves and they're marching them through Goblin Town, there's constant shoving and anger, both towards their captives and also each other.

In cases where there's a lot of pushing and shoving of the Dwarves going on it made sense to replace the live-action Dwarves with digital doubles so that we could integrate them more easily. It also meant we could be more violent, so the Goblins could really be rough with their captives, making them appear more nasty and thereby ensuring their escape comes as a genuine relief.

As the Company is fleeing and fighting their way out of Goblin Town, carving up Goblins as they go, we had to make sure that our animation painted the heroes in the best possible light. The actors were all filmed on the set, cutting their way to freedom. As we went in and added our Goblins for them to kill, we had to make sure that each one that dies was posing a threat to the Dwarves. They're not just slicing and dicing random Goblins for the fun of it. For example, in one of the live-action plates Kili goes out of his way to chase down and kill a Goblin. We didn't want Kili to look like a jerk, so it was important that the Goblin was threatening him. How could he do that if he's more than six feet away? We gave him a bow. If he'd only been armed with a dagger then Kili would have been going out of his way to kill him needlessly, which wouldn't be consistent with his honourable character, however we as the audience might feel about Goblins.

David Clayton, Weta Digital Animation Supervisor

As to who gets chosen to be featured in a given shot really comes down to who looks cool at the end of the day, so we build all our characters to the same standard. There's no such thing as a background character anymore. We build every character to the level that Peter could pick them and use them in a close-up and we can be sure they will hold up to scrutiny.

James Jacobs, Weta Digital Digital Creature Supervisor

Goblin 01

Goblin 03

There's one Goblin in particular that keeps popping up again and again because he looks so good. His face 'puppeteers' very well and he has a lot of expression: Goblin 10. We call him the Oaf because he's bigger than the others. He pops up in the background of all the crowd shots. In the end Gandalf beheads him. He was one of our custom Goblins, built to allow head decapitation, which is something we have to build specifically into our models.

David Clayton, Weta Digital Animation Supervisor

You wouldn't build all that internal tissue unless you're going to show it. He's got quite a thick neck and the beginnings of a double chin, which made him the ideal guy for decapitation.

James Jacobs, Weta Digital Digital Creature Supervisor

Goblin 10

Goblin 09

THE GOBLIN KING

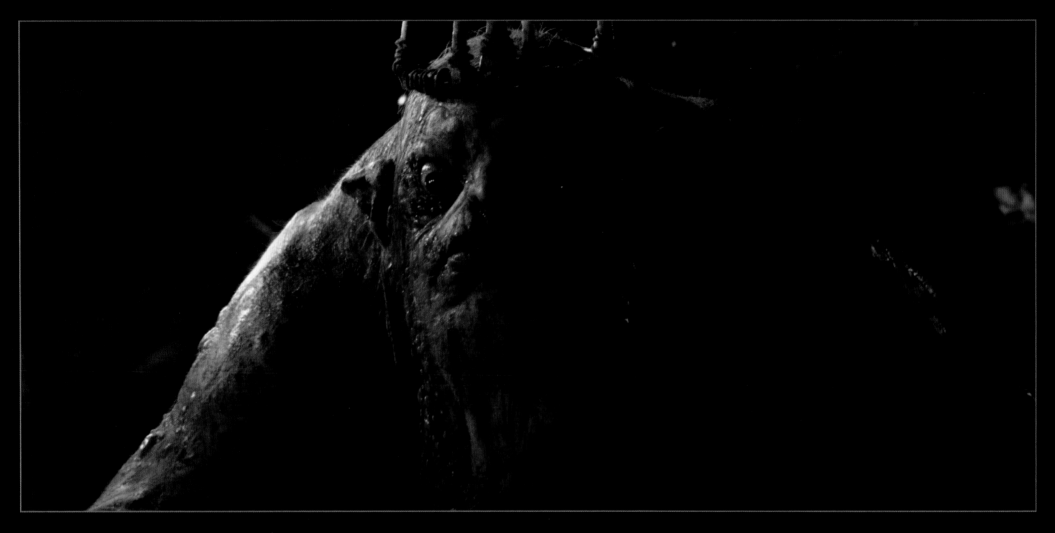

The Goblin King is a complex character. He's an attention whore, but at the same time evil and conniving, while running under all that there is an unexpected innocence about him. It all comes out in little fleeting moments, but then he's back to being king, evil and mean, then the next moment he's jealous. The emotions whip through him so quickly.

He's enormous and fat, which was great fun to personify physically. I worked with Barry Humphries for a few hours, getting a sense of who he is as we worked on movement and just by watching him do his thing. I helped with some of the character's movement, so I got in a motion capture suit and got to play a bit, translating Barry's physicality into the weight of the character. In that sense I'm like a stunt double or like a movement double, and hopefully I have done him justice.

This huge character is like a freight train. Once he gets going, he's driven by momentum. When he's moving about, it's as if he's clawing his way along, heaving himself and throwing his massive weight around. In a sense the Goblin King is like a cheesy, aging lounge singer who has had a few too many martinis and is a bit past his day, but as far as he's concerned he's still got it. He indulges himself when he's doing his thing, but then he's also glancing around, looking to make sure everyone is adoring him, always aware of everything, and then pulling back in.

He's just like the classic bully in the sandpit. It's all about him. There's nothing else that exists. It's just me, me, and me. It's coming from a pain. It's coming from emptiness. It's coming from the sadness. There's a lot of that depth there. He's really a sad, pathetic and funny character, a roller-coaster of emotion that was fun to play because there's so much to him. I watched what Barry was doing; those were the things he was playing with. The character has an almost feminine vanity, and then he sinks into this terribly dark place. There's a moment of a little lost boy and then he's a bullying, biting character again. Taking cues from Barry and jumping between those states physically was a lot of fun for me.

Terry Notary, Movement Coach

Inset: Facial capture of Barry Humphries' performance (above) driving the Goblin King animation puppet (right).

The Goblin King's extreme physicality limits his flexibility. If he raises his legs there's his belly in the way. There's only so far he can bend or twist before the simulation is pushed too far. We try to make it flexible, but the design only permits so much. Anything good is usually defined by the constraints that are built into it. With no limitations a character might end up moving in ways that would be inappropriate, given his physiology.

James Jacobs, Weta Digital Digital Creature Supervisor

We're always trying to squeeze as much performance as possible out of the creature models in a way that is funny and compelling, but without breaking them. It's important that a creature not be completely freeform of course, and have stiffness and limitations that confer a particular character. The Goblin King has a disgusting, giant wattle that connects partway down his front and adds so much value to him as a character. It's his defining feature and it jiggles about as he moves and talks with weight and realism.

David Clayton, Weta Digital Animation Supervisor

As good as the motion capture data is, we don't stop work there. The Goblin King, for example, was fantastic but we slowed it down, smoothing out any quick movements or direction changes, preserving the intent and essence of the performance, adding extra frames to help convey the appropriate sense of mass.

David Clayton, Weta Digital Animation Supervisor

The Goblin King is a giant mass of a character whose sheer size and bulk define him, performance-wise. He's not physically capable of chasing people around, so he has built a society around himself based on fear. He has relied on his minions for so long that he has become almost ineffective. When he realizes that the Dwarves are gaining the upper hand he is compelled to do something for himself and actually throw himself into the fight.

Joe Letteri, Weta Digital Senior Visual Effects Supervisor

To the Goblin King, his subjects are literally just furniture. He has no regard for them. He squishes them into the ground when he mounts and dismounts his throne. He just ploughs through them and if they're in the wrong place at the wrong time, too bad. As for the Goblins themselves, they have a strange kind of admiration for him, so even though he's flattening them, they're happy they somehow helped him get back on his throne.

David Clayton, Weta Digital Animation Supervisor

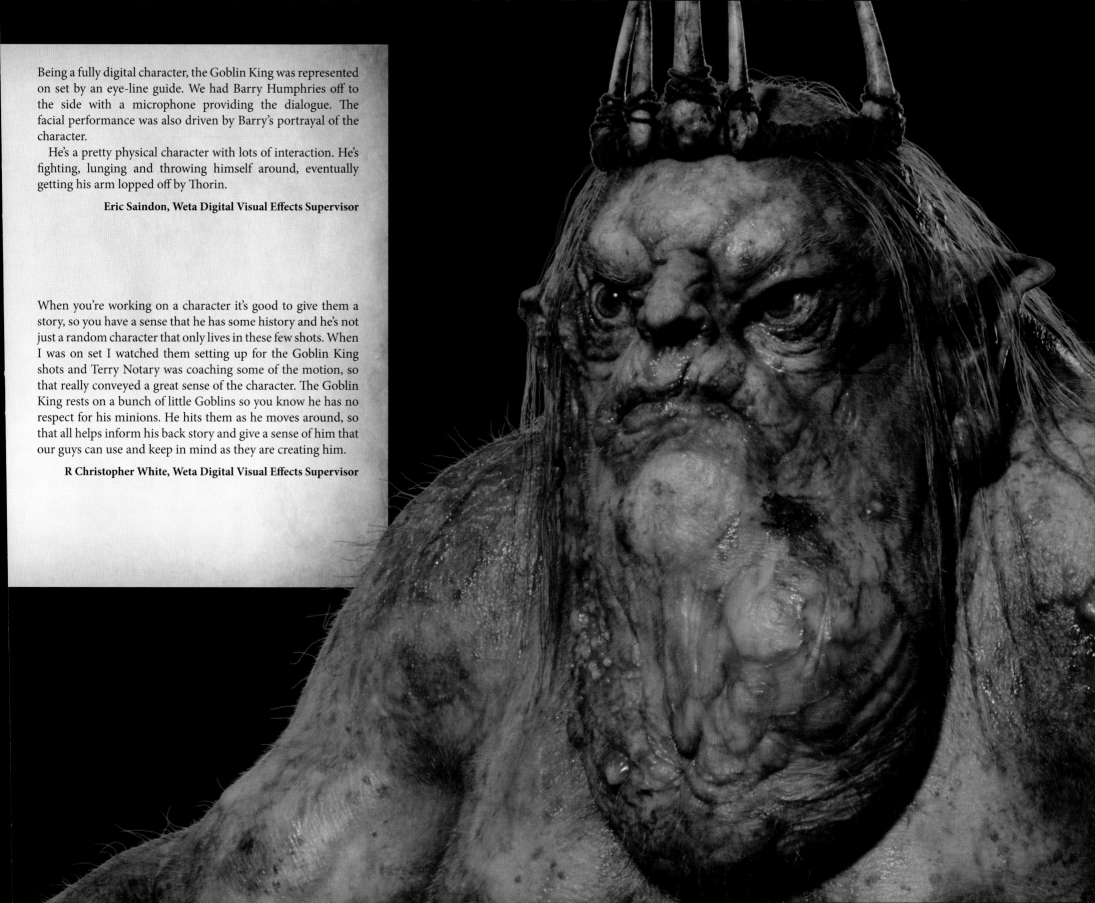

Being a fully digital character, the Goblin King was represented on set by an eye-line guide. We had Barry Humphries off to the side with a microphone providing the dialogue. The facial performance was also driven by Barry's portrayal of the character.

He's a pretty physical character with lots of interaction. He's fighting, lunging and throwing himself around, eventually getting his arm lopped off by Thorin.

Eric Saindon, Weta Digital Visual Effects Supervisor

When you're working on a character it's good to give them a story, so you have a sense that he has some history and he's not just a random character that only lives in these few shots. When I was on set I watched them setting up for the Goblin King shots and Terry Notary was coaching some of the motion, so that really conveyed a great sense of the character. The Goblin King rests on a bunch of little Goblins so you know he has no respect for his minions. He hits them as he moves around, so that all helps inform his back story and give a sense of him that our guys can use and keep in mind as they are creating him.

R Christopher White, Weta Digital Visual Effects Supervisor

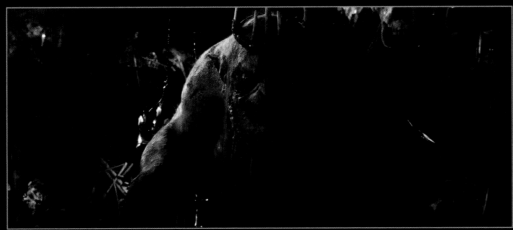

The Goblin King's skin is very translucent, especially his boils and little pustules. The shader artist has done a gorgeous job.

As part of my role, I will get a render from the shader person or texture artist assigned to a creature and work up a Photoshop painting on top of that where I think we can add more detail. If it gets approved it can get handed to a texture artist to match. It's a great time saver to do it this way, in Photoshop. I'm always looking for interesting and cool skin textures. There is some pretty gross stuff out there on the internet that we sometimes reference.

One of our techniques, which has worked extremely well in the past, is using life-casting techniques. We'll take physical elements and scan them to get all the fine wrinkles and pore detail, and we have some excellent ways of getting even finer detail into our displacements now. Daniel Bennett and I work together on the colouration, painting big sheets of illustration board with mixes of alcohol and water or methylated spirits and other products to create really cool, organic blends and colours. These are scanned at a high resolution and shared with our texture artists so they can use them to work from. There's so much you can get for free from organic processes and reality that would be impossible to sculpt or paint from scratch. We source a lot of stuff this way and it has worked very well.

Gino Acevedo,
Weta Digital Textures Supervisor/Creative Art Director

One of the Goblin King's eyes is particularly diseased. It's open wide all the time in a very creepy way, and it's something we kept going throughout his animation. His right eye is always a lot more open than his left. He can't really even blink it properly. If he blinks his left eye closes completely but his right can only manage a partial blink with some of the white still showing. It adds to his creepiness. Just before Gandalf takes him down, when he leans forward with his big creepy eye, Gandalf pokes him right in it with his staff. That eye was just begging for it. It had to be done.

David Clayton, Weta Digital Animation Supervisor

GRINNAH

Nasty little Grinnah heads up the Goblin mob that hauls the Dwarves before the King. He's also part of the interrogation squad that dresses down the trespassers to learn what business they have in the mountains. He seems to take to that kind of work with enthusiasm.

R Christopher White, Weta Digital Visual Effects Supervisor

Grinnah is the Goblin King's toad. He's a little more upright and carries himself with a bit of pride in front of the masses.

James Jacobs, Weta Digital Digital Creature Supervisor

He only has a few lines, but Grinnah says enough for us to get the sense that he's a bit more intelligent than most of the other Goblins in this sick little society, perhaps more evolved. In each case, he thinks of himself as more intelligent and evolved. He has a sword and a whip and gets to boss everyone else around. He's nasty and takes great enjoyment in whipping Thorin, which is all build-up because in the end Kili stabs him in his gut, and that had to be earned. It had to be a, 'Yeah!' moment and not an, 'Awww.'

David Clayton, Weta Digital Animation Supervisor

THE BRUTE

'It had to be hate at first sight or it wouldn't work.'

There's a grotty little piece of work in Goblin Town who was referred to as the Brute in the script. He's the little troglodyte Goblin that takes on Bilbo but, unfortunately for him, ends up going down the hole with him, eventually ending up as a prospective meal for Gollum.

Richard Taylor,
Weta Workshop Design & Special Effects Supervisor

The intention with any of the Goblins is that audiences dislike them immediately. The Brute that fought with Bilbo was one hideous little Goblin. He had an Elvis-like blow-wave hairdo and big wiry eyebrows. He dies over and over again too. He goes over the cliff with Bilbo and takes a big fall. It looks like he breaks his neck as he cartwheels off the rocks. He lands in the pit and Gollum finds him and bashes his head. Then Bilbo sees him lying there and bashes him again so then he's finally really dead, but through all this the audience can't be feeling sorry for him. It had to be hate at first sight or it wouldn't work.

David Clayton, Weta Digital Animation Supervisor

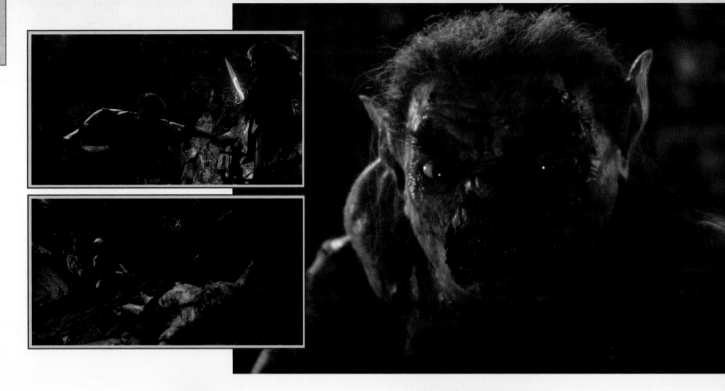

THE SCRIBE

The Scribe is a particularly unpleasant-looking little Goblin who works in the Goblin King's court. He's the jotter, taking down everything his master says, making notes, running message errands and keeping a detailed inventory of their acquisitions.

R Christopher White, Weta Digital Visual Effects Supervisor

In his brief appearance the Scribe is tasked with taking a message for his King. The Goblin King tells him to get a message to his Orc pal. He's in a little sling that has been adapted to work like a flying fox so he can hurtle away on his mission.

He's a great little character with a creepy, long fingernail that he uses to write. He has a very specific look. His diminutive legs make it impossible for him to walk, so we have had to make sure his performance is interesting despite him being stuck in a sling.

David Clayton, Weta Digital Animation Supervisor

On *The Lord of the Rings* I was tasked with helping portray a great many different characters. On any day I could be stood in as the scale double for any of four or five different hobbits. In *The Hobbit* I was brought in to be the scale guy for just one, Bilbo, so that has been my role for the most part, but because I was here and available I ended up doing a few unexpected and different things. I looked for opportunities to do more wherever I could.

When I was back in England looking at signing my contract to be Bilbo's scale double, we asked if there were any other roles I could play that would make the most of me being in New Zealand. The answer came back from the Production, 'If you can find anyone else in the book, let us know.' So, before coming over, I spent time going through the book, looking for opportunities, and one that I found was this character described as a Goblin Scribe. There was just one line. I didn't know it at the time but the writers already knew about him, so when I said, 'Look up page so and so, line number so and so,' they knew who I meant, and when I arrived they told me I had the part. It was great to have a character who is so different to Bilbo to perform. He's only in the movie for a very short time, but I hope people enjoy him.

Kiran Shah, Scale Double, Stuntman and Actor, Goblin Scribe

OF GOLLUM

' IN THE HOBBIT, WE MEET GOLLUM AT A CRYSTALLIZING MOMENT IN HIS LIFE THAT WILL HAVE PROFOUND EFFECTS. '

- Andy Serkis, 2nd Unit Director & Actor, Gollum

Concerning Gollum

'Gollum's look and performance embody so much of what is at the heart of these films and what these stories are about.'

Above: Gollum as he appeared in The Lord of the Rings: The Two Towers *and* The Return of the King. *Facing Page: Gollum in* The Hobbit: An Unexpected Journey.

Hopelessly lost and alone in a labyrinth of tunnels, Bilbo inadvertently stumbles into the realm of the creature Gollum, setting in motion a series of events that will change the course of Middle-earth's history. Gollum, of course, is well known to audiences from *The Lord of the Rings*, but in *The Hobbit: An Unexpected Journey* the story of how he meets Bilbo and the much-loved riddle game of the book is played out. Gollum is master of this subterranean world and Bilbo quickly appreciates he must depend upon him to escape. Though not yet the desperate creature of the previous trilogy when introduced, bereft and enraged by the 'theft' of his precious Ring, Gollum has nonetheless begun that journey by the end of the game when he realizes the true depth of his loss. His familiar dual personality, however, is already present, even at this time in his life, and Bilbo finds himself riddling with two competing personalities – one enjoying the game and the other eager to enjoy tasting him.

Gollum's look and performance embody so much of what is at the heart of these films and what these stories are about. He is so nuanced. We only spend a short time with him in *The Hobbit*, but there is so much that comes through in terms of what we learn about him and setting up what is to come for him, for Bilbo, and for all Middle-earth in the rest of the movies.

Joe Letteri, Weta Digital Senior Visual Effects Supervisor

The Hobbit was one of my favourite books as a kid and Gollum was my favourite character. He was the coolest: a bipolar, unpredictable, slimy character. He's scary, but you feel sorry for him at the same time. It has been a real pleasure to work on him.

Jeff Capogreco, Weta Digital Digital Effects Supervisor

'This scene is the genesis of the war between Gollum and Sméagol.'

Gollum's split personality is not in the book of *The Hobbit*. The notion of the Sméagol part of his personality was something that appeared in *The Lord of the Rings* and we emphasized it when making the film trilogy, mining his schizophrenic nature for that relationship. Sméagol, this young and innocent side of his personality, had been dominated by Gollum for many, many years while he hid beneath the Misty Mountains. He was an innately weak person so the Ring was able to exert a very powerful hold over him. Outcast from his society and set to wander, his child-like innocence was fading as he was subsumed by Gollum, the ruthless, hard-edged part of his personality that protected and kept him alive.

Audiences were introduced to Gollum and immediately mistrusted him because he was a vicious, vain and nasty creature, but they would feel pity for Sméagol. As the trilogy evolved it turned out that Sméagol was actually the more manipulative, passive-aggressive and sly. He was actually the darker and much more dangerous of the two, though these two different aspects of his character were at war with one another most of the time.

This duality of character was so firmly established in the trilogy and so much a part of the character's appeal that we didn't want to ignore it in *The Hobbit*, even if it wasn't strictly written that way in the book. This is the case with the movies as a whole. The lore, mythology and legendarium of *The Lord of the Rings*, which was written later, have been infused into the adaptation of *The Hobbit*. Peter, Fran and Philippa have been writing the films this way, honouring the source material while also making it work within what we know of the larger world of Middle-earth and what audiences have become familiar with thanks to the trilogy. The filmmakers have been very sensitive about finding that balance.

In *The Hobbit*, we meet Gollum at a crystallizing moment in his life that will have profound effects on the course of history. It's sixty years before he will meet Frodo and Sam, and he has been living in his cave, beneath the Mountains, alone with his *Precious*. Removed from the world in this sealed-up tomb of a home, he has been kept alive by eating fish and dead Goblins. He knows every stone and crevice. For more than five centuries this has been his existence and suddenly into this world comes Bilbo, a hobbit. Gollum doesn't know what a Baggins is, but it awakens long-dormant snatches of memory from Sméagol's past, before the Ring, when he was something quite similar, a river-dwelling Stoor hobbit. Gollum thinks a Baggins is something to eat, but Sméagol wants to play.

This scene is the genesis of the war between Gollum and Sméagol. One is bent on survival while for the other suddenly the thought of company and the kindling of ancient, dream-like memories is a game to be savoured. The riddle game they end up in with Bilbo is a means to an end for Gollum, who sees a meal at the end of it and wants to trick and catch Bilbo as quickly as possible, whereas Sméagol actually wants to uphold the rules. As Gollum's impatience grows, the riddles become darker and darker: 'Gnaws iron, bites steal, grinds hard stones to meal'. The answer of course is *Time*, which is what is on Gollum's mind. Sméagol's riddles and answers come from his past – memories of his old life in the sun and his grandmother, bubbling up in response to Bilbo.

At the end of the scene, Bilbo asks what has he got in his pockets. Sméagol finds himself completely stumped and can't answer. He loses the riddle game, at which point Gollum takes over and goes crazy. What he realizes at that very crucial moment is that he has lost the Ring, which collapses his world and catapults him into a loss-driven madness.

One of the most pivotal moments of the stories comes in the scene that follows, with Gollum chasing Bilbo to catch him and Bilbo slipping the Ring on to his finger and vanishing. Bilbo finds himself just inches from Gollum's face. Gollum can sense his presence but can't see him. At that point Bilbo could kill him with Sting and escape, but something happens there. It's not in Bilbo to do it. He can't kill this wretched creature, despite Gollum having no qualms about killing and eating him. That very act, the sparing of Gollum in that moment, allows the end of the trilogy to unfold as it does. A small act of mercy by a compassionate soul saves the world.

Gollum has just lost everything he cared about and his desperation to get it back is what drives him to endure so much during what follows. He is a hero, ultimately, because he helps Frodo and Sam and inadvertently fulfils the quest in the end, but he is also completely craven and egocentric, the most morally ambiguous character in the canon. Gollum is one of these characters in literature that holds a mirror up to the reader or viewer and shows them their own moral compass reading. I think that's why he's a challenging character – you might want to just hate him, but somehow you can't.

Andy Serkis, 2nd Unit Director & Actor, Gollum

Capturing Gollum

'It started with Andy and Gollum and now on The Hobbit we've come full circle.'

It has been great coming back to Gollum ten years on from *The Lord of the Rings* and benefiting from everything that has been learned and developed since then. He is hugely performance-capture driven. When we first brought the character to the screen, we were still figuring out if it could be done at all; subsequently each project we used the technology on allowed us to take it a stage further. For *The Lord of the Rings* it was the body we were capturing. On *King Kong* we were capturing the face. On *Avatar* we were doing all of it, while on *The Rise of the Planet of the Apes* we brought performance capture on stage.

It started with Andy and Gollum and now on *The Hobbit* we've come full circle and applied everything we have learned. Andy's Gollum and Martin's Bilbo were together on the set, and we've captured it all live. We didn't have to capture Gollum's performance separately, as we did in the past when Andy would have to go back to a dedicated motion-capture stage to perform his movements. Now we could get it all at once while he was in the scene with Bilbo, with all their interaction and Peter there directing it. It was a huge leap forward and made for a much more fluid and seamless filmmaking process from Peter and the actors' perspective.

Joe Letteri, Weta Digital Senior Visual Effects Supervisor

Performance capture is a technique that utilizes the recorded movements and expressions of an actor in the computer-driven animation of a character. The movement data from the capture session is brought into the computer, edited and translated for use on a given digital character. Animators are then able to use this movement data as a starting point for the animation of that character and combine it with more traditional animation techniques like key-framing to bring a fully CG/digital character to life.

The way in which we do performance capture has changed since we began back on *The Lord of the Rings*. At that time it was a completely virginal experience for me and for a lot of people, so there was no *modus operandi*. I had been hired to come and do three weeks of voice work for Gollum, but Peter was watching what I did on set and saw merit in filming it. Reference passes then became actual takes, with Rotoscoping and studio-based motion-capture elements to be overlaid later. It was a new tool that we were using in the hope it would bring value to the character, but it was early days in terms of the technology and its application. It evolved over the course of the time we were shooting the trilogy.

The technology was embraced beyond these studios too and by the time of *The Adventures of Tintin: The Secret of the Unicorn* and *The Rise of The Planet of the Apes* performance capture had really become the main means of production and principal photography for some films. For *Apes* we were shooting on location, shooting outside with full motion capture. That was a breakthrough.

Now we are back with Gollum again, in his cave, and there is no disconnect between me playing Gollum via performance capture and Martin playing Bilbo. It's just the film cameras filming Martin and the motion capture cameras filming me in the same moment. It is a significant change, not only technically, but also in the way it is perceived and used. It has been an amazing journey.

Andy Serkis, 2nd Unit Director & Actor, Gollum

REBUILDING GOLLUM

Gollum has been completely upgraded since *The Two Towers*, a decade ago. Our techniques have been honed so that many of the things that previously required a lot of hand work are simpler now and more physically accurate. There is more realism thanks to the advances we've been able to make in translating what Andy is doing more directly into the digital character.

Though he looks the same as audiences will remember from the first trilogy, he is more detailed, nuanced and real thanks to what we have been able to do with his skin texture, pores and translucency, and the way his muscles move beneath the surface and react with his bone structure. All these things are more grounded in reality because we know so much more about the body and how it works than we did a decade ago.

Gollum was a groundbreaking character in terms of how far he pushed the technology last time around and he is doing it again in *The Hobbit*, taking it to the next level.

Joe Letteri, Weta Digital Senior Visual Effects Supervisor

While we were giving Gollum an upgrade, we really wanted to hold on to the spirit of the original. The design itself changed very little. He's still pretty dirty, but he doesn't have the marks from the whippings and beatings yet that he endures in Sauron's dungeons. We also gave him a little bit of a haircut, though it's minor, and added a few more strands of hair. Overall we didn't want to go too far with changes. He looked so good in the first movies, we just wanted to take this success and build upon it without reinventing him.

The biggest changes came from improvements that we have been able to make with the technology, so that he more accurately replicates what Andy does in performance, and how real bodies move, so his eyes are more realistic as are his muscles and skeletal system. When he's crawling on the ground the muscles are firing where they should be; his spine is stretching along the back the way it should. He doesn't wear much, but what little clothing he does wear is also simulated a lot more accurately.

Jeff Capogreco, Weta Digital Digital Effects Supervisor

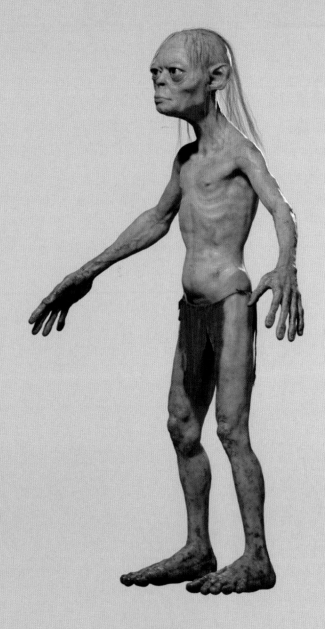

> *'He looked so good in the first movies, we just wanted to take this success and build upon it without reinventing him.'*

A creature like Gollum is built with its own basic internal skeletal system to which we graft tissue and muscles. These structures push and swim under the skin very realistically when the character moves. On a given model there may be many, many different layers that all influence the way the skin moves and drives it in different directions, that is to say tendons and the way muscles connect into a character's shoulders, pulling into the clavicle area or other complicated pieces of anatomy. As a Supervisor, it's part of my role to identify whether this is looking right in our creature.

Jeff Capogreco, Weta Digital Digital Effects Supervisor

There is always a chance that a character is going to end up filling the screen, so we have to build everything to an incredible level of detail because it might end up under intense scrutiny. We could have a shot in which Gollum's fingers reach into frame to pick up the Ring or something equally close, in which case the digital creature has to hold up, revealing fingerprints and even dirt under the nails.

R Christopher White, Weta Digital Visual Effects Supervisor

OF ORCS

'*IT WOULD BE A MISTAKE TO THINK OF THE ORCS OF MIDDLE-EARTH AS ONE SPECIES WITHOUT REGIONAL VARIATION, CHARACTERIZED BY A SINGLE LOOK AND CULTURE.*'

- Richard Taylor,
Weta Workshop Design & Special Effects Supervisor

CONCERNING ORCS

Cruel, unnatural creations, Orcs owe their origin to the corruption of captured Elves in the distant past. Now they exist as a race of ruined beings, twisted and misshapen by hate and abuse until they can take pleasure in little other than the mistreatment of others. Children of darkness, they fear the sun and rarely cross open ground in its light unless compelled or threatened.

Spreading like a plague across Middle-earth these creatures have become the bane of peace-loving peoples. Elves despise them, men fear and hate them and the Dwarves have gone to war against them in an effort to eradicate them from beneath the mountains both call home. Covetous creatures, the Orcs and their smaller Goblin cousins are drawn to the Dwarves' delvings by the wealth and accomplishments of the bearded folk. Many fierce battles have taken place deep beneath stone in caverns and mines as the Orcs seek to steal what Dwarven hands have shaped.

A particular enmity exists between Durin's line and the Orcs of the Misty Mountains. Displaced from Erebor by the Dragon, Smaug, King Thror and his family, Thrain and Thorin, fought a war with an Orc horde under the leadership of the great pale Orc, Azog. Referred to ever after his defeat and maiming of the Dwarf king as The Defiler, Azog was huge by Orc standards, a full head taller even than a man, and uncommonly clever for a member of his species. By terror and might he amassed a great army of Orcs and took the Dwarf stronghold of Khazad-dûm, also called Moria, no small task considering unity among Orcs was a rare and fleeting thing. Only a leader with sufficient force of character and strength could muster such an army and seldom could such an individual be found from within the species.

In the battle that saw his grandfather fall and Moria lost, Thorin repaid the great Orc by cutting off his arm, but while the Dwarf survivors of that day believed Azog dead, in truth he lingered on, recovering his strength and replacing his severed limb with a jagged metal proxy. The thought of revenge upon Thorin and the final destruction of the line of the Longbeards gnawed at Azog, but he bided his time until late in the Third Age, when the emergence of the Necromancer and commencement of Thorin's Quest to retake Erebor saw him lead a troop of hunters in a chase across Middle-earth in pursuit of the Dwarven Company.

Azog's followers in the hunt were a hardened group of Warg-riding Orcs. Atop their rapacious mounts the Orcs tracked Thorin and his friends, moving in for the kill when they cornered the Company on the eastern slopes of the Misty Mountains. Only the timely arrival of Gwaihir and the Great Eagles saved the Dwarves that day, but Azog's thirst for Thorin's blood means the hunt is far from over.

Coming back to Middle-earth again it has been interesting re-approaching familiar cultures like the Orcs and giving them a new spin. It would be a mistake to think of the Orcs of Middle-earth as one species without regional variation, characterized by a single look and culture. The Orcs are in fact even more diverse than our own incredibly variable species on this planet, so in *The Hobbit* we are introduced to new types and groups of Orcs as distinct from those we have seen as the Orcs of Gorgoroth were from those of Moria, maybe even more so.

Azog's troop are more like rangers, a fast-moving, mobile pack of predators who live on their Wargs' backs and cover great distances at their master's bidding.

Richard Taylor,
Weta Workshop Design & Special Effects Supervisor

This Quest doesn't mark the first time Nori's come up against Orcs, hence the daggers he carries secreted all about his person. I think he has had reason to slit a few Orc throats over the years that he's lived rough, and, having played an Orc, I know they're clumsy. It wouldn't take much for a Dwarf to sneak up behind an Orc and stick him. Orcs think they're sneaky, but they're really not. They're quite loud and they're quite smelly. You can smell Orcs coming from a distance.

Jed Brophy, Actor, Nori

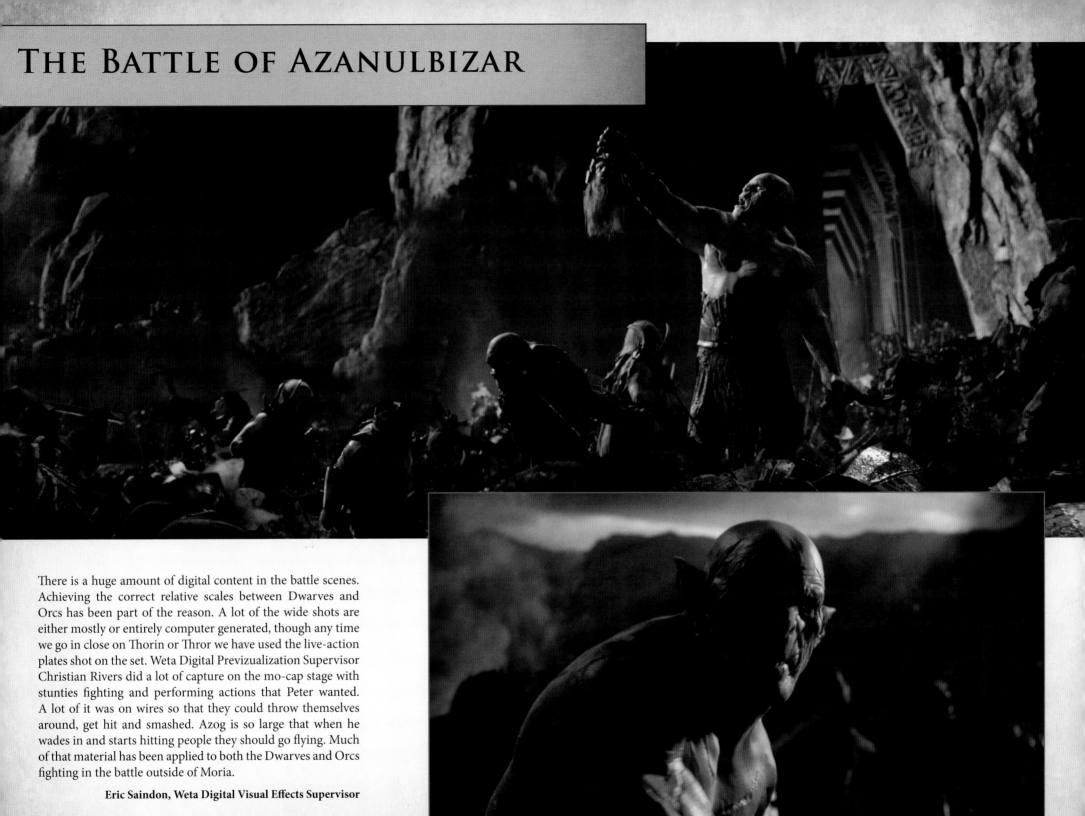

THE BATTLE OF AZANULBIZAR

There is a huge amount of digital content in the battle scenes. Achieving the correct relative scales between Dwarves and Orcs has been part of the reason. A lot of the wide shots are either mostly or entirely computer generated, though any time we go in close on Thorin or Thror we have used the live-action plates shot on the set. Weta Digital Previzualization Supervisor Christian Rivers did a lot of capture on the mo-cap stage with stunties fighting and performing actions that Peter wanted. A lot of it was on wires so that they could throw themselves around, get hit and smashed. Azog is so large that when he wades in and starts hitting people they should go flying. Much of that material has been applied to both the Dwarves and Orcs fighting in the battle outside of Moria.

Eric Saindon, Weta Digital Visual Effects Supervisor

AZOG'S ORC TROOP

'Going digital with the Orcs and Goblins meant it was possible to go beyond the constraints of what is possible on a suited performer, removing the physical limitations that basing any creature on the human body imposes.'

Our Orcs in *The Hobbit* were planned as a mix of performers in prosthetics, digitally enhanced prosthetics and fully digital characters. The way it has turned out, they are mostly digital but with some notable prosthetic Orcs like Yazneg and Fimbul. Even they have digital counterparts in some shots. There are also prosthetic Orcs in the background of some of the live-action battle plates, but they're mixed in with digital Orcs as well. Having that mix allows us to make the most of the freedom that digital technology affords in terms of creature design.

Weta Workshop provided around ten designs for wholly digital Orcs, which we have realized. We get a sense of the diversity of the Orcs and having guys in there who are entirely achieved through prosthetics means there's also a visual and stylistic connection to the Orcs that we saw in *The Lord of the Rings*. We're still in the same Middle-earth, even if we're seeing some new types of Orcs.

Eric Saindon, Weta Digital Visual Effects Supervisor

Going digital with the Orcs and Goblins meant it was possible to go beyond the constraints of what is possible on a suited performer, removing the physical limitations that basing any creature on the human body imposes. While the level of realism they have been taken to might make someone think they could be actors, the proportions they exhibit would be physically impossible to achieve on a person. The digital Orcs aren't limited in the way they can pose or in the kind of masses we can play with on their bodies and faces in pursuit of character. We can be wholly led by the intent of the character design and carve away faces, make jaws and mouths really pointed or eyes sharp – the kinds of things that can't be done in a make-up over an actor's head. The back can be bent over without sacrificing the ability to perform in a very violent fashion, as these Orcs need to. They can have proportions that diverge from human and still give battle and be dangerous. It has given them a unique character, presence and personality as a race.

Joe Letteri, Weta Digital Senior Visual Effects Supervisor

We track our featured Orcs for the sake of continuity and if one is killed then we remove him from use in subsequent scenes. Hero Orc 03, for example, is killed off in scene 88. We started out with ten featured Orcs. The designs are very strong, which is great because they're cool, but it also means that when we've used one guy we can't really use him again as a different Orc because he's too recognizable. So, we always need new ones.

Eric Reynolds, Weta Digital Animation Supervisor

Hero Orc 17

Hero Orc 21

The Orcs have body proportions that are close to human, but slightly off, which makes them all the more disturbing. They have very mangled faces. It's easy for us to do that digitally, plus once we have a group of Orcs we can very easily extrapolate and expand upon them, creating fifty more. Subtle tweaks with skin and hair colour, and variations in costume elements all make a difference. Before you know it, you've got a thousand different guys.

Kevin Andrew Smith,
Weta Digital 2nd Unit Visual Effects Supervisor

Hero Orc 01

Hero Orc 18

ORC PROSTHETICS

The Orc prosthetics created for *The Hobbit* were similar to those we made a decade ago for *The Lord of the Rings*, in the sense that it was decided to run the make-up appliances and suit parts in foam latex again, rather than silicone as per the Dwarves. We embarked on the same process, bringing in actors or stunt people and life-casting them, generating plaster cores based on their appearance that we could sculpt on.

The make-up concepts were sculpted over the top in Plasticine, with revisions as necessary until each was approved by Peter. We had a few designated Orcs, specific characters with certain roles to play in the story, but for the most part they were rank and file bad guys and sculpted for the members of the stunt team. We actually sculpted specific make-ups to fit each stunt performer's unique features, but there was also a bit of swapping that went on during the shoot to help create variety, so while they were made to be specific, they worked well generically too.

The Orcs had generic foam latex arms and legs that they slid on like sleeves, very much as we did for all our Orcs and Uruk-hai on *The Lord of the Rings*. They were attached to body suits, which were covered by their costumes. The foam skin of their arms was only visible from wrist to shoulder as they wore leather gloves.

Each stuntie always had their own Orc teeth, however, even if they weren't scheduled at the time to be playing an Orc, because there was always the chance they'd be required to do so at short notice. We took casts of all the stunt team member's mouths and sculpted custom Orc dentures for them all. It was important each one had their own custom-fitting set for safety reasons. It's possible to make generic Orc teeth that have a soft lining so that they can change to suit the mouth they are in, but for a stunt person an exact fit is essential purely because of the work they do and the risk of something rattling around inside their mouths either injuring or choking them.

I had a system that allowed me to create a set of teeth for one stunt person and then run them in soft plastic and modify them to fit the next person's set, thereby creating custom teeth for every individual, but not having to sculpt them from scratch each time, which was good because we had to generate between forty and fifty custom sets very quickly.

The stunt performers' teeth were designed with looks in mind, but for an Orc actor who might have lines to deliver, we had to be sure they could deliver lines with a mouthful of projecting false teeth. Yazneg's, for example, we designed not to impede his ability to speak. If all a character has to do is yell or growl, then we could get away with a lot more.

Yazneg was also the only exception to our foam prosthetics rule for the Orcs. His prosthetics were actually produced in silicone, like the Dwarves' faces. This consisted of a head cowl with his ears, a neck piece, chin, face and silicone chest. It was quite an elaborate make-up, and heavy. The chest alone weighed three kilograms and the head weighed two.

Silicone is heavy, but it also looks great. In Yazneg's case we used it because he is such a pale character and silicone is translucent, so it looks very much like skin. Fimbul, by contrast, was so dark that we could get away with foam. There was no gain in using silicone for his appliances.

The moulding techniques for both silicone and foam latex are similar. We use the same materials to create the moulds, but the techniques differ slightly. The main difference is in the flashing, the thin material around the edge of the appliance. There's a flash area outside the make-up that we tend to make a lot tighter when using foam. When we close the mould it really cuts through the foam and leaves a very fine blending edge. With silicone we can afford to let that flashing be a little wider because it provides a more generous blending edge that we can melt away when applied so that the edge is as subtle as possible and harder to see.

In saying that, if a mould is made specifically for running silicone, foam can also be run out of it and vice versa. The only thing to be aware of is that once one of these moulds has been run in foam latex it is very difficult to go back to silicone again because the sulphur from the latex permeates the mould somewhat and can cause an undesirable reaction in the silicone. We tend to try to avoid that scenario if we can.

Jason Docherty,
Weta Workshop Special Make-up and Prosthetics Supervisor

Left, from top: Weta Workshop Sculptors and Designers Michael Asquith, Lindsey Crummett, Jamie Beswarick and Greg Tozer sculpt Orc facial prosthetics in Plasticine atop cores cast from faces of actors and stunt performers.

Above: Weta Workshop crew discuss an Orc prosthetic test with stuntman Shane Rangi. From left: Special Make-up and Prosthetics Supervisor Jason Docherty, Workshop Supervisor Rob Gillies (behind), Prosthetics Painting Team Leader Dordi Moen, and Prosthetics Technician Simon Rose, and inset, right: Hair Technician Warren Dion Smith applies hair.
Right, from top: Prosthetics Make-up Artist Rachelle O'Donnell puts the finishing touches on her Orc in preparation for shooting, Weta Workshop Prosthetics Technician Fiona Walsh cleans up a raw, freshly cast foam latex slip-on background or stunt Orc mask, Weta Workshop Prosthetics Painting Team Leader Dordi Moen airbrushes Stuntman Shane Rangi's test prosthetics.

When painting creatures, we would get a general direction from the designer, and then we would apply that to what we were doing, drawing on our experience with what works and looks realistic. Sometimes there's scope for us to make stuff up, which is fun too. Workshop Supervisor Rob Gillies and Richard Taylor would sign off on it and then it would go to set to make sure it worked for what they require.

We painted masks for background Orcs and their body suits, as well as screaming gag masks that had jaws that could open wider and look really frightening. Designer Gus Hunter established a palette for us, but we had a lot of latitude to work within that and push the colour so we had a lot of variation with blues, red, purple, yellows and greys all within an overall colour family, and we got to play with some different skin patterns. We looked at realistic skin patterns but applied them using less conventional colours, and then added birthmarks and scars. We had to be mindful of the costumes and not go too extreme because then we'd be competing, so our body suits tended to be fairly basic. They shouldn't attract attention to themselves but work as a base for the rest of the make-up and costume design to sit on.

Dordi Moen, Weta Workshop Prosthetics Painting Team Leader

MOVEMENT COACHING ORCS

Orcs drive with their egos. The biggest Orcs lead from their chest and surge forward. Where Goblins are sly and dart from side to side, the big Orcs are much more linear, moving straight forward. As I tell the guys portraying Orcs, these creatures cut forward when they move, breaking the crust of the earth, cutting their way as if they have to fight their way through the air with each step. They use more effort than a person does in moving. It's almost like their feet grab at the ground when they walk. They're in constant conflict with everything around them.

Like the Goblins, who are their cousins in movement sense, they dart, but with an Orc there is a grinding quality. It's as if everything that they do is like a ball and chain that's got sand and grit in it. There's no fluidity. Imagine taking a long metal bar and driving it in to big pile of gravel, then dragging it through that gravel – it's that feeling.

Orcs have demons that live inside them, welling up and propelling them into action. Their consciousness kicks in moments behind those impulses and takes over, but the demon leash, it's instinct and fear that drives them. They're nasty, ruthless killers who would break right through a door and, only once they're in, figure out if there was any danger inside. They're not calculating. They are militaristic, but their society is held together by fear and that's what stands in for structure. They obey, but not willingly, and if they can stab you in the back, they absolutely will.

Somewhere between the Goblins and the soldiers that we see in the battle sequences are Azog's hunters. They are more like raptors, combining the ego-driven surge and pull of the soldier Orcs with stealthy athleticism. When they stop, it's as if they're pulled up short, so I have worked with the actors, telling them they have to trick themselves into stopping so that it doesn't look rehearsed or as if they're planning to hit a mark. Instead, the same demon that drives them to go also pulls them up short. There are surges that go through them, driving their actions – I call them the 'piss-shivers'. Their dim consciousness comes through moments behind, dragged along for the ride, but it's the impulsive demon in their core

There's no getting around it – being an Orc is exhausting. You can't be thinking like a human. You can't be second guessing because it totally kills the point of an Orc or a Goblin – that they live in the moment, driven rather than driving, reacting to something inside them rather than being in control, so nothing that you do can appear to be driven by a thought. That would kill the performance. The best thing to do is to rehearse the sequence and know exactly what you're going to do, and then go back into the basics of the creature and feel it, knowing the specific beats to the action and where to look, but letting the eyes and mouth lead. If you slip and lead with your thoughts it immediately ruins the character you're trying to be.

It's very challenging because Orc performers have to be in a constant state of tension. They're not breathing normally, they're breathing in, sipping the breath, keeping that tension. It's very hard to keep up, but when it works it looks great. It's not something that can be cheated. It's just hard work.

Terry Notary, Movement Coach

STUNT ORCS

The stunts team were responsible for anything that is action oriented or could present a safety or physical capability issue for the actors or performers. Even if it's not action but involves someone finishing a move high or in some risk we might be called upon to troubleshoot the situation and ensure no one was going to fall or injure themselves.

For any Orc performance that required a lot of physical exertion; 99% of the time we had our stunt guys double the actors for the sake of their safety. It was especially necessary out on location where we had all kinds of hazards. It was easier if the actors didn't have to worry about their safety. We also used stunt performers at times when our Orcs had to run. That is pretty tough to do in suits and costumes unless you are used to it or in very good physical condition. You heat up very quickly.

We have clocked up thousands of man days of stunts. We had a crew of as many as eighty at certain times, but always at least 95% of our stunt workers were New Zealanders. The country has a reputation for sword-fighting work so many of our team members have that background. We supplemented the group with Australians as well. It was essential that we had people with experience, because we couldn't afford the risk of using unpolished stunties. It was too complicated a job and hard enough even on those experienced stunt performers, let alone new recruits.

Many of our stunties were on *The Lord of the Rings*, some even started their careers on those films, so they knew what they were in for, although the 3D aspect of *The Hobbit* changed the way we did a few things.

What we have learned is that, in some situations, where before we could get away with a convincing near miss, now there's such a sense of realistic depth that we can't miss by six inches and still have it look real. To 'sell' a hit now we have to be much closer, and that can mean some risks, especially when we have people wearing masks and armour with limited visibility or working in very close quarters. That's another aspect of 3D – in order for a battle to feel full, we have to be much closer together. To get around this in some instances we replaced full weapons with just handles, and the actual blades were added digitally later. It looked better in the long run too, and meant we could have characters fighting in very congested scenarios in which backswings might otherwise have resulted in people getting hurt.

Glenn Boswell, Stunt Co-ordinator

FIMBUL AND YAZNEG

Among Azog's lieutenants are the cunning Fimbul and ambitious Yazneg. Both Orcs were portrayed by performers wearing macabre costumes and prosthetics, complete with contact lenses and dentures.

I was lucky enough to follow Fimbul all the way through the process at Weta Workshop. I produced the initial design, which was done in ZBrush and Photoshop, and then translated it onto Stephen Ure's head cast when he was chosen for the role. Stephen worked on *The Lord of the Rings* and fans might know him better as Grishnákh or Gorbag as he played both roles. It was the plan at the beginning that his eyes would be digitally enhanced to make them extra creepy so his prosthetic make-up was sculpted with them very sunken. The notion was they would be enhanced and changed later.

Something else we tried to make allowance for was breathing tubes. Sometimes masks that cover the nose don't allow for nasal breathing, but in order to make this as comfortable as possible for Stephen and not limit his performance options we designed the make-up to have surgical tubing that ran from his nostrils, through the cheeks and down to the prosthetic's mouth.

Greg Tozer, Weta Workshop Designer and Sculptor

I have always thought Stephen Ure brought something very special to his roles in *The Lord of the Rings*. Consequently, when Peter was in the process of considering characters for *The Hobbit* and talking about possible casting we were quick to bring Stephen's name into discussion, knowing that, even playing a third Orc, he could find a totally new character and we'd be able to distort his features through prosthetics sufficiently that there would be no risk of anyone mistaking him for Grishnákh or Gorbag. We were thrilled when he was cast.

Stephen has an astonishingly mobile face and ability to express with great intensity through his prosthetics, but he also has a wonderful physicality in his whole performance, so his entire body is performing at the same time, to great effect. As a make-up artist, it's everything you could hope for in your creature-suit actor, because you know he will sell the character and make it real, so the audience never for a moment thinks of a man wearing a mask.

Richard Taylor,
Weta Workshop Design & Special Effects Supervisor

Fimbul's prosthetic make-up consisted of a head cowl, neck and face. His ears were separate. We do the ears separate so that we can run them in slip latex. Unlike foam latex, it is translucent, so if an Orc is ever backlit the light would come through his ears the way it does with skin. Like the rest of our Orcs, Fimbul also had foam latex arms and legs.

The character's facial makeup was designed with exaggerated eye sockets because the intention was to enhance his eyes digitally, moving them apart or changing their size. He was also a little more challenging because it was also intended that his features would be offset a little. His mouth was slightly off centre as if at some point he'd been smacked in the side of the face and his jaw had healed askew. His teeth were offset as well. It posed a few problems because with offset features it is less clear where a blending edge should go.

For scenes in which he wasn't seen close to camera we had a very simple slip-on mask made too, something which could be very quickly pulled on or off and not require gluing, or that Fimbul's stunt double could use.

Jason Docherty,
Weta Workshop Special Make-up and Prosthetics Supervisor

Although for some of their wider shots and anything involving extreme action or interaction with other digital craetures and characters Fimbul and Yazneg would be entirely digital, both were achieved live on the set as physical make-up with prosthetics.

Eric Saindon, Weta Digital Visual Effects Supervisor

With his sunken eye sockets and braised skin Fimbul looks like he's been out in the sun for too long. He was achieved using prosthetics for his close-ups, including when he's laughing along with Azog, his boss, but we had a digital version for some of his shots such as when he's riding his Warg.

Eric Reynolds, Weta Digital Animation Supervisor

Yazneg is a low-level leader amongst the Orcs. He serves Azog, but when his commander isn't around he asserts himself. He drives his guys and the Wargs hard as they chase down their quarry. He's very brutal, but when we meet Azog he cowers in submission. He's thinking to himself that he'll have this Orc's job one day, but he dares not let that sentiment show, so he sucks up his pride and ambition and submits because he has to. It's not out of respect, but fear, because Azog is in another league to Yazneg and just being around him reminds Yazneg of his own inferiority, despite what he might think of himself when he's not within Azog's sight. He's no equal to Azog, who has survived this long by being so physically superior to everyone around him. He's pathetic and weasely and apologetic because he has bad news to bring, which doesn't go down well, unfortunately for Yazneg.

Terry Notary, Movement Coach

The lighting in the Orc meeting scene that takes place at Weathertop was beautiful. Azog is there with his huge Matriarch Warg, and of course it's here that Yazneg meets his fate for having lost the Dwarves. The character was shot live and we added the Wargs, Azog and Orc riders. If you're an Orc your life is probably going to be short and violent. The scene makes me think of *The Untouchables* when Al Capone is going around with a baseball bat. That's how it is being an Orc. Sooner or later you'll displease Azog and that will be how you die. The others all know Yazneg has it coming, but their days are coming too, because now they're one Orc closer to meeting the same fate. There's always a level of nervousness when you're an Orc. The Goblins at least have some sort of community going, and there's the sense that as long as you keep out of the Goblin King's way you might be able to scratch out some kind of a life there in your own safe little corner, but Orcs don't even have that.

Eric Reynolds, Weta Digital Animation Supervisor

ORC LANGUAGE AND SPEECH

There were two forms of Black Speech in these movies set in Middle-earth, that which Sauron uttered in *The Lord of the Rings* which we referred to as Black Speech, and its derivative, Orcish, which was a more basic form. Tolkien described it as a very unattractive language, very guttural. It's certainly not the easiest to speak when you are wearing prosthetics and a mouthful of fake teeth.

Leith McPherson, Dialect Coach

We had begun our journey with these languages during *The Lord of the Rings*. For the Black Speech that we required in those films we started with the inscription on the One Ring. It had to sound very different to the Elvish languages. Tolkien intended Black Speech to be something difficult to listen too, that sounded uncomfortable on the ear. In the Council of Elrond, when Gandalf speaks it, Elrond is deeply unhappy, not so much because of what he said but because he uttered the Black Speech in Rivendell.

With that in mind we chose sounds that were very foreign to a Western ear, an accent that was produced in the back of the throat. It's very dark, but at the same time there something hypnotic about it, whereas Orcish, by contrast, which is heard for the first time in *The Hobbit*, is guttural and spat out. The Orcs are a twisted, deformed race, so there had to be something in the way they spoke that reflected their nature. It's a more vulgar or base form of Black Speech.

The dialect team would practice Orcish lines together. It almost sounded like someone speaking backwards. Azog, being a rare, intelligent Orc, uses both the Black Speech and Orcish depending on who he is addressing. His hunters speak Orcish. The sentences are simple or incomplete, little more than utterances and insults like, 'spit their blood,' or 'filthy wolves,' and all very violent.

Roisin Carty, Supervising Dialect Coach

In addition to speaking their own languages, we have villains in *The Hobbit* speaking Mannish, or English. The Orcs did so in *The Lord of the Rings* as well, but one of the nice shifts in *The Hobbit* versus *The Lord of the Rings* is that now it's not only bad guys who speak with London accents. We have not only Orcs and Trolls speaking this way, but Nori too. It's something that seems to be equitable with coming from a more mechanical environment, an urban one perhaps? It seems to stem from an association with industrialization, which Tolkien contrasts against the pastoral nature of the hobbits or loftiness of the Elves, classical Gondor and other cultures. In that sense, Nori being more worldly and travelled is justified in having a similar accent. It has that cheeky chappy, geezer quality to it that suits his character so well.

That said, it is also an example of an instance where we want to be clear and consistent, but not get too specific with our accents. They are intended to be clues that help define a character, telling an audience something about them just as in the way that we form opinions about people when we hear them speak for the first time; but we didn't want them to be distracting to the point where people sit down and try to map out *The Lord of the Rings* over the British Isles by dialects. It wouldn't hold and was never intended to. We use accents to infuse individual qualities that contribute to the overall acoustic spectrum of our cast of characters.

Leith McPherson, Dialect Coach

Azog the Defiler

Having bested every opponent, Azog has risen to dominate the Orcs of northwest Middle-earth and by the time of the Battle of Azanulbizar his reign was absolute. Having slain Thror, king of the Dwarves, Azog seemed invincible, but he would be humbled by Prince Thorin.

What I like about Azog is his very realistic feel. At first glance I think people could almost think he's an actor and then quickly realize that he can't be, because his proportions aren't human. He's entirely a digital creation, from head to foot. The level of realism he has means he can sit in a scene with live-action actors and not stand out. I really like that about what we've done with this character.

He has tremendous screen presence. He is very intense and commanding, so it's easy to accept him as the leader of the Orcs and having the strength of character to unite and drive them. Some of that comes from his sheer size and bulk, which is partly why we ended up creating him as a fully digital character in the end and not an actor in make-up. As a computer-generated character he can be larger than life, and ironically, more physically imposing. Even after what happens to Azog in the early scenes, losing his arm, his power is just as commanding. If anything it makes him even more menacing.

Azog was motion-captured, but there was also a lot of hand animation that was done on him to bring him to life on screen.

Joe Letteri, Weta Digital Senior Visual Effects Supervisor

Azog's motion capture was provided by actor Manu Bennett. We did lots of work with him on the motion capture stage and he was a really good physical actor who comes across very well. It's nice to get a strong physical performer, just like many of our Orcs from *The Lord of the Rings* were, being that many of them were stunt men. Manu is a good, solid performer and plays the character with a very powerful and imposing presence. He's very menacing and over the top with his growls and snarls. He's really in your face and makes a fantastic villain. When Azog loses his arm Manu taped his hand up on the motion capture stage so that he wouldn't be able to use it and you would see that come through in more subtle ways through the performance.

Eric Saindon, Weta Digital Visual Effects Supervisor

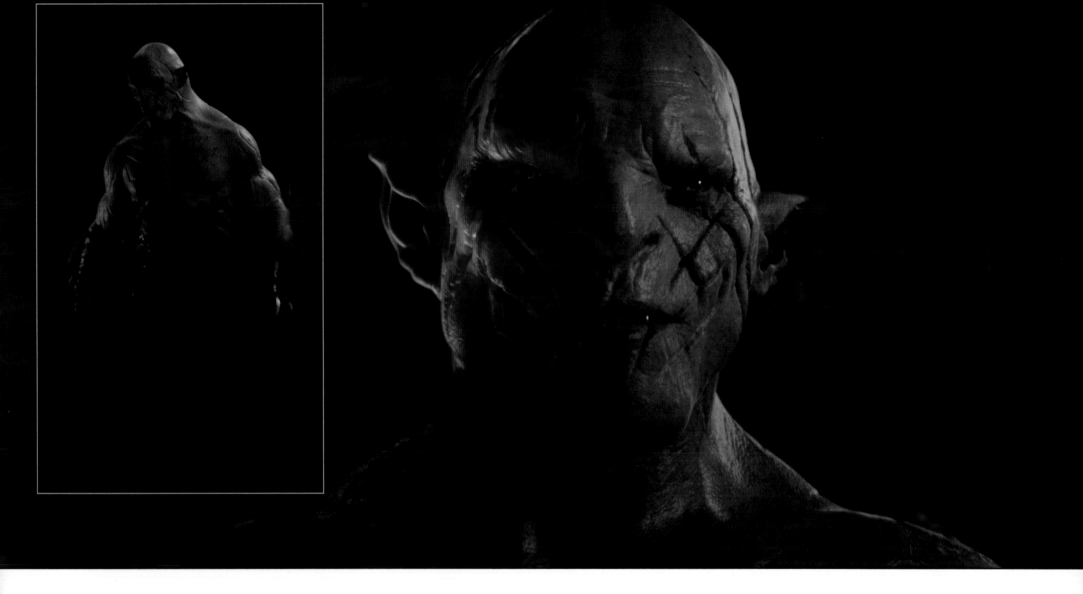

The scene in which Azog's riders chased the Dwarves up their trees was a great showcase for the character. He didn't have a lot of lines and those he did have were in Orcish, but I think he came across as a very strong character and one that people are going to want to see more of in the subsequent films.

He's a good villain in the sense that he doesn't just sit there and growl and bark at people. There are other facets to his character. He talks and smiles and teases Thorin.

When Bilbo jumps in to save Thorin, Azog doesn't rush to get involved. He just watches with disgust as this Orc from his group of hunters struggles to deal with the tiny halfling. He doesn't step in to save the Orc, which he could do easily. Instead he waits to let that little scene play out and only when

the Orc is killed does he get ugly and act, bringing in all his other henchmen to take out Bilbo. He's a scarier villain because he holds back and plays it cool and keeps his composure so much of the time.

In his final scene in *The Hobbit: An Unexpected Journey* he is enjoying himself right up until the end. The Dwarves are hanging on to a burning tree over the edge of the cliff. Azog is savouring his victory when it is all ripped out of his hands – er, hand – and it's only then that he starts screaming because his plan is unravelling and he has lost control.

Eric Reynolds, Weta Digital Animation Supervisor

Azog loses a limb in battle with Thorin, but survives and comes back to hunt him through the film. Instead of a hand, now he has this cruel-looking, hooked metal barbeque spit thing that goes into his stump and projects out the back of the forearm in a jagged spike. It's very nasty.

Fran decided Azog should be hairless. He has self-inflicted scars all over him that all help make him look even nastier. Orcs go in for that kind of thing. He's very cool-looking and an interesting villain.

Eric Saindon, Weta Digital Visual Effects Supervisor

The sequence in which Azog loses his arm was shot on a stage with suited performers playing all the Orcs and Dwarves in slow motion; it looked great. It was up to us to insert Azog, who is seven feet tall. Given the relative heights of the Dwarves and this massive Orc, it has meant that often Azog's head isn't even in frame and Thror is just fighting his chest, but it's great because it really drives home the size difference and makes his predicament even more threatening. We have enough shots that show Azog's full body that it wasn't essential to have his face in every shot. I think it's cool to see just how huge Azog is and what Thorin and Thror are really up against, from a Dwarf's perspective.

We also stuck lots more Orcs in the background, fighting Dwarves, so the scene could become deeper than was shot and felt bigger.

Having their animation driven by motion capture, our digital Orcs still have certain human qualities to their movement. That ties in well when we have physical Orcs sharing the screen with them in the same plate. Even Azog, being entirely digital and such a huge character, is nonetheless very human in his mannerisms. It's always more interesting if these kinds of villains are a bit more human.

Eric Reynolds, Weta Digital Animation Supervisor

OF BEASTS

'*WE STRIKE A BALANCE BETWEEN FAITHFULNESS TO NATURE AND PRESENTING CHARACTERS THAT CAN PERFORM.*'

- Joe Letteri, Weta Digital Senior Visual Effects Supervisor

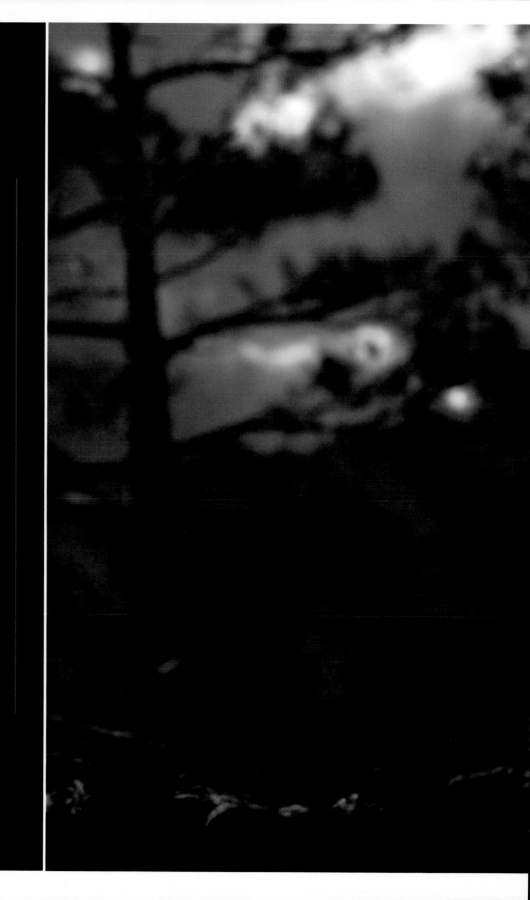

Concerning Beasts

As numerous as the speaking roles in *The Hobbit* were the whinnying, tweeting or bleating kind. Most of the film's characters required riding beasts and Radagast was supported by a menagerie of animal companions.

There were also more sinister animals. As the Company made its way deeper into wild country they were harassed by slavering evil creatures including bats and Wargs. Were it not for rescue by the most resplendent of Middle-earth's fauna, the Great Eagles, the Quest might have ended with the gnawing of charred Dwarf and hobbit bones upon the eastern flanks of the Misty Mountains.

Whether flesh or pixel, the movie's animal cast was full and diverse, sporting coats of feathers, fur and, in some instances, fabrication. Both animatronics and digital wizardry were called upon to bring Middle-earth's fauna to life for the screen.

Radagast's Animal Friends

Radagast communicates with his bird friends by whistling. Through them, he is able to detect changes in the forest, so they are his eyes and ears, but he is also very protective of them. He has sparrows that live under his hat (doing their business down his cheek) and he has a beautiful red-breasted robin that acts as a messenger. Both the sparrows and the robin are digital creatures that we have built and animated, though if we have done our jobs no one will be able to tell. Our ability to simulate feathers has come a long way.

Radagast also becomes a living haven for the mice living in his house, who take shelter in the folds and holes of his tattered clothing when the Spiders attack – lots of mouse animation for us to do as these are all digital as well.

Matt Aitken, Weta Digital Visual Effects Supervisor

Until very recently we didn't understand how to make feathers look like feathers and how to calculate all the millions of interactions that actually happen to a bird's plumage when they're flying or landing or even just sitting, moving their head around. Now we have a much better understanding of this. We've built a whole new system of feathers to allow us to handle all these calculations. All the movement and feather interaction is much more realistic, which is great because between the Great Eagles, the robin, sparrows and others, we have a lot of birds in *The Hobbit*.

Joe Letteri, Weta Digital Senior Visual Effects Supervisor

Our little birds like the sparrows and robin are all driven off the same feather simulation technology that we have applied to the Eagles, so they're pretty complex.

**Kevin Andrew Smith,
Weta Digital 2nd Unit Visual Effects Supervisor**

While we use performance capture a great deal for humanoid digital characters, our non-human creatures are generally key-framed, which means they are animated by artists from start to finish. We will key-frame humanoid characters if they need to perform big actions that defy or push what could be performed on a stage. As good as the performance-capture software is, we will also have an animator finesse the work to make sure the intent behind the performance is coming through. Even in a film like *Avatar* or *The Adventures of Tintin*, there was a combination of motion capture and key-frame animation. It's not something we can entirely rely on software to do for us, so there's still plenty of work for animators in what we do!

Our animals, however, tend to be entirely key-frame animated. They have their own way of moving and behaving that really demands an animator. Examples of that in *The Hobbit* would include all of Radagast's animal friends, his bunnies, the birds, mice and the hedgehogs.

Matt Aitken, Weta Digital Visual Effects Supervisor

THE HEDGEHOGS

Sebastian is one of Radagast's closest animal friends. He plays an important part in the scene that introduces Radagast and his compassion. As the last vestiges of old Greenwood the Great around the Wizard's home become more and more infected by the spreading evil little Sebastian falls ill. Radagast finds him and takes him back to Rhosgobel to cure him with various wizardry potions. Unfortunately, it doesn't go so well for the hedgehog and sadly he passes away, much to the distress of his family. Fortunately, Sebastian isn't real.

No hedgehogs were harmed in the filming of this movie. Our prickly insectivore is in fact a digital character. Sebastian was our first experience with a digital hedgehog, but we're all very proud of how he turned out. He's very believable. While we can get away with a lot because the hair and fur on him is so fine, to tackle his quills we had to go through some extra steps, working out how the light interacts with the surface. We ended up using a modified version of our fur code to do it, and it worked very well. We had some very good people working on that and they came up with a great scheme that allows us to get very close to the hedgehog and still have him hold up to scrutiny, looking completely believable.

I think there's a certain type of person that is naturally drawn to this kind of work because they get to play in that space – the combination of the math, the physics and science of it, but also art. It has to look good. You're using your eyes to judge whether or not what you're doing mathematically is successful or not. It's a special skill-set but fortunately we have some very clever and talented people doing it.

In addition to our digital Sebastian, there was a little puppet hedgehog made by Weta Workshop. Radagast needed to have something there that he could wrap his hands around and pick up, cradling him as the poor little creature struggles for life.

The end of Sebastian's story is a happy one though, for when the house is attacked by giant Spiders Radagast realizes there is witchcraft at work and is able to draw on a spell to bring his friend back to life. It's one of the most tender moments in the film.

Matt Aitken, Weta Digital Visual Effects Supervisor

'Sebastian was our first experience with a digital hedgehog,
but we're all very proud of how he turned out. He's very believable.'

While very true to real-world hedgehogs, there was a leve
of characterization that we brought to the digital characters
because they had to be expressive. We strike a balance
between faithfulness to nature and presenting characters tha
can perform, conveying emotion or condition and evoking
empathy from the audience.

Joe Letteri, Weta Digital Senior Visual Effects Superviso

We built a tiny animatronic hedgehog with a curling
mechanism in its belly, moving arms, blinking and nose
wiggles. It gave Radagast something physical to interact with
that wasn't inanimate. We found a stuffed hedgehog and soaked
it to remove the skin, then built an internal structure with th
mechanisms. Basically he was a real hedgehog with real hair
bristles and claws over a robotic interior with a cable running
out his bottom. No hedgehogs were harmed for the film, bu
we weren't above using one who was already dead.

Rob Gillies, Weta Workshop Superviso

RADAGAST'S RABBITS

Radagast moves about at speed on a sled drawn by a team of tethered rabbits. Much bigger than any rabbit species or breed from our own world, the Rhovanion bunnies of Middle-earth were entirely digital creations.

We based Radagast's rabbits on giant German rabbits because we wanted to know what a really big rabbit looks like. Simply scaling up a small bunny doesn't work. Proportions of certain body parts change as size increases and they move differently. We have taken liberties with them, however, because our rabbits are even bigger than the biggest real-world varieties and are a wild Middle-earth kind that lives in the woods, so they're not groomed and fluffy like pets. They're more like sled dogs, so we've made them look more powerful like working or wild animals.

Joe Letteri, Weta Digital Senior Visual Effects Supervisor

Though they were entirely digital, I actually went looking for the biggest real bunnies we could find for Radagast. We found a giant Flemish rabbit and the idea was briefly tossed around that they might motion capture it, but that didn't happen.

Steve Old, Lead Animal Wrangler

Radagast's sled-team bunnies were each the size of Labradors and because they were so huge they had to be entirely digital.

The challenge here was that in a number of their shots both they and Radagast were ducking and diving to avoid branches and trees. Sylvester was pretending on the day because there were no physical obstacles. We then created a digital forest environment around him that fit his actions as he and the bunnies careened wildly through the woods, dodging and crashing through foliage and limbs in their haste to escape the bats.

Weta Digital Digital Effects Supervisor

Some of the shots of Radagast on his sled were filmed using a physical sled on a stage, pulled by a vehicle standing in for the bunnies with a more or less even rate of speed; but rabbits hop, so if they were pulling a sled we might expect it to similarly move in jerks and bounces. We came up with a way of staggering the rabbits' movement and having a certain degree of slackness in the harnesses at times to iron out the up and down effect it would have on the sled that they were pulling as a team. The result was a sled that was still careening along in a manner much like it would be if pulled by a running dog-sled team rather than hopping bunnies, but not in a way that looked like it would be jerking up and down too much.

For other shots we had a completely digital Wizard and sled, so we have been able to play up the hopping of the rabbits a little more strongly. In a wider shot we can afford to play the motion a little bigger than we might in a close-up in any case, because in close-up that bobbing would be distracting.

Joe Letteri, Weta Digital Senior Visual Effects Supervisor

THE GREAT EAGLES

Gandalf and his companions are narrowly plucked from a fiery death by Gwaihir and the Great Eagles who patrol the Misty Mountains and hate Orcs and Wargs with as much bitterness as the Dwarves. Using real eagles to achieve the shots was never a realistic option, given the scale and performance requirements of the scenes, so just as they were a decade earlier the great birds would be rendered digitally.

We've had lots of fun with feathers, especially when there's interaction occurring. The Dwarves jump into the air and some land on Eagles swooping past, so there's a lot of interaction going on there between hairy, clothed Dwarves and feathered Eagles.

The technology has moved on by light years since *The Lord of the Rings*, but birds are tough because they're feathered, and feathers are pretty complicated things. We have some code that we tried on *The Adventures of Tintin* with the falcon from that film and we've improved it for use on the Eagles in *The Hobbit*. There are also ways to sometimes cheat that can work. Sometimes it's possible to create little cards with feathers painted on them or some have tried to simulate feathers with hair. What we've done is build our birds with actual digital feathers. We have new technology that lets us solve the challenge of feather interpenetration, so that the feathers don't go through each other. It looks pretty good.

When you study birds of prey their feathers are always moving when their wings are splayed. There are little ruffles as the wind buffets them. Even when they are standing still they can fluff out their neck feathers and they always lie correctly on top of each other. That's the hard part. A person can't do it – you just can't. You would lose your mind, trying to go through the bird in every shot and make sure that all the feathers are in the right place. That is why we have techniques for simulation. It's quite intensive, but the computers have become faster and faster, and the code has got better and better. We've reached a point now where our animator can animate the bird and then the feathers go on and just naturally do the right thing.

It's all predicted on real physical properties and physical equations, but as with any simulation that we run it also has to be able to be art directed, so we the animators also have the ability to dial the effect up or down in different ways. These are massive birds, after all, and we have to factor that in, meeting the audience's expectation of how a bird should look in flight, but also acknowledging that these are birds the size of small aircraft with wing feathers as big as people, so some things are going to be a little different. In that sense sometimes we are fighting the scale. It's all about finding a balance, which again means things like our feather simulations have to be controllable so we can adjust them to suit.

Although the feather technology has come a long way, our Eagles should be aesthetically similar enough to those seen in *The Lord of the Rings* so that audiences would have no reason to think they're not the same – they'll just look even better.

Kevin Andrew Smith,
Weta Digital 2nd Unit Visual Effects Supervisor

'These birds are the size of small aircraft
with wing feathers as big as people.'

WARGS

Pursuing Thorin and his Company is a murderous pack of Orc hunters and their allied mounts, the vicious Wargs. Cruel creatures akin to but distinct from wolves, the Wargs are huge carnivores led by a matriarchal alpha who had aligned herself with the Orc chieftain Azog.

Differing in design from the Wargs previously seen by audiences in *The Lord of the Rings*, Azog's pack represents a related variety. Their design was very strongly driven by the narrative context and specific shots in which they would appear.

The Wargs' design moved around a bit, starting out very much like the Wargs we saw in *The Lord of the Rings* then becoming radically different, based on artwork by designer Gus Hunter. Developing away from that, they eventually became something closer to a dog, and then more like a lion, finally settling as something that blends characteristics of both. Peter's driving comment was for us to make them look like something that an audience wouldn't feel sympathy for. They couldn't be pets. The lion aspect was a result of the kind of movement Peter wanted to see.

Eric Saindon, Weta Digital Visual Effects Supervisor

Dogs tend to let their heads loll around when they're running, but as soon as you lock that head movement, like how a big cat does when it's stalking, it gives your Warg focus and intent. It immediately makes them predatory, calculating creatures.

Eric Reynolds, Weta Digital Animation Supervisor

Make the Warg too dog-like and people are going to think, 'Aw, he's just a big misunderstood puppy-dog. Don't kill him, he's cute.' Dogs carry their heads higher and have a lope that isn't necessarily all that scary.

So, our Wargs have slitted pupils like cat's eyes and move in a very lithe and predatory, feline manner, which is very threatening on screen. They have dog-like claws but a musculature that's much more influenced by lion video reference that we were studying. They're smaller across the chest and carry their heads low and menacingly. It's all driven by the demands of the scene and what role they play in the story. What's the impression they have to make on the audience? While we always refer to real-world biology when we're building these creatures and trying to make them as believable as possible, in the end they have to serve a very specific function in the story that Peter is telling and what matters is what is seen in their final shots.

Where we settled in terms of design is something that feels very natural and in keeping with the menagerie of creatures that we've established for this world, such as Goblins and Orcs and Trolls. Their hair is short for the most part but longer on the trailing edges such as behind the elbows and jaw, down the back and in the mane area, which creates an interesting shape in profile.

Kevin Andrew Smith,
Weta Digital 2nd Unit Visual Effects Supervisor

We had different classes of Warg, ranging from scouts, through regular Wargs, to the Matriarch, who stands out as the biggest and leads the pack. She's the clever one. All our Wargs are pretty big, though – horse-sized, and when compared to the scaled-down Dwarves they're massive.

For the sake of efficiency we try to minimize the amount of work we have to do as far as building lots of different assets, so we've achieved variation in our Warg pack partly by applying different grooms, of which we had around a dozen, but mainly by using colour to distinguish individuals. We also have a library of scars and cuts that we can draw upon to mix up the variations and create unique individuals so no two are exactly the same. Most of the shots involving large numbers of Wargs are from a distance, so in those cases colour has offered us the best tool as far as establishing variation. Our Wargs range the gamut of wolf colours, so we have browns and greys, dark and light, and variation in blotchy patterning.

Kevin Andrew Smith,
Weta Digital 2nd Unit Visual Effects Supervisor

We had thinner Wargs, bigger ones, stronger ones – all sorts, each adapted from the basic Warg model. As far as basic anatomy goes they were all the same, but, like any pack, some look better nourished than others. The Matriarch was of course the strongest.

James Jacobs, Weta Digital Digital Creature Supervisor

For the sake of more variation we designed six or seven different teeth configurations for our pack.
David Clayton, Weta Digital Animation Supervisor

The Wargs of *The Lord of the Rings* had a brutal, hyena-like quality to them. Although our Wargs in *The Hobbit* are very clearly a different breed, we tried to bring a little of those qualities back. They needed to look like they were very feral, living out in the wild but obviously scraping and fighting all the time, so their hides were mangled and scarred.

Joe Letteri, Weta Digital Senior Visual Effects Supervisor

Warg fur isn't pretty. They're ridden by the Orcs so it's safe to assume they're not treated well. We've made their coats patchy with lots of scars. They probably fight with each other all the time too so we've beaten them up as much as we could and given them nasty, greasy pelts. It has helped avoid them being in any way cute or fluffy.

Wargs are basically killing machines. They're all teeth and claws and viciousness, built for chasing down and tearing apart prey. They don't have harnesses or reins, but some are nonetheless ridden by Orcs, who grab fistfuls of fur in their claws and hang on.

Kevin Andrew Smith,
Weta Digital 2nd Unit Visual Effects Supervisor

When we're seeing Wargs in shots with Dwarves their massive size becomes very apparent. It's like a Dwarf fighting something with the mass of a horse. They're huge and we have between seventeen and twenty in every scene, so they are very worthy adversaries for our heroes.

Eric Reynolds, Weta Digital Animation Supervisor

The amount of direct physical interaction between digital Wargs and physical Dwarves has been minimal. We had Wargs being swung at and struck with swords and axes during the chase, but otherwise most interaction came when the Matriarch grabbed Thorin and shook him like a chew toy. In situations where there's a lot of interaction often it's easier for us to use digital doubles of characters like the Dwarves rather than trying to marry digital creatures to a performance shot on set.

The same is true of Orcs riding on Wargs. Some very simple practical Warg stuff was shot using very basic stand-in Warg rigs, but we haven't been slaved to that material, so we had free rein with the Wargs to push them wherever they needed to go.

Kevin Andrew Smith,
Weta Digital 2nd Unit Visual Effects Supervisor

There were two practical Warg riding rigs made. One we built at Weta Workshop that was spring-based, and the physical effects team built a hydraulic powered one as well, both for tightly framed live-shot Warg riders. They gave quite a lively performance, but once the decision to go fully digital with the Warg riders was made, these were no longer needed.

Rob Gillies, Weta Workshop Supervisor

No matter how well we might shoot a guy in an Orc costume sitting astride a green-screen Warg stand-in, when it comes time to paint that digital Warg under him we are constrained by what was able to be achieved physically on the day of the shoot. Basically, that's a bull ride, so the guy goes up and down a bit and maybe side to side, but in the end there is a big difference between that and what a character looks like riding a real running beast.

For that reason, among others, going fully digital for both rider and beast offered clear advantages, and that's what we ended up doing for the majority of the Orc and Warg scenes, barring maybe some close-ups of specific prosthetic-wearing Orc actors like Yazneg and Fimbul. Going all digital meant the animators could do what they needed to do unfettered to make the performance work, and it's probably more efficient too, as they're not having to match live-action movement. The result is dynamic and cool action with Orcs riding Wargs at speed over rough terrain as they chase the Dwarves down. We could throw our digital Orcs around in ways you wouldn't want to try with a real person, like throwing a guy off a Warg running over jagged ground at forty kilometres per hour.

Kevin Andrew Smith,
Weta Digital 2nd Unit Visual Effects Supervisor

Inset, above: Weta Digital motion capture stage manager Jake Botting at the motion capture studio with Bebe in her motion capture suit.

I was initially concerned about the Wargs because we're very geared up for motion capture. It's a process that is very helpful when we need to get a lot done very quickly. There's no really good motion capture for dogs, but we did it. We had explored the possibility of using police dogs but, understandably, there would have been a problem with using taxpayer-funded police dogs for movie work, so we hired a crew from Wanganui. We didn't have the motion capture suits for dogs at the time so we ordered some from the United States – full Lycra suits that fit and strapped on to the dogs. We captured a lot of material including running, jumping and stopping. It was early days so the way the movement mapped onto the Warg model wasn't perfect. The legs would pop around a lot, but we could get the basics for motion. My initial thought was that we'd at least have it available for reference. The Wargs were so huge that I wasn't convinced it would work, being directly used to drive animation.

We had a stage dog, Bebe, who came to work with Weta Digital motion capture stage manager Jake Botting. She was there a lot, just being low key and following him around. I wanted to get more material because I noticed the animators were grabbing motion capture that I had made available to them for reference and were using it and getting it to work. One quick way to do so is to slow it down fifteen to twenty per cent. That instantly makes the creature seem larger.

In any case I needed more, so we arranged to have Bebe put in the motion capture suit. After all, she was free! We captured her running around and jumping. It was all usable – even her skittish behaviour – and it saved us because we could use her captured performance to inform things like what happens when our Wargs change direction or where their legs might touch down when running, the kind of stuff that takes forever to key-frame accurately. With Bebe's capture that information came automatically.

We had to remove her tail wagging from the capture, of course, because Wargs aren't cheerful, but once we had done that, slowed her down and made a few other little tweaks we had a pretty viable Warg performance that could be employed in a lot of shots.

Eric Reynolds, Weta Digital Animation Supervisor

THE MATRIARCH

Towering over her pack-mates is the giant white Warg Matriarch, Azog's ally and personal choice of mount. Similar to him in many ways, she is scarred and pale, out-sizes her underlings and instils terror in them with a glance.

The Matriarch is a little better taken care of than her pack, so she looks more well fed than the rest. She has her share of scars and she's definitely grimmer than the others. Being so big she commands respect and deference from the other Wargs and even the Orcs.

Eric Saindon, Weta Digital Visual Effects Supervisor

The Warg Matriarch doesn't see a lot of action in the first film, so we have key-frame animated her. Like Azog, she holds back, letting her pups do the dirty work and only getting involved when she has to.

Eric Reynolds, Weta Digital Animation Supervisor

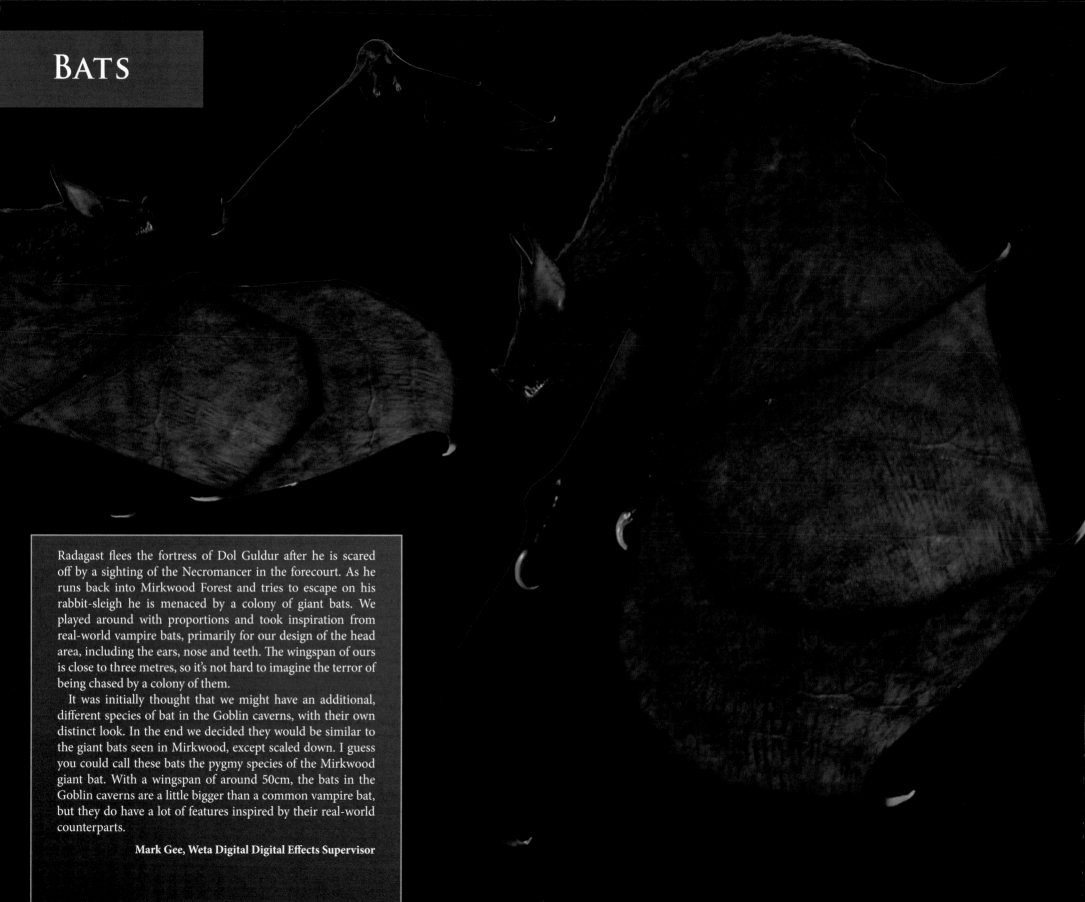

BATS

Radagast flees the fortress of Dol Guldur after he is scared off by a sighting of the Necromancer in the forecourt. As he runs back into Mirkwood Forest and tries to escape on his rabbit-sleigh he is menaced by a colony of giant bats. We played around with proportions and took inspiration from real-world vampire bats, primarily for our design of the head area, including the ears, nose and teeth. The wingspan of ours is close to three metres, so it's not hard to imagine the terror of being chased by a colony of them.

It was initially thought that we might have an additional, different species of bat in the Goblin caverns, with their own distinct look. In the end we decided they would be similar to the giant bats seen in Mirkwood, except scaled down. I guess you could call these bats the pygmy species of the Mirkwood giant bat. With a wingspan of around 50cm, the bats in the Goblin caverns are a little bigger than a common vampire bat, but they do have a lot of features inspired by their real-world counterparts.

Mark Gee, Weta Digital Digital Effects Supervisor

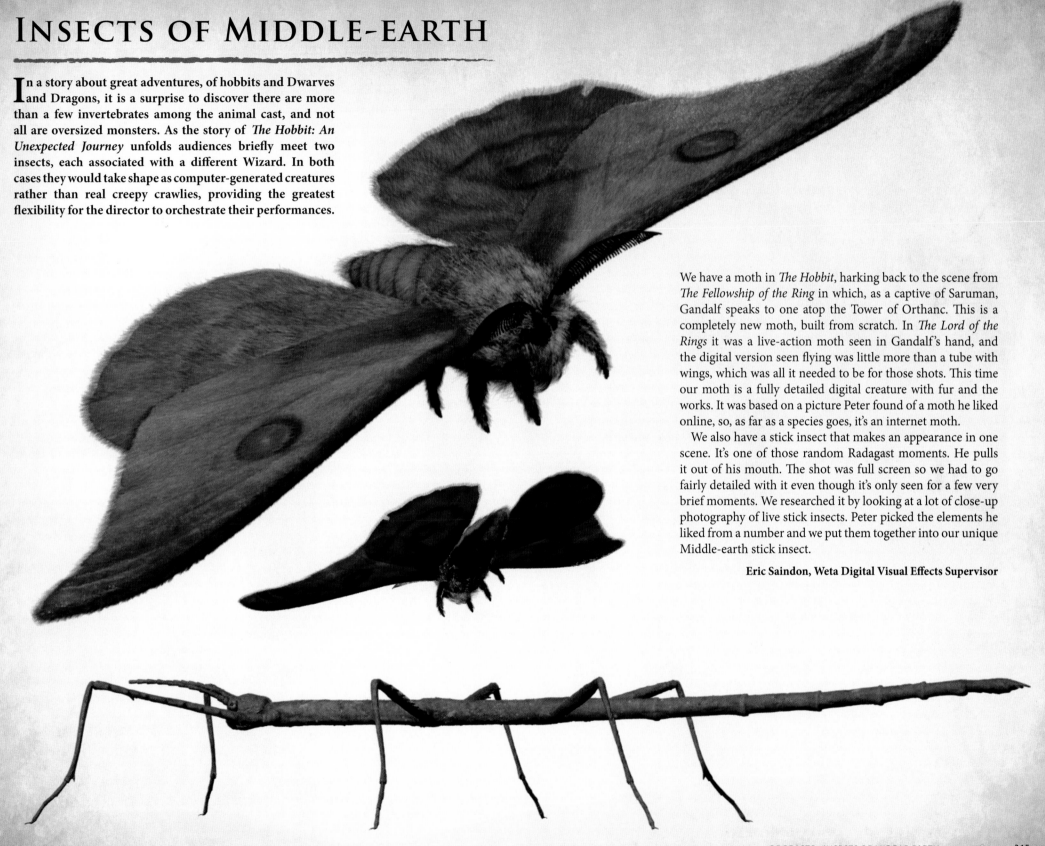

INSECTS OF MIDDLE-EARTH

In a story about great adventures, of hobbits and Dwarves and Dragons, it is a surprise to discover there are more than a few invertebrates among the animal cast, and not all are oversized monsters. As the story of *The Hobbit: An Unexpected Journey* unfolds audiences briefly meet two insects, each associated with a different Wizard. In both cases they would take shape as computer-generated creatures rather than real creepy crawlies, providing the greatest flexibility for the director to orchestrate their performances.

We have a moth in *The Hobbit*, harking back to the scene from *The Fellowship of the Ring* in which, as a captive of Saruman, Gandalf speaks to one atop the Tower of Orthanc. This is a completely new moth, built from scratch. In *The Lord of the Rings* it was a live-action moth seen in Gandalf's hand, and the digital version seen flying was little more than a tube with wings, which was all it needed to be for those shots. This time our moth is a fully detailed digital creature with fur and the works. It was based on a picture Peter found of a moth he liked online, so, as far as a species goes, it's an internet moth.

We also have a stick insect that makes an appearance in one scene. It's one of those random Radagast moments. He pulls it out of his mouth. The shot was full screen so we had to go fairly detailed with it even though it's only seen for a few very brief moments. We researched it by looking at a lot of close-up photography of live stick insects. Peter picked the elements he liked from a number and we put them together into our unique Middle-earth stick insect.

Eric Saindon, Weta Digital Visual Effects Supervisor

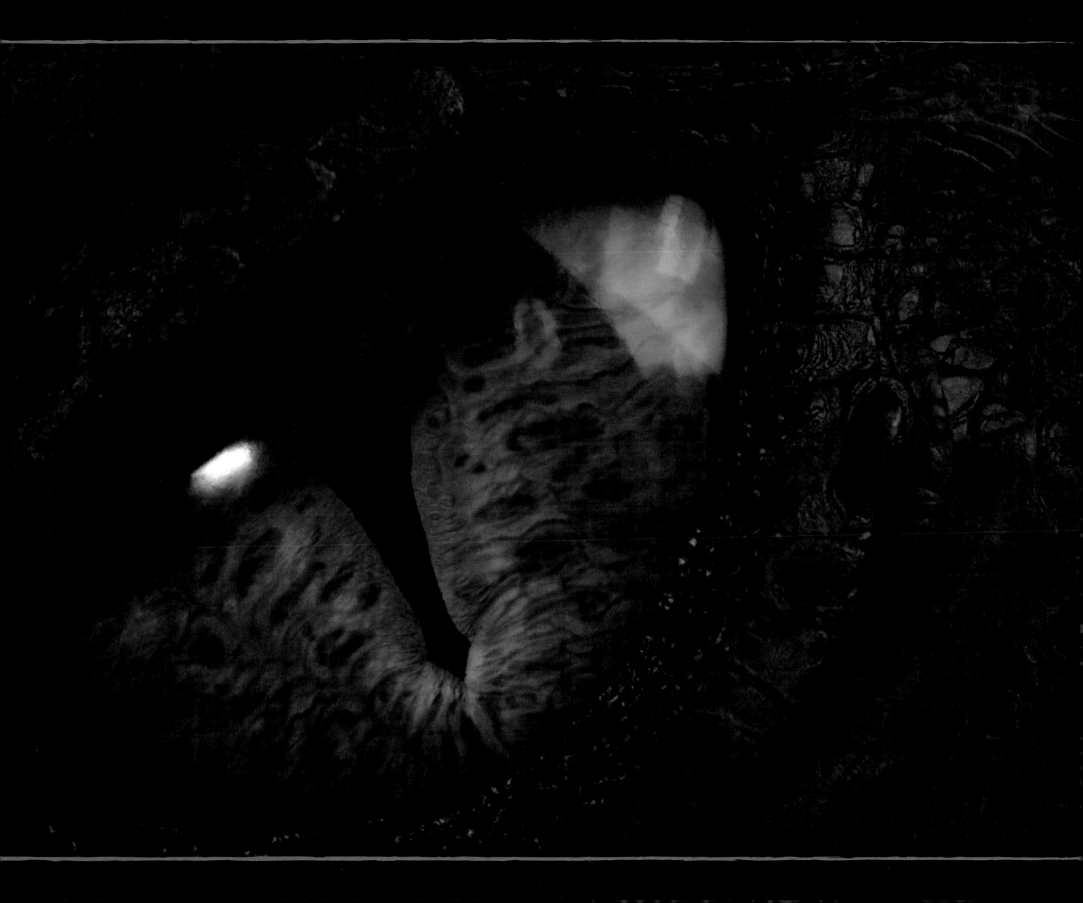

ABOUT THE PENINSULA

CASTING

A number of international casting agents and entities were called upon to fill the many roles required for *The Hobbit: An Unexpected Journey*, including offices in the United States and United Kingdom. The New Zealand casting department was made up of five people with an on-site office at Stone Street Studios, and an office in Park Rd with an adjacent studio where auditions were held. The extras department had a separate on-site studio office and would also work from the Park Rd location when more space was required. Local venues such as Toi Whaakari in Newtown were hired when large public casting calls were needed.

The department was responsible for auditioning local actors, co-ordinating Australian auditions, finding exceptionally tall and short people to play scale doubles, looking for picture doubles for all lead cast, and casting and co-ordinating extras. This included visually identifying suitable people and taking them through the process of auditioning in order to determine who was the most suitable in terms of 'looks' and talent. The department coordinated individual requirements, liaised with the make-up and costume departments for fittings, co-ordinated movement and weapons training, and generated necessary paperwork, while constantly on the lookout for new faces.

MAKE-UP & HAIR DEPARTMENT

The 3 Foot 7 Make-up Department created characters by designing and applying make-up, prosthetics, wigs and the beards to the cast. Every cast member, including extras, wore some form of wig and all the lead actors and their various doubles wore prosthetics. Four make-up department bases managed the large number of artists and extras. All activity was coordinated through the make-up room based at Stone Street Studios. This was also where wigs were made and mended, and hair was prepared for inclusion in the wigs, including dying and curling. Seven five-seater make-up trucks positioned on the back-lot were used for applying prosthetics, make-up and hair on principal actors, some taking three hours to complete each day, under the eye of two supervisors. Offsite was another 18-station make-up facility for extras. There were 34 permanent staff though the department swelled to as many as 60 during periods calling for large numbers of extras and stunt people.

STUNT DEPARTMENT

Where action was indicated in the script, the stunt department was tasked to translate those words into a tangible reality for filming. The stunt coordinator and his department were responsible for the action adhering to the director's vision and performed safely, with minimum fuss. Action in *The Hobbit* was always involved due to the numerous facets of the production: prosthetics, costumes, fat-suits, wigs, armour, weapons, and the cumulative effect of doubles and stunt performers in addition to the actors, the safety of all of whom was the responsibility of the stunt department. This responsibility also extended to include the crew working immediately in and around the action.

The Hobbit films required a team of up to a hundred stunt performers from various countries. Alternate teams were sometimes rostered on day and night shifts to meet the demands of filming. Choreography of all the action sequences and preparation of sets for specific action were also the responsibility of the department, including placement of wire work to accentuate any throws or impacts.

Prior to shooting beginning on the physically challenging production, the fitness of the actors was assessed and they underwent extensive physical and technical training with the stunt team for the work ahead. Working with other departments, costumes and make-up elements were refined and improved to allow the actors to more easily execute special movements and fight sequences.

DIALECT COACHES

The Dialect Coaches provided support and training for films' actors in preparatory sessions, on set and during additional dialogue recording. During preproduction their services included working with the filmmakers and cast members to help find key accents for specific characters. With the help of translations provided by Tolkien language expert David Salo, the Dialect Coaches also instructed cast members in the correct pronunciation of the invented languages of the Dwarves, Orcs and Elves, as well as helping them master and maintain their character's unique accent when speaking English. On set they also provided offline dialogue for characters whose actors were not present during that particular day of shooting.

WETA WORKSHOP

Weta Workshop is a multi-award winning conceptual design and manufacturing facility based in Wellington, New Zealand, servicing the world's creative industries. Weta Workshop's crew draws upon more than twenty-five years of film-making experience and is led by five times Academy Award® winner, Richard Taylor. The company's crew members are expert in a diverse range of disciplines and enjoy engaging in all aspects of each project, from preliminary technical analysis and conceptual design through to manufacture and final delivery of product, anywhere in the world. Weta Workshop's crew provided design and manufacturing services on *The Hobbit*, designing creatures, armour and weapons, as well as building armour, weapons, prosthetics and physical creature effects.

WETA DIGITAL

Weta Digital is one of the world's premier visual effects companies. Led by Senior Visual Effects Supervisor Joe Letteri, Weta Digital is known for uncompromising creativity and commitment to developing innovative technology. From groundbreaking performance-driven digital characters like Gollum, Kong and Caesar, to the revolutionary virtual production workflows of *Avatar* and *The Adventures of Tintin*, Weta Digital's team continues to break down barriers between live action and computer-generated imagery and expand what is possible in film. Weta Digital established its reputation for cutting edge visual effects with work on blockbusters like *The Lord of the Rings* trilogy and *King Kong*. The company began work in 1993 on co-founder Peter Jackson's film *Heavenly Creatures* and is based in a number of facilities spread around Wellington, New Zealand. Weta Digital is creating all digital visual effects on *The Hobbit* films.

Keep up to date on all our new releases as well as all the Weta news, including *The Hobbit: An Unexpected Journey*, by signing up for our free email newsletter at: www.wetaNZ.com

COLLECTIBLE CREATURES AND CHARACTERS

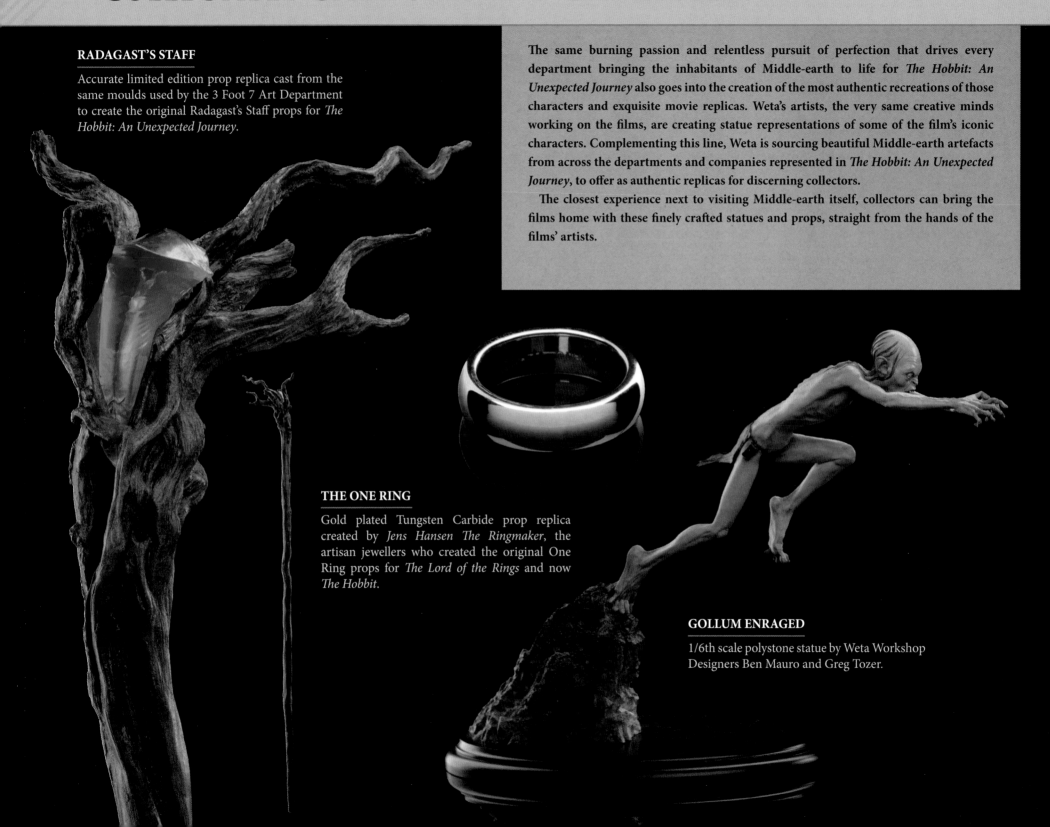

RADAGAST'S STAFF

Accurate limited edition prop replica cast from the same moulds used by the 3 Foot 7 Art Department to create the original Radagast's Staff props for *The Hobbit: An Unexpected Journey*.

The same burning passion and relentless pursuit of perfection that drives every department bringing the inhabitants of Middle-earth to life for *The Hobbit: An Unexpected Journey* also goes into the creation of the most authentic recreations of those characters and exquisite movie replicas. Weta's artists, the very same creative minds working on the films, are creating statue representations of some of the film's iconic characters. Complementing this line, Weta is sourcing beautiful Middle-earth artefacts from across the departments and companies represented in *The Hobbit: An Unexpected Journey*, to offer as authentic replicas for discerning collectors.

The closest experience next to visiting Middle-earth itself, collectors can bring the films home with these finely crafted statues and props, straight from the hands of the films' artists.

THE ONE RING

Gold plated Tungsten Carbide prop replica created by *Jens Hansen The Ringmaker*, the artisan jewellers who created the original One Ring props for *The Lord of the Rings* and now *The Hobbit*.

GOLLUM ENRAGED

1/6th scale polystone statue by Weta Workshop Designers Ben Mauro and Greg Tozer.

HOBBIT

RIDDLES IN THE DARK

Art print by Weta Workshop Designer Gus Hunter.

BILBO BAGGINS

1/6th scale polystone statue by Weta Workshop Sculptor Brigitte Wuest.

DWALIN THE DWARF

1/6th scale polystone statue by Weta Workshop Designer and Sculptor Greg Tozer.

Purchase these and many other great Weta collectibles at our online shop :

www.wetaNZ.com

You can also keep up to date on all our new releases as well as all the Weta news, including *The Hobbit: An Unexpected Journey,* by signing up for our free email newsletter at:

www.wetanz.com/mailinglist

Writer and Art Director	Daniel Falconer
Layout Artist	Monique Hamon
Image Retouching	Stuart Thomas
Transcribers	Candace Little
	Darinie Johnston
Size Chart Illustrator	Nick Keller
Weta Workshop Design & Special Effects Supervisor	Richard Taylor
Weta Workshop Manager	Tania Rodger
Weta Ltd General Manager	Tim Launder
Weta Publishing Manager	Kate Jorgensen
Weta Workshop Design Studio Manager	Richard Athorne
Weta Workshop Photographer	Steve Unwin
Weta Workshop Assistant Photographers	Wendy Bown
	Simon Godsiff
Unit Photography	Todd Eyre
	James Fisher
	Mark Pokorny

HarperCollins*Publishers* UK

Chris Smith	Series Editor
Charles Light	Production Director
Terence Caven	Design Manager

ABOUT THE AUTHOR

Daniel Falconer has been a designer at Weta Workshop for more than sixteen years, producing conceptual art as part of the design team on many of the company's high profile projects including *The Lord of the Rings*, *King Kong*, *The Chronicles of Narnia*, *Avatar*, and now *The Hobbit*. Daniel has written a number of books for Weta; *The World of Kong*, *The Crafting of Narnia*, *Weta: The Collector's Guide*, *The Art of District 9* and *The Hobbit: An Unexpected Journey: Chronicles: Art & Design*, each showcasing the creative works of the Miramar Peninsula based companies.

Daniel lives and works in Wellington, New Zealand with his wife Catherine and two daughters, reveling in his dream career of playing in imaginary worlds every day.

CREDITS

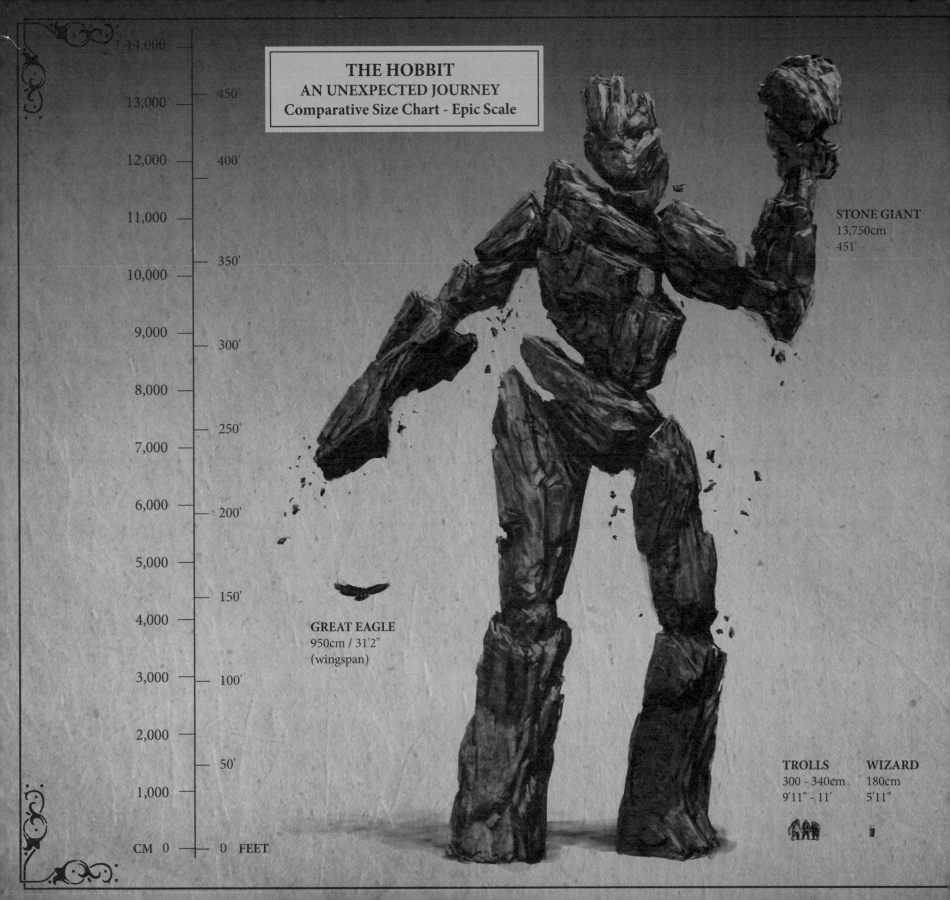

THE HOBBIT
AN UNEXPECTED JOURNEY
Comparative Size Chart - Epic Scale

STONE GIANT
13,750cm
451'

GREAT EAGLE
950cm / 31'2"
(wingspan)

TROLLS
300 - 340cm
9'11" - 11'

WIZARD
180cm
5'11"

		CM	FEET
		200	6'
		150	4'
CM	FEET	100	
	12'		2'
350		50	
	10'	0	0
300			
250	8'		

WARGS

Warg Scout
180cm / 5'11"
(at shoulder)

Warg Matriarch
212cm / 7'
(at shoulder)

ORCS

Azog
215cm / 7'

	CM	FEET
200	150	4'
6'	100	2'
150	50	
4'	0	0
2'		
50		
0		

HOBBIT **DWARVES**

HOBBIT	DWARVES									
Bilbo Baggins	**Balin**	**Dwalin**	**Kili**	**Thorin**	**Fili**	**Oin**	**Gloin**	**Bombur**	**Bofur**
127cm	138cm	150cm	143cm	149cm	135cm	145cm	141cm	135cm	145cm
4'2"	4'6"	4'11"	4'8"	4'10½"	4'5"	4'9"	4'7½"	4'5"	4'8"

GREAT EAGLE

Gwaihir
950cm / 31'2"
(wingspan)

Fimbul
169cm / 5'6"

Robin
28cm / 11"
(wingspan)

Sparrow
15cm / 5¾"
(wingspan)

WIZARDS   ANIMALS   ELVES

Bifur	Nori	Dori	Ori	Saruman	Gandalf	Radagast	Sebastian	Rhosgobel Rabbit	Galadriel	Elrond
135cm	136cm	136cm	135cm	200cm	180cm	163cm	22cm / 8"	85cm / 2'9"	180cm	188cm
4'5"	4'5½"	4'5½"	4'5"	6'7"	5'11"	5'4"	(length)	(length)	5'11"	6'2"

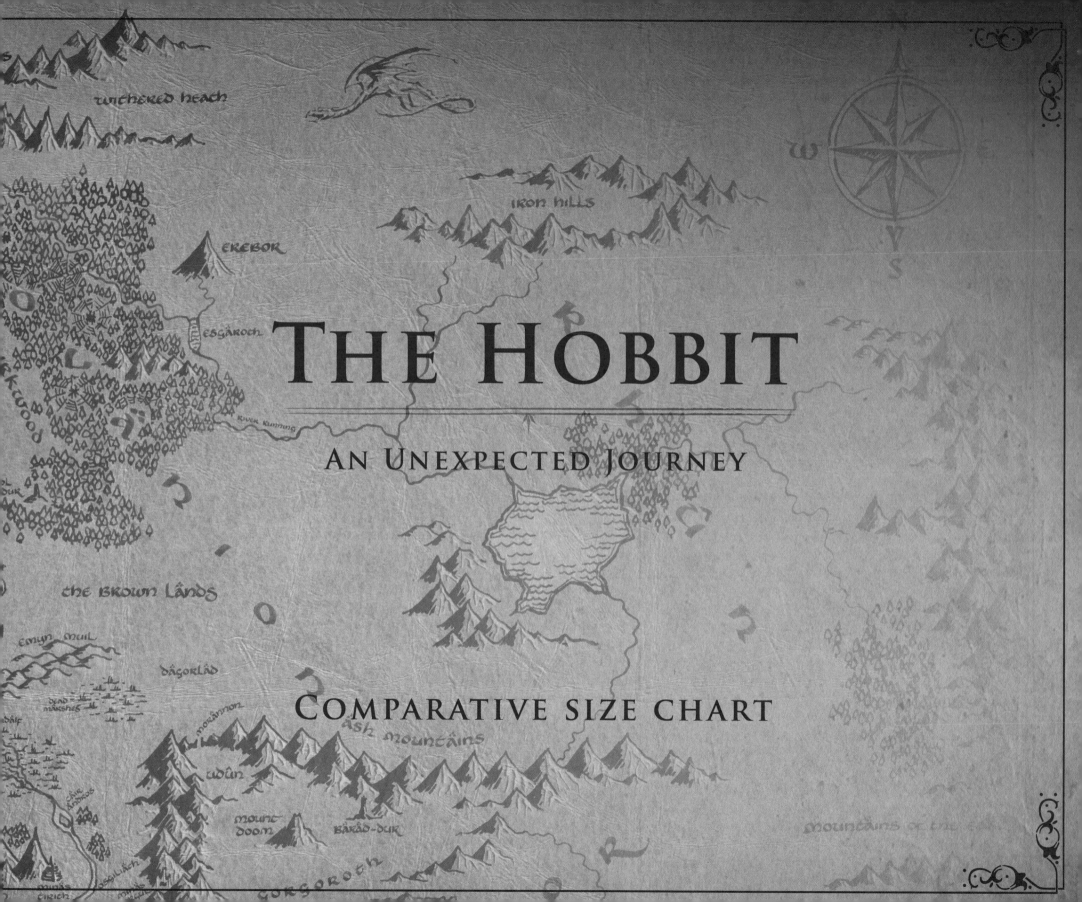

THE HOBBIT

AN UNEXPECTED JOURNEY

COMPARATIVE SIZE CHART